THE BRONTËS AND NATURE

THE BRONTËS AND NATURE

Enid L. Duthie

MACMILLAN

First published 1986

Published by
THE MACMILLAN PRESS LTD
Houndmills, Basingstoke, Hampshire RG21 2XS
and London
Companies and representatives
throughout the world

Printed in Hong Kong

British Library Cataloguing in Publication Data
Duthie, Enid L.
The Brontës and nature.
1. Brontë. (Family)   2. Nature in literature
3. English fiction — 19th century — History
and criticism
I. Title
823'.8'0936   PR4169
ISBN 0–333–39848–3

To the Memory of Eleanore Waldock

Contents

vii

Acknowledgements

The author and the publishers wish to thank the following who have kindly given permission for the use of copyright material: Macmillan, for extracts from Edward Chitham's *The Poems of Anne Brontë: a New Text and Commentary* (1979); to the Folio Society, for extracts from Charlotte Brontë's *Five Novelettes*, edited by Winifred Gérin (1971); and to Columbia University Press, for extracts from *The Complete Poems of Emily Jane Brontë*, edited by C. W. Hatfield (1941).

Thanks are also due to John Murray for the use of the Haworth edition of the Brontë works and Mrs Gaskell's *Life of Charlotte Brontë*; to Hodder & Stoughton for extracts from *The Complete Poems of Charlotte Brontë*, edited by Clement Shorter; and to the Brontë Society for references to valuable material in their *Transactions*.

I should also like to express my sincere gratitude to the staff of the University Library, Exeter; to the staff of Howard Print, Exeter, for their competence and courtesy in dealing with the typescript; and finally to Mr T. M. Farmiloe, and also to Miss Frances A. Arnold, of Macmillan, to whose help and unfailing consideration I am deeply indebted.

Introduction

Critical works on the Brontës are so numerous that it seems as if any fresh study must inevitably risk discussing questions already examined. The present study has, however, been undertaken in the belief that its subject has not yet received all the attention it merits. It has long been recognised that nature plays an important part in the works of the Brontë sisters. But its role has not yet been fully considered, nor has it been generally realised that their approach to nature offers one of the surest criteria for distinguishing the originality of each as artists, an originality necessarily connected with their individual temperament and outlook.

They had inevitably much in common, for they shared the same Celtic ancestry, the same Pennine background, the same Parsonage upbringing. They were all avid readers, and authors from childhood onwards, and they grew up at a time when, with the triumph of Romanticism, the concept of nature had gained a new significance, a significance embracing the whole of human life.

The Romantic concept of nature was essentially poetic, and all the Brontës were poets, though Emily alone attained greatness in the medium of verse. But they also brought the Romantic approach to nature, at once metaphysical and profoundly human, into the novel, an achievement the more memorable because it took place in an era of growing industrialisation. Each did so, however, in their own way, Anne modestly, but not ineffectively, Charlotte with most variety, Emily with most elemental force. English literature, which owes so much to the Romantic vision of nature, is the richer today for the distinctive contribution of each.

Part I
Nature and Background

1   The Common Heritage

When Patrick Brontë brought his wife and family to the moorland village of Haworth in the early spring of 1820, he came to a
place well suited to nurture the genius of his children. It is
sometimes assumed, however, that for the father of the family
the step was a retrogressive one, taking him into a bleak environment alien to his nature and his tastes. Increased knowledge of
his character and background has shown that this was far from
being the case.[1] He was a man who, from childhood, had been
accustomed to country life and for whom the hills and moors
that surround Haworth were among its chief attractions.

He had been born in a cottage in County Down, and he was
not unduly concerned with his father's claim that the family
were not originally of peasant stock. Certainly their lot in life
depended, as he said, not on family descent but on their own
exertions. The cottage in the quiet valley of Emdale was in fact
no more than a cabin:

A neat Irish Cabin, snow-proof,
    Well-thatched, had a good earthen floor,
One chimney in midst of the roof,
    One window, and one latched door.[2]

Even when the young couple and their child moved to less
cramped quarters, theirs was still a life of hard work and plain
living. By the time Patrick was twelve, his parents had five
children to support and, as the eldest, he went to work as a
blacksmith's assistant and then as a linen weaver, becoming
proficient in both skills. When, years later, he addressed his
Cottage Poems to those who "turn the sturdy soil, or ply the loom
with daily toil", he was speaking to those who belonged to the
same world in which his boyhood had been spent.

But there was another side to his boyhood. Somehow he
learned to read, and found in the new world opened up for him

3

an engrossing interest. It was the boy's enthusiasm for books which attracted the notice of a schoolmaster in a neighbouring village, who generously gave him a couple of hours' teaching in the early morning before he walked the five miles to the linen draper's to work at his loom. Thanks to his help, Patrick, at sixteen, became a schoolmaster himself in a village school and later graduated to the larger church school in nearby Drumballyroney, becoming tutor at the same time to the vicar's sons. But the schoolmaster remained a countryman: he encouraged his pupils to make excursions into the countryside and in the summer holidays explored the Mourne mountains, sometimes with them, more often alone, developing his love and understanding of nature.

But he was not destined to spend his life within sight of the mountains of Mourne. The vicar of Drumballyroney, the Rev. Thomas Tighe, was a priest whose outlook had been decisively influenced by his friendship with John Wesley, who stayed with him during his preaching tours in Ireland. He shared Wesley's concern for the people, and he and his curate aimed at making every adult in their parish literate. One can imagine the appeal this liberal outlook had for the young schoolmaster, and on the other hand how Mr Tighe saw in his sons' tutor a potential recruit for the evangelicals within the Anglican ministry. It was owing to his encouragement and help that, at twenty-five, the young man took the decisive step of leaving Ireland to become an undergraduate at St. John's College, Cambridge, where Tighe himself had studied. Helped by some college assistance on grounds of poverty, but also by grants won by his own ability, he graduated in 1806, and was ordained deacon of the Church of England a few months later and priest the following year.

While at Cambridge he had remained in contact with the evangelical movement through the influence of men like Henry Martyn, then a Fellow of St. John's, and Charles Simeon. The Mecca of young evangelical clergymen was the West Riding of Yorkshire, and it was in this northern region of England that most of Patrick Brontë's future life was to be spent. His first charge, however, was at Wetherfield in Essex, and his next curacy at Wellington in Shropshire, but in 1809 he became curate of Dewsbury, and the West Riding remained his place of residence for the rest of his life. From Dewsbury he moved to Hartshead, a few miles away, in 1811. In 1812 he married, and his two eldest children were born at Hartshead, but three years later the family moved north-west to Thornton, near Bradford, where the four younger children were born. The youngest was only an infant when, in 1820, Mr Brontë was appointed to the living of Haworth, a moorland parish eight miles away across the hills, famous among evangelicals through its association with the pastor William Grimshaw, the friend of Wesley, who during his ministry had made it the centre of revival in Yorkshire.

By the time he came to Haworth, the father of the Brontës had proved his eminent fitness for the life of a country parson. He loved the countryside, whether it was the upland country round Hartshead or the bleaker hills about Thornton. And he was well able to play the part expected of him in the life of the community, a demanding one at a time when the parish priest had often to intervene in secular matters. The beginning of his curacy at Hartshead coincided with one of the most serious of the Luddite riots, the attack by the frame-breakers on nearby Rawfolds Mills, later to become the source of his daughter Charlotte's novel *Shirley*. It is probable that it was at this unsettled time that he began to carry a loaded pistol in his pocket. He was not a man to be intimidated by violence or to condone the breaking of the law. Yet he must also have been keenly aware of the situation of the weavers. It is said that he turned a blind eye when he accidentally witnessed the secret burial by night in his churchyard of the bodies of rioters brought there by their friends, when they had died in hiding from their wounds.

Popular with his people, and known for his vigour and courage, Patrick Brontë was also happy at this time in his domestic life. He was married to a wife who shared his outlook, though she came from a different social background. Maria Branwell belonged to a Cornish merchant family with an established position in Penzance society. They were Methodists, and it was while on a visit to her uncle John Fennell, head of the new Wesleyan boarding-school Woodhouse Grove near Bradford, that she met Patrick Brontë, then acting as the school examiner. They were married a few months later and, first at Hartshead and then at Thornton, their home was a happy one. Thornton, though not so attractively situated as Hartshead, had the advantage, for Mrs Brontë, of being nearer to Bradford, where her relations the Fennells and their daughter Jane, married to

Patrick's friend and fellow curate, William Morgan, were now living. Here, too, the Brontës enjoyed the friendship and hospitality of the Firth family, whose home Kipping House, with its extensive garden, was only a short distance from the parsonage.

The five years at Thornton were happy ones, but Mr Brontë's appointment as perpetual curate at Haworth marked an advancement; it was an honour to occupy the pulpit from which the famous Grimshaw had preached; it meant security of tenure; in addition, the situation of this hillside village, backed by mile on mile of rolling moorland, made a strong appeal to the nature-loving parson. He soon received proof of the sturdy independence of his future parishioners, though this was not a characteristic to daunt him. The appointment was in the hands of the Vicar of Bradford, but the church trustees at Haworth, in virtue of an Elizabethan charter, had power to veto his choice. Not having been consulted, they objected to the appointment. Mr Brontë confronted the difficult situation wisely, understanding their feeling and actually giving in his resignation. But his firm and dignified attitude convinced the trustees that he was in fact the man they wanted, and the Vicar of Bradford's attempt to make them accept a second choice of his, the Rev. Samuel Redhead, resulted in a riot in Haworth church, the precipitate departure of Redhead and, ultimately, the appointment of Patrick Brontë.

When this storm had been safely weathered, it seemed as if a secure and happy future lay ahead. But less than a year later Maria Brontë suddenly became dangerously ill, and she died of cancer in September 1821. Her husband had lost an ideal companion and was left with six small children, of whom the eldest was only seven. His wife's elder sister Elizabeth Branwell had come from Cornwall some months before to help the stricken family. Patrick Brontë made two attempts to remarry, but without success. His children were not destined to have a stepmother, and his sister-in-law stayed on in Yorkshire to keep house for him and look after the family.

It is at this stage that he is often thought to have undergone a transformation from a vigorous and sociable man, passionate by nature but strong-willed and normally self-controlled, into a morose recluse who kept himself aloof both from his parishioners and his children. For this view Mrs Gaskell's biography of his daughter Charlotte was partially though unintentionally responsible. Recent research, in particular the full and illuminating biography by John Lock and Canon W. T. Dixon, has conclusively proved how mistaken it was. Patrick Brontë remained essentially the same man he had always been. He had lost his wife after only nine years of marriage, and the irreparable loss shadowed his life and took away his buoyancy. But his faith was unshaken and his outlook on life unaltered. Religion and nature remained his primary sources of inspiration and consolation, and for him the two were indissolubly connected.

This basic attitude is clear in the two volumes of verse he published while still at Hartshead, *Cottage Poems* and *The Rural Minstrel*. Critics have usually adopted a highly condescending attitude to these poems but here, as so frequently, Patrick Brontë has had less than justice. He made no high claims himself for his "rustic Muse". His intention was to write as simply as possible for the benefit of "the unlearned and the poor", and to offer them help and encouragement. At the same time it is important to realise that he did not in any sense look down on his humble audience. He respected and admired them, and gave them the place of honour in *Cottage Poems*. The old man and his daughter in "The Happy Cottagers", the family in "The Irish Cabin" have accepted the restrictions of their lot with courage and cheerfulness. It is true that his cottagers are shown as meriting admiration primarily because their virtues are "a consequence of Grace". Nevertheless there is a connection between their piety and the spartan conditions in which they live. "Some circumstances are certainly more favourable to piety than others, and in this respect the poor man has generally the advantage."[3] This is amply illustrated in *Cottage Poems* as a whole. "Winter-Night Meditations" evokes the corruption rife in the city, the misery of the prostitute, once a rural beauty, the plight of the rich man in whom self-indulgence has bred apathy, disease or hypochondria. The "Epistle to the Labouring Poor", while it does not minimise the physical hardships they endure, emphasises the corroding effects of wealth and pride.

The didactic aim of these verses is evident, but it is noticeable that the best of them are those in which the writer's descriptive talent asserts itself. There is little that is novel in the plight of the merchant whose ship founders at sea, but there is vigour and freshness in the description of the actual shipwreck. In Patrick Brontë's next collection of verse, *The Rural Minstrel*, it is by evoking "rural scenery in all its forms" that he expresses the truths he wishes to convey. In "The Sabbath Bell" the sounds and fragrance of spring form a pastoral prelude to the summons to prayer. "Rural Happiness" celebrates the beauty of the countryside as the mirror of divine creativity:

> As roves my mind o'er nature's works abroad,
> It sees, reflected, their creative God . . .[4]

In "Winter" the plight of the birds during the season of storms makes a particular appeal to the heart of the observer:

> Ah! may you light on friendly sheds,
> To hide your drooping pensive heads,
>   From winter's chilling roar . . .[5]

The Rural Minstrel shows a deep love of nature and sometimes finds the accents to match it. It was the description of the morning sky in "The Sabbath Bell" which caused Christopher Fry to say: "There was a poet in him, too, fumbling to find a way to match sound with spirit", and he adds: "These are not negligible contributions to his children's birthright."[6]

It is interesting to see in these verses the instinctive sympathy with, as well as for, animals which is part of the writer's understanding of nature. This had always been a characteristic of Patrick Brontë. Years before, when a young curate, he had promised his vicar's wife at Dewsbury to let her know how her dog, Tweed, was faring during the temporary absence of herself and her husband. The dog pined to an alarming extent, and his friend became his interpreter in a verse epistle, "Tweed's letter to his mistress". Tweed, no aristocratic among the "barking gentry", comes to life in these charming verses, as he describes with suitable humility his present sorrowful vigil, and the crux of his dilemma:

> But mankind change,
> As round they range –
> A dog, he changes, never![7]

The conversational tone half conceals the real depth of feeling. A much graver note is struck when the writer is concerned with an unexpected experience of nature in a mood of elemental fury.

In September 1824, during a violent thunderstorm, the marsh at Crow Hill on the moors near Haworth erupted, sending a seven foot high torrent of water, mud and slime rushing down into the Ponden Valley, carrying huge stones and boulders in its course. At the time when this took place, the early evening of 2 September, Patrick Brontë's three younger children, Branwell, Emily and Anne – the eldest only seven – had been taken walking on the moors by the parsonage servants. Their father, warned by the suddenly threatening skies, watched anxiously for their return and, unaware that they had found shelter, noted every detail of the ensuing storm. Ten days later he preached in Haworth Church on the event. In the interval he had visited and observed for himself the scene of devastation at Crow Hill. The sermon showed his concern as an evangelical that his hearers might profit spiritually from having so nearly escaped disaster. At the same time he was anxious that they should have an intelligent understanding of the natural causes that had contributed to it. He also wrote an account in verse for children, "The Phenomenon", which, like the sermon, was subsequently printed, and which is the clearest indication of the poetic vein in Patrick Brontë.

After an explanatory introduction in prose, the poem narrates the actual course of events, from the oncoming of the storm, and the dramatic emergence of the turbid mass of water from the riven moor, to the flooding of the valley below. Clearly there is a fascination for the writer in the sheer force of elemental nature. He compares the eruption to a storm at sea, and finds the same wild grandeur in both:

> But, see! the solid ground, like ocean driven,
> With mighty force by the four winds of heaven,
> In strange commotion rolls its earthy tide . . .

But the most impressive part of the description is that of the uneasy period before the storm breaks. Here the apprehension of the moorland creatures and the uprush of the wind as the tempest approaches seem to reflect a personal knowledge of such sudden storms, frequent on the moors:

> Now kawing rooks on rapid pinions move,
> For their lov'd home, the safe sequester'd grove;

> Far inland scream the frighten'd sea-gulls loud,
> High the blue heron sails along the cloud;
> The humming bees, sagacious, homewards fly,
> The conscious heifer snuffs the tempest nigh . . .[8]

This poem, and his sermon on the same subject, offer the clearest example of Patrick Brontë's approach to nature. He was a keen observer, and took an intelligent interest in whatever observation or modern science – as far as it was accessible to him – could offer in the way of explanation of natural phenomena. He did not choose that even children should be mystified where no mystery existed. But, more than this, he was keenly sensitive to the beauty of nature, to which the poet in him responded. Above all, he was one of those who, in his own words, "in deep contemplative mood . . . saw by faith through nature to nature's God". For him the Psalms were "the most sublimely simple of all pastorals", and it was from them that he took the text of his sermon: "His lightnings enlightened the world; the earth saw, and trembled. The hills melted like wax at the presence of the Lord of the whole earth." If he could not himself achieve the sublime, he understood what it was and saw in a regional cataclysm a cosmic significance. This, too, was part of his children's birthright.

The story *The Cottage in the Wood*, a prose tale published in 1815 while he was minister of Thornton, also has the rural setting he preferred. It seems probable that he was inspired to write it by the sight of a small cottage in a wooded valley near Thornton which may well have evoked early memories, for it was "of the cabin type, not unlike those of the Irish peasantry".[9] In this tale, as often in his verse, he contrasts the cottagers with the idle rich, greatly to the advantage of the former. Mary, the only daughter of the cottagers, refuses to become the mistress of a young aristocrat who is a waster and a drunkard. He is sobered, however, by a narrow escape from death, when, one night, as he and his riotous companions are going through a wood during a thunderstorm, a nearby oak is struck by lightning. Having lingered behind the others to reflect on the situation, he escapes death a second time when they are attacked and shot by robbers, and as a result of this dual experience he finally reforms. Eventually he meets Mary again and the story ends, predictably, with their marriage.

One cannot claim much literary distinction for this simple tale, but it is followed by two poems, the second of which, "The Nightly Revel", includes a description of the fateful thunderstorm and so provides the author with another opportunity for describing nature in tempestuous mood. However, it is the restoration of calm to the night sky, as the storm subsides, which is the most telling part of the description. Here, as previously in "The Phenomenon", where he had described the onset of a tempest, he chooses a theme to be developed with more mastery by his children, fascinated, like himself, by the glory of the constellations:

Now, the exhausted lightnings harmless play,
With lambent flame, pale as the milky way,
That track serene, which by their mingling light,
Remotest stars shed on the lovely night.
The mellow thunder scarcely heard to roll,
Far distant, mutters round the brightening pole;
Hush'd are the winds, the breaking clouds retire,
And countless stars light up their twinkling fire . . .[10]

During the period at Thornton Patrick Brontë also wrote a narrative entirely in prose, *The Maid of Killarney*, published in 1818. The story itself is again basically a simple one. Albion, a young Englishman visiting Ireland, meets and falls in love with Flora, "the maid of Killarney", only child of Captain Loughlean. She returns his love, and the only real threat to their happiness comes from a night attack on Loughlean Hall, while he is a guest there, by an insurrectionary group, which is foiled by the courage of the defenders and the quick wits of Flora. Here, for the first time, Patrick Brontë is not writing for "the unlearned and the poor" but for educated readers. Albion is "a man of family and influence" and Flora the daughter of the master of Loughlean Hall, the chief house of the neighbourhood. The Loughleans, who combine high principles with plain living, have little in common, it need hardly be said, with the wealthy hedonists whom Patrick Brontë contrasts so unfavourably with the patient cottagers. It is when Albion, as a traveller interested in new scenes, visits an Irish cabin that he first meets Flora, who has come on an errand of mercy to its dying inhabitant.

The old woman's wretched dwelling presents a very different appearance to the "neat Irish cabin" of *Cottage Poems*:

> The cabin was now in full view, and within a few yards of them. Part of a mound of earth, the boundary between two farms, constituted one of its sides; its front wall and gables were of mud hardened by the sun; it was covered on the roof with thin green turf, which the Irish peasantry denominate scraws; a sooty coloured goat, and a few smoky hens, strutted serenely upon it. The smoke from a dark peat fire urged its way out of a hole in the middle of the roof, and through the door. . . . The interior of the building corresponded perfectly with its outside. The whole furniture consisted of an old table and chest, falling to pieces, two or three low stools, and a bed of straw . . .[11]

In *Cottage Poems* Patrick Brontë had endeavoured to evoke the poetry of the Irish cabin; here he gives the prose, and shows his intimate knowledge of the primitive conditions endured by many peasant families. But his point of view has not changed, only his audience. To the "unlearned and poor" he counselled resignation and the consolations of religion. To those more fortunate he shows by implication the urgent need of the poor for help, both spiritual and practical. Flora Loughlean does her best to comfort the old woman dying in the wretched hovel, both with Bible reading and with the provision of food and of a nurse in the shape of a "little rough-headed girl" entirely at home in such surroundings.

The best writing in *The Maid of Killarney* is, as usual, descriptive, but its interest lies also in the conversations which are interwoven with the narrative. Albion likes to discuss "men and manners" and, at an early stage, launches on the well-worn comparison between the English, the Scots and the Irish, and asks his companion, with some complacency, whether he has not drawn a very fine picture. The reply is unexpected:

> "Let me see, Albion; here is the sombre English picture, there the grave Scotch picture, there the variegated Irish picture. Most assuredly I have seen worse portraits. But I think they are better calculated for high, than low life; more suitable for hanging up in the palace than adorning the cottage. Whenever

you would draw a character truly national, make a peasant sit for it."[12]

Here speaks the understanding and appreciation of the simple life, of human nature face to face with the stern realities of existence, which was the heritage of the Irish cabin.

As has already been seen, however, Patrick Brontë did not think that the simple life in itself was enough to make one virtuous. Nor did he think there was any virtue in being illiterate, and he did all he could to provide reading matter within the grasp of the "labouring poor", though his primary aim here was religious instruction. The opinions expressed in conversation at Loughlean Hall would have pleased neither advocates of the "noble savage" nor those of social revolution, but there is liberality and, above all, humanity blended with the basic belief in a firm social order founded on religion.

The Maid of Killarney was the last of Mr Brontë's published works, with the exception of pamphlets and "fugitive pieces". Perhaps if he had still had the sympathetic companionship of his wife, and of the congenial circle at Thornton, it might have had a successor. But at Haworth he was in charge of a moorland parish of considerable extent, whose affairs would not in any case have left much leisure to a priest as conscientious and as energetic as himself. Henceforth he gave himself up to the manifold duties of a country parson, which he was to discharge faithfully for forty-one years. These included not only preaching and visiting, though these were priorities, but ceaseless efforts to improve the conditions in which his people lived. Disease was rampant in Haworth because of the appalling lack of sanitation and the poor water supply, which made cholera and tuberculosis endemic. The situation was made worse by the housing congestion in the village; the population included many weavers in cottage workshops, as well as workers in the mills at the foot of the valley. It was he who took the initiative in a fight for healthier conditions which, after encountering every kind of obstacle, ultimately proved successful. Under his leadership stronger measures were also taken to secure law and order in the community. But he was always on the alert to oppose any suggestions of tyranny, particularly at the expense of the poorer classes. It was for this reason that, in February 1837, he opposed the new Poor Law in an impassioned speech in a public meeting held in Haworth for the purpose of petitioning Parliament to repeal the Act. It was this speech, made "not to promote the interests of party, but to plead the cause of the poor" which, at a moment when many such protests were being made, earned special notice from *The Times* of the day. As can be seen from this, his ceaseless concern for his parishioners did not blind him to the wider issues of the period. He kept abreast of current affairs, and communicated his interest in them to his children. He also retained his lasting belief in the value of the classical education which he had himself acquired, at the cost of so much effort, and which he was able to pass on to his son.

Fortunately for Patrick Brontë the duties of the incumbent of a moorland parish also included visits to the widely scattered cottages and farms within its bounds, of which many more were inhabited then than now. He was consequently able to maintain that vital contact with nature which meant so much to him. "No farmstead was too far across the moors for him to visit, no night too wild and stormy to preclude his holding a cottage meeting, if one had been requested."[13] He was "an insatiable walker in the cause of his people", but those walks must have been exhilaration and balm to the man himself. He delighted in them and, till age and blindness overtook him, could with ease walk forty miles a day. They took him into a world which was also to delight his children, and his knowledge of it must have acted as a spur to their own desire to explore it. Mrs Gaskell's allusion to his keen-eyed observation on these walks bears the stamp of authenticity and suggests that she is repeating what she had heard from Charlotte or possibly from her father himself:

> Mr Brontë was an active walker, stretching away over the moors for many miles, noting in his mind all natural signs of wind and weather, and keenly observing all the wild creatures that came and went in the loneliest sweeps of the hills. He has seen eagles stooping low in search of food for their young; no eagle is ever seen on those mountain slopes now.[14]

But a father with a love of nature and an understanding of country folk could not have communicated these qualities to his children if they had not been able to experience for themselves the spell of the moors and to meet those who had been formed by such an environment. The initiation of the Brontë children into the secrets of a world unknown to the townsman really began with their arrival at Haworth parsonage.

The situation of their new home, on a narrow plateau at the top of the village, went far to determine the pattern of their childhood existence. The view from the front windows, then unobstructed by trees, looked over the strip of garden and the tombstones in the graveyard to the church tower and beyond it, over the Worth valley, to the hills and the more distant moors. From the back windows the view was directly on to the moors rising immediately behind the house. The strength of the wind must often have been eloquent of their nearness, as it beat on the unsheltered stone parsonage standing foursquare to the elements. There could be little question of the direction their steps would take when they began to explore the world outside its walls. "From their first going to Haworth their walks were directed rather out towards the heathery moors, sloping upwards behind the parsonage, than towards the long descending village street."[15] Wherever they might later travel as individuals, it was this particular landscape that first cast its spell upon them, and to which they always returned.

It was a landscape which, as part of the sweep of the moors on a spur of the Pennines, must have awed them at first with its vastness. The heathery slopes stretched, fold on fold, to the horizon. There was no single spectacular feature, no soaring mountain against the skyline, for the eye to focus on. Such landscapes have an enigmatic quality, a mystery which sometimes proves more challenging to the imagination than the more spectacular scenic beauty which is easier to define.

It was an elemental landscape. Its foundation was the millstone grit whose presence was evident in grey rocks and crags and in the heather, bracken and hardy grasses which were its natural covering. There were marshes and bogs among the heather, and dark rivulets which the rains had channelled in the peat. There were becks in the deep valleys hidden in the folds of the moors, whose mellow flow became a torrent when they were swollen by winter rain and melting snow. The wind was a constant presence, except in halcyon summer days, chasing the clouds so that there was an ever-varying play of light and shade on the hilly slopes, twisting the sparse trees, whistling through the heath or rising to the fierce blasts of the autumn and winter gales. The sun could shine warmly on the moors, but the sultry heat might be the precursor of sombre or copper-coloured skies, of clouds charged with electricity, the roll of thunder and the vivid flashing of lightning.

This moor country to which they had come was, as the children discovered, a place of "wonders beyond the counting, surprises beyond the telling". They had only to follow the lane at the back of their home which led to the mounting swell of the heath, and Haworth village vanished from their sight. The valley of the Worth lay on their right and for a time they were accompanied in their walk by the presence of fields. But soon the fields began to fall away as they moved on to the open moor. They found themselves in a land of wide spaces, of heather and bilberry clumps, of black-faced sheep, a place where the larks sang and the lapwings called. Only an occasional farm building spoke of the presence of man.

This was but the prelude to further discoveries. It cannot have been long before they descended the sloping path which led to that pleasant spot in the Sladen Valley which they christened "The Meeting of the Waters", the "oasis of emerald-green turf, broken here and there by small clear springs" where they were to spend many hours. A boulder of millstone grit, shaped rather like a chair, did duty for a seat, and close at hand the water cascaded over the rocks from the higher level of the moor to join with the beck which ran through the valley. But they had not yet reached the heart of the moor. From the further side of the sheltered dell a rougher path led upwards to the wilder region where the remote farmstead of Top Withens dominated immense vistas. Yet even the country surrounding Top Withens was less awe-inspiring than the stern grandeur of the moors stretching towards the Ponden Valley. Here were dark cliffs and, at the head of the clough, the towering crag of millstone grit known as Ponden Kirk.

There were times, however, when the moors were hidden by a shroud of mist or rain or when, in winter, they were impassable because of snow and ice. At such times the young Brontës must have been thankful for the sheltering walls and the cheerful fires of the parsonage. It was round the kitchen fire that their evenings were chiefly spent and, fortunately for them, the presiding genius of the kitchen was Tabitha Aykroyd – the faithful servant

Tabby – a woman who possessed all the sterling qualities which Mr Brontë admired in countryfolk, and who was steeped in the lore of the countryside.

Tabitha Aykroyd, a widow of fifty-three when she came as servant to the parsonage, had relatives and friends in Haworth, though she had been away from it for some time, and had been assisting at a farm immediately before she entered the service of the Brontës. Forthright and sharp-tongued on occasion, she was also warm-hearted and generous, and found time to mother the children as well as dealing with the work of the household. When she arrived in 1825 only Branwell and Anne were at home, the others having been sent to the newly founded and highly recommended Clergy Daughters' School at Cowan Bridge. But in the course of the spring the two eldest, Maria and Elizabeth, were brought home ill and died of tuberculosis within a few weeks of each other. Charlotte and Emily were fetched in haste by their father during the same spring and brought back to the parsonage. One can understand the appeal that the four remaining children, the eldest not yet ten, made to Tabby's sympathies. She saw to it that their material needs were catered for, but she did more for them than that. Her kitchen fireside became a place of comfort and entertainment where they could hear stories of the village and the countryside, and the fact that these stories were told in dialect increased their fascination for her youthful audience.

Since Tabby could look back over half a century, her tales had something of the quality of folklore. She could recall the days when there were no mills in the valley at Haworth, and claimed to have known people who had seen "fairishes" by the beck-side on moonlight nights. She knew local legends like those of the phantom Guytrash, the ghostly Dog who was one of the best-known figures among the moorland superstitions, and could tell of the wild doings of the owners of the ancestral homes in remote upland districts. Though no longer young, she was still able to accompany the children on their walks. In her they had a natural link with the life of a moorland village, past and present.

Their aunt Elizabeth Branwell, already middle-aged when she left her home in distant Cornwall to come to Yorkshire, was obviously unable to fulfil such a function, but her influence was felt in other ways. Skilled in all the household arts, she organised the domestic life of the parsonage and trained her nieces in "a

perfect knowledge of all kinds of household work". But the
routine of the household left scope for the children's own activities. When they had learned their lessons, for which their father
and their aunt were responsible, they did not lack for possibilities of entertainment in their leisure hours.

They enjoyed the freedom of the kitchen, unless Tabby was
too busy for their company. There were vaulted cellars beneath
the parsonage, and a yard behind it with a dovecot. The peat
store once housed two tame geese and feathered guests also
included, at different times, a pheasant, a wild goose and a hawk
rescued from its abandoned nest on the moors. A permanent
inhabitant was the house-dog, first "Grasper" and then his
successor the faithful "Keeper". There was the inevitable spoiled
cat. The companionship of animals was an essential part of the
Brontës' daily life, if it did not add to the pleasure of Miss
Branwell's. In front of the house was a small garden with bushes
of elder and lilac and a square plot of grass. Above all, behind it
was the path that led to the moors.

The children's main resource, when they were not on the
moors, was reading. Like their father they were compulsive
readers, and the small upstairs room over the hall, where Charlotte and Emily slept, became known in the day as "the children's study". For them books opened doors into new worlds,
and helped to inspire the games from which their childhood
writings developed, while later they were to leave lasting traces
in their mature works. What books they read is a question which
has often been discussed.[16] Clearly they enjoyed more liberty of
choice than the heroine of *The Maid of Killarney*, whose father
strictly censored his daughter's reading. To Mr Brontë's credit
be it said that his children had free access to the books which
made up his own small library, and these included the works of
Byron. He was also a member of the Keighley Mechanics'
Institute Library, founded in 1825, and his family often walked
the four miles to Keighley with this as their objective.[17] There
was in addition an extensive private collection to which they had
access, that of the Heatons of Ponden House. Robert Heaton was
one of the Haworth Church trustees. His family library included
travels, essays and much poetry and drama, predominantly of
the eighteenth century, as well as technical works. The young
Brontës were able to keep in touch with contemporary writing
through the medium of *Blackwood's Magazine*, a constant source

of interest and pleasure throughout the whole of their childhood and youth. As children of an evangelical parson they were familiar with the Bible from their earliest days, and also with *The Pilgrim's Progress*. Inevitably Shakespeare and Milton were part of their literary background. But above all they responded to the attraction of the leading writers of their own century, the century whose first decades saw the richest creative period of English Romanticism.

This era of high achievement was the result of evolution rather than revolution. The Preface written by Wordsworth for the 1800 edition of the *Lyrical Ballads* was not, like Hugo's Preface of *Hernani*, a declaration of war. Its aim was to forestall criticism rather than to impose a new technique. Nevertheless, the poems, with their significant Preface, represent one of the foundations of the Romantic school. Nature, and the countryman, then acquired an importance, never afterwards to be lost, as one of the richest sources of inspiration for the modern writer. This was of vital significance at a time when an age of growing industrialism was succeeding an age of predominant rationalism. It offered an outlet to those writers who, however much they might differ in temperament, were united by their hatred of the artificial and their belief that the senses and the imagination, no less than the reason, had their place in art, as in life. It was in part the example given by the Lakeland poets in returning to "a more simple and natural style of poetry" which inspired Sir Walter Scott to write his first verse romance, *The Lay of the Last Minstrel*. But it was still more the scenic beauty, the history and the legend of his own native country, where so much that was primitive still survived. His subsequent verse romances and the first and Scottish group of the Waverley novels had a similar source. If he is now considered by many as much an Augustan as a Romantic, for his contemporaries, and for Europe at large, he was supremely "the Wizard of the North". Similarly it was the unspoilt beauty of the landscapes he saw on his travels through Europe, and the freedom he enjoyed as a traveller, which were the inspiration for the first cantos of Byron's *Childe Harold*. Though he is now thought of chiefly as the poet of *Don Juan*, it was those cantos which made him famous overnight in the England of the early nineteenth century. For the young Brontës, these three were the great masters of the Romantic literature of their own time, those who had most to offer because they themselves had learnt most from nature before they attempted to realise an art of which it was the foundation.

Of these three, their earliest favourite was Scott. In 1828 his *Tales of a Grandfather* were a New Year's gift to her nephew and nieces from Miss Branwell. They were intended for his grandson, Johnny Lockhart, and that they appealed to the young Brontës is evident from Emily's choice of "Walter Scott, Mr. Lockhart, Johnny Lockhart" as the leading inhabitants of her imaginary island in the children's play of "The Islanders". Scott's verse romances and his Waverley novels, of which there was a complete set in the library at Keighley, had no more loyal admirers than at Haworth parsonage. For them he was both novelist and poet. Charlotte, at eighteen, writing to her school-friend Ellen Nussey, after a second and this time a happy experience of boarding-school at Roe Head, can still praise "Scott's sweet, wild, romantic poetry" in the same letter in which she says: "For fiction, read Scott alone; all novels after his are worthless."[18]

Scott's descriptions of nature were an integral part of his verse. As a young man he had travelled on foot through the Border country, to which his own clan belonged, collecting by word of mouth the ballads which gave him the material for his *Border Minstrelsy*. He knew the scenes of which he wrote, the lochs, the glens, the wild passes, the hillside caves. For the young Brontës such landscapes offered affinities with their own moorland surroundings;

> Land of brown heath and shaggy wood,
> Land of the mountain and the flood . . .

Descriptions of wild and rugged scenery remained an essential characteristic of his art when he turned to the writing of novels. The grandeur of the Highlands is the background to *Waverley*; the wildness of the Macgregor country is at the heart of *Rob Roy*, and the bleak expanse of Mucklestane Moor a fitting introduction to *The Black Dwarf*.

In no case, however, is the role of landscape in Scott purely descriptive; it is also the theatre of the action. The moors and lochs, the precipitous hillsides and impenetrable thickets are the stage for the forays and chases, the ambushes and conflicts which are part of the existence of his mountaineers. The excitement and drama of such action had a strong attraction for the young Brontës, and the greater extent and variety of the Scottish landscape offered wider scope for its development.

But it was not only a congenial setting and dramatic action which they found in the work of Scott; it was the painting of a whole way of life which had a natural appeal for them. The wild, primitive existence of his Highlanders and his Borderers offered striking affinities with the tales they had heard of the wild doings of bygone generations of yeomen farmers on their own Yorkshire moors. At the heart of such a primitive society was the same unremitting struggle for existence in a stern environment.

One of the concomitants of such a world was the important place given to animals, another attraction for the Brontës. Animals were a necessary part of the community and as such had their own status. In *The Lady of the Lake* Douglas avenges a blow to his dog as he would an insult to a friend. Hunting was inevitably part of such a primitive existence, but the stag is shown by Scott less as a quarry than as a gallant foe. It is no mere figure of speech on his part when, in the same poem, he compares the noble animal alerted by the noise of the distant hunt to the

. . . Chief who hears his warder call,
"To arms! the foemen storm the wall."

The analogy is clearer still in memorable episodes of the Waverley novels. The affinity between a wild and free creature at bay and the plight of the dispossessed chief of an ancient race is even more powerfully implied by the last stand of the hunted stag in *The Bride of Lammermoor*, "his stately head bent down . . . his eyes strained betwixt rage and terror", still formidable enough to be "an object of intimidation to his pursuers" moments before his inevitable end.

Of particular interest is the unusual degree of compassion for animals felt by Ellieslaw, the misanthropist who is the central character in *The Black Dwarf*. While watching a Border thief ruthlessly mastering his rearing horse, he bitterly reflects: "That villain . . . has thews and sinews, limbs, strength and activity enough, to compel a nobler animal than himself to carry him to the place where he is to perpetrate his wickedness."[19] The dwarf's compassion for animals is a salient feature of his character. The verse heading to chapter three of *The Black Dwarf* comes from "The Cout of Keeldar", a ballad by Scott's friend John Leyden, based on "the characteristic detestation of the chase" felt by that order of fairies said to appear among the Border wilds in the form of dwarfs.[20] They consider the wild animals as their subjects and never fail to avenge their destruction. It is "The Cout of Keeldar" which, with Scott's poem "The Death of Keeldar", is thought to have suggested the unusual surname of Charlotte Brontë's Shirley,[21] a character modelled partly on recollections of her sister Emily, and the derivation seems perfectly consistent with Emily's known love of the creatures of the moors.

Inseparable from a primitive culture, as Scott well knew, is a strong belief in the supernatural. This, too, struck a responsive chord in the young Brontës, who had listened to Tabby's tales and who grew up in a milieu still permeated with folklore. The apparitions and omens of local legend had their counterparts in the world of Scott's peasants and mountaineers. *The Lay of the last Minstrel* had its origin, according to Scott's introduction, in the tale of Gilpin Horner, a malicious goblin who suddenly appeared at a farm house in the Border country and remained there till recalled by the evil spirit to whom he owed allegiance.[22] In the Waverley novels the supernatural remains part of the climate in which the characters live. Fergus Mac-Ivor believes that he sees the Bodach Glas, or grey spectre, always a portent of death to his family, on the eve of his capture and on the night before his execution. Of *The Bride of Lammermoor* Scott himself said that it could not be called a Scottish tale unless it showed a tinge of Scottish superstition. It may be added that Scott's love of folklore was shared by one of *Blackwood's* leading contributors, James Hogg. The author of "Kilmeny" contributed a series of articles on "Fairies, Devils and Witches" to the young Brontës' favourite periodical in 1828.[23] Charlotte referred to him admiringly as "a man of most extraordinary genius, a Scottish shepherd", and he must have helped to confirm their interest in the realm of gramarye.

An indispensable factor in Scott's evocation of a more primitive civilisation was his use of dialect. When he wrote in verse, he respected the eighteeth-century requirements for poetic diction, but with *Waverley* he introduced dialect where he judged it appropriate, and he continued to do so with consummate mastery throughout the Scottish novels. To readers as used to the vernacular as the Brontës, eager auditors of Tabby's stories in a Yorkshire kitchen, this was a further guarantee of the authenticity of his peasants, farmers and family servants, never more convincing than when arguing, gossiping or telling the tales of their countryside.

But Scott's total achievement was not only to reveal the wild beauty of his country and the stern and often heroic existence of clansmen and peasants, expressed in their own forceful idiom: he was also the creator of the historical novel. His verse romances were set in a past already remote, his Scottish novels in a more recent past, where the currents of change were already becoming clearly perceptible. Scott shows folk and peasant culture, and Jacobite allegiance, with fidelity and affection, but he shows them in perspective and in relation to evolving civilisation. This was not the least valuable part of his legacy to the Brontës.

It was indeed fortunate for them, as future writers, that their youth should coincide with the still continuing popularity of a master so congenial and with so much to offer them. Inevitably his impact was at once evident in their juvenilia. But his example was also to bear fruit in the works of their maturity, and they made no secret of their lasting admiration. Jane Eyre describes the pleasure of reading *Marmion*, "one of those genuine productions so often vouchsafed to the fortunate public of those days – the golden age of modern literature".[24] It is also the book given by Gilbert Markham to Helen Graham – who has expressed the wish to read it – in Anne Brontë's *Tenant of Wildfell Hall*.

As eloquent as these direct tributes are the quotations from Scott's verse romances which find their way into the Brontë novels. Jane Eyre quotes directly from the description of "Norham's castled steep" which opens the first canto of *Marmion*, while phrases from *The Lay of the last Minstrel* occur in the course of her narrative.[25] There are echoes from the same works in *Shirley*.[26] Scott is also the author of "the old Scotch ballad" which Frances Henri recites to herself in *The Professor*.[27] In *Wuthering Heights* it is an authentic ballad, translated from the Danish and grimly appropriate in the circumstances, "The Ghaist's Warning", which Nelly Dean starts to hum as she rocks her orphan nursling to sleep:

"It was far in the night, and the bairnies grat,
The mither beneath the mools heard that"

But Emily Brontë owed her knowledge of it to Scott, who quotes
it in full in his notes to *The Lady of the Lake*.[28]

Scott's affinity with the ballad obviously had a strong attraction for the Brontës, and echoes of his essays in this genre blend
in their own verse with those of the Border balladists. Charlotte
was less successful than her sisters in catching the spontaneity of
the ballad tone, though she admired it and valued the kindred
qualities in the songs of Burns. But Anne, in early poems like
"The Parting", is close to the ballad or its adaptation by Scott.
It is Emily, however, who is closest to Scott, and to his *Minstrelsy
of the Scottish Border*. Her most sustained narrative in this style,
"Douglas's Ride", has been thought by John Hewish to stem
from the scene in *Old Mortality* where the Covenanter Balfour,
hiding in the Black Linn, hurls a tree bridge into the chasm
which safeguards his place of refuge.[29]

The mature art of Scott in the Waverley novels left less
obvious traces in the work of the Brontës than his verse, as far as
direct quotation is concerned. None the less there are textual
echoes. When Rochester tells Jane Eyre, who sees Thornfield as
a splendid mansion, that "the glamour of inexperience" is over
her eyes and she sees it through a charmed medium, he is using a
dialect word introduced by Scott, and in its original sense.[30]
Sometimes textual resemblances are sufficiently striking to warrant the supposition that a work of Scott was one of the sources
of a Brontë novel. Florence Dry drew attention to the similarities
of nomenclature in *The Black Dwarf* and *Wuthering Heights*, and to
textual similarities between the dwarf's bitter outbursts and
Heathcliff's invective which are too close to be accidental.[31]

Parallels exist, too, as she argued, between incidents and traits
of character in the two novels. It is possible, however, to push
such parallels of detail too far. More significant for the relationship between Scott and the Brontës are their choice of subject
and method of treatment as a whole. In her important study of
Wuthering Heights Mrs Leavis showed that Emily's novel, set in
the latter part of the eighteenth century, depends for its structure
on the contrast between a primitive and a more sophisticated
way of life, and that such a contrast had already provided the
main theme in *The Black Dwarf*, set at the beginning of the

eighteenth century, where the existence of the rough Border farmers is compared with that of a refined but corrupt upper class. In the opinion of Mrs Leavis Scott's influence was seminal here:

> The inspiration for this structure . . . comes from observation . . . In the Brontës' youth and county the old order visibly survived. But the clue to making such perceptions and sympathies into a novel was found, I suspect, in Scott, whose novels and poetry were immensely admired by Charlotte and Emily. His own sympathies were with the wild rough Border farmers . . . Emily and Charlotte were genuinely attached to their moorland country, but Scott's example was what made it usable for them as literature and gave it rich associations . . .[32]

Emily's novel of moorland life is the most forceful representation of the contrast between the primitive and the sophisticated in the Brontë works. It is natural that it should also be the one where, as with Scott, folk superstitions are closely interwoven with daily life and where dialect is used most frequently and most effectively. But Charlotte too is concerned with a similar opposition between the natural and the sophisticated, though she presents it with more ambivalence. Anne Brontë presents a less romantic contrast between the two ways of life than either of her sisters, but *The Tenant of Wildfell Hall* depends none the less, for much of its effect, on such an opposition.

Inevitably a primitive background breeds characters with salient traits in common, even though they may differ widely as individuals. Here again it is the general affinities with Scott, rather than resemblances of detail, which are most significant. To claim, as Florence Dry does, that the servant Ellen Dean in *Wuthering Heights* has her origin in Jeanie Deans, of *The Heart of Midlothian*, is to do less than justice to Emily's powers of observation. She is much more likely to have had her origin in Tabby Aykroyd. But Scott had shown just how resourceful and courageous an intelligent countrywoman, bred to hard work and heavy responsibility from early childhood, can be, and it is probable that Emily profited from his masterly delineation, though Ellen Dean retains none the less her own very distinct individuality. When she portrayed the mistress rather than the maid, Emily was less able to find a prototype in her immediate

environment. Winifred Gérin has remarked how much her Gondal heroines owed to "the inspiriting example of Diana Vernon,
Flora MacIvor, and the others, close to hand". Something of the
imperiousness of Scott's Jacobite heroines survives, too, in the
two youthful Catherines. It survives also in the Diana Rivers of
Jane Eyre and in the masterful Shirley, while Helen Huntingdon,
who takes her mother's name of Graham when she escapes to
Wildfell Hall, has some affinity with the proud and tragic Flora
MacIvor.

It was Scott himself who, with his customary good humour,
acknowledged that, in turning from verse romance to the novel,
he was influenced by the appearance, in the former field, of "a
mighty and unexpected rival", Lord Byron. If Scott was loved
by the Brontës from childhood onwards, Byron dazzled their
adolescence, and was to exert an influence no less lasting on the
development of their genius. As early as 1829 Charlotte's juvenilia showed the repercussions of a first reading of *Childe Harold*.
The 1833 edition of the poet's works, with engravings by Finden,
was on their father's bookshelves. In 1834, counselling Ellen
Nussey on her reading, Charlotte advises her to read Byron
freely, with the exception of *Don Juan* and possibly *Cain* –
"though the latter is a magnificent poem" – and, where biography is concerned, includes Moore's *Life of Byron*. She does not
hesitate to place him on a level with Shakespeare: "Both these
were great men, and their works are like themselves."

Childe Harold's Pilgrimage, the work that first made its author
famous, was written "for the most part, amidst the scenes which
it attempts to describe".[33] The first two cantos delighted a public
debarred by war from touring the Continent. Brilliant glimpses
of Portugal and Spain were succeeded by descriptions of Byron's
Albanian journey and his stay in Greece. In the last two cantos,
written after his final departure from England, the pilgrimage
was continued along the Rhine and through the marvels of
Alpine scenery to reach its final stage in Italy. If the Waverley
novels brought Scotland to Haworth parsonage, Byron's poetry
brought all Europe to dazzle the imagination of the young
Brontës with a kaleidoscope of more vivid and more varied
colours.

It also evoked for them "the clime of the East . . . the land of
the Sun". Byron's travels in the Levant brought him into touch
with the Orient, which had fascinated him ever since, as a child,

he had been an avid reader of the *Arabian Nights*, of histories of the Turks and travel books about the East. *The Arabian Nights* had also been one of the major delights of the Brontës' childhood and tinged their juvenilia with exotic colours. For Byron the dream had become a reality:

> Childe Harold saw, like meteors in the sky,
> The glittering minarets of Tepalen . . .

In the course of his travels through the Mediterranean lands, he came to know something of their inhabitants. He described his mode of living as "To-day in a palace, to-morrow in a cow-house – this day with the Pacha, the next with a shepherd".[34] He thus saw more of the conditions of primitive life than most of the English aristocrats who toured Europe. The variety of the mountain races at the court of Ali Pacha fascinated him, and he was struck by the resemblance in "dress, figure and manner of living" between the white-skirted Albanese and the Highlanders of Scotland, his mother's country, where his early childhood had been spent. But he did not know them intimately, as Scott knew his Highlanders and Borderers. Childe Harold watches with interest the wild dancing of the Suliotes round their open fire, but his attitude is very much that of the patrician bystander:

> Childe Harold at a little distance stood
> And view'd, but not displeased, the revelrie,
> Nor hated harmless mirth, however rude . . .[35]

Whatever scene he surveys, Byron interprets it in fact through the medium of his own personality. He appreciates, if with some condescension, the wild vigour of the Suliotes because it strikes a kindred chord in his own nature. In a landscape he looks for qualities that correspond to the dominant need of his own temperament for force, for splendour, for movement:

> Where rose the mountains, there to him were friends;
> Where roll'd the ocean, thereon was his home;
> Where a blue sky, and glowing clime, extends,
> He had the passion and the power to roam;
> The desert, forest, cavern, breaker's foam,
> Were unto him companionship; they spake
> A mutual language . . .[36]

But in the dialogue with the elements, his is the most articulate voice. Even when, in the third canto of *Childe Harold*, he tries to forget his personal dilemma by an attempted merging with nature, one cannot but be aware how perfectly the Alpine landscape reflects the tumultuous passions of his own heart, above all when the lightnings and thunders of not one but many storms flash and reverberate among the mountains:

> . . . Most glorious night!
> Thou wert not sent for slumber! let me be
> A sharer in thy fierce and far delight, –
> A portion of the tempest and of thee![37]

The personal colouring of Byron's descriptions was recognised by Scott, who rarely sought to draw attention to himself in his own. To the youthful imagination of the Brontës it opened up new possibilities of self-expression at the very time when adolescence made this most desirable. Their instinctive response to the wildness of their surroundings and the play of the elements acquired thus a new significance.

Byron's affinity with nature, and especially with its most tempestuous moods, was closely interwoven with the most fundamental passion of his own nature – the passion for liberty. The glories of Alpine scenery were enhanced for him by the freedom of the Swiss mountaineers. In Greece, on the other hand, he was haunted by the contrast between her heroic past and her present subjection under Turkish rule, and could not celebrate the beauty of country and climate without a deep sense of departed glory:

> Apollo still thy long, long summer gilds,
> Still in his beam Mendeli's marbles glare;
> Art, Glory, Freedom fail, but Nature still is fair.[38]

This love of liberty found an instant response in the Brontës, accustomed to the freedom of the moors, and proud of the freedom enjoyed by their own country.

It was clearly a more complex approach to nature than that of Scott that Byron offered. Before Childe Harold sought the "pathless woods" and the "lonely shore", he was, on his own admission, prematurely wearied by a life of reckless indulgence and deeply disillusioned, like many of his generation, by the situation of Europe in the epoch succeeding the French Revolution. To the melancholy stemming from these sources was added, in the later cantos, the violence of the emotional upheaval which followed the break-up of his marriage and his self-exile. The overtones of melancholy in many of his descriptions did not come from his contact with nature. But there was in him an immense resilience which responded to nature's most tempestuous moods, and delighted in its splendour and its ceaseless movement.

It was not only, though primarily, through his poetry that the Brontës knew the landscapes of Byron. In 1833 Thomas Moore's *Life of Byron* was acquired by the library of the Keighley Mechanics' Institute, and the engravings by Finden included a number of the scenes mentioned in *Childe Harold's Pilgrimage*. The interest they had for the parsonage family is shown by the fact that when, a year later, the Leeds artist William Robinson came to Haworth, at their father's request, to give them drawing lessons, these were among the models they chose to copy.[39]

More significant, however, for these eager readers than any pictorial representation was the portrait offered by Moore's life of the poet himself. It was to a large extent a self-portrait, based on his incomparable letters and journals. In this way they came to know his complex personality more intimately than they could possibly have done otherwise. They learnt thus, from his own account, how much nature had meant to him, particularly in its most grandiose aspects. It was from his early childhood in Scotland, where he came to love the sight of Loch-na-gar, that Byron himself dated his fondness for mountainous countries. In Switzerland he saw at first hand the heights he celebrated in *Childe Harold*, and that were to be the setting of *Manfred*. In the mountains he was always conscious of exhilaration, whatever the physical hazards. But even in these surroundings he could not forget his personal tragedy, and a scene of natural desolation became instantly the mirror of his own experiences: "*Passed whole woods of withered pines, all withered*; trunks stripped and barkless, branches lifeless; done by a single winter, – their appearance reminded me of me and my family."[40]

It was to be expected that such a lover of nature should have a fondness for animals. This characteristic, always one particularly congenial to the Brontës, emerges clearly both from his poems and from Moore's *Life*. His admiration of wild, untamed

creatures, and his sympathy for them when they are victimised
by man, are evident in such passages as the description of the
bull fight in *Childe Harold* or of the young, desert-born horse in
Mazeppa, as much a victim of tyranny as the captive bound on
his back. The same wildness is admired by Manfred in the eagle
he sees soaring above him in the Alps. So necessary was the
companionship of animals to him in general that a selection of
them always shared his home, wherever that might be. The
similarity between the laconic references to them in his journals
and Emily Brontë's diary entries on the same subject have been
noted more than once.[41] Her first diary-paper begins: "I fed
Rainbow, Diamond Snowflake Jasper pheasant (alias) . . .".
Typical of Byron's references is an extract from his account of a
wet evening in Ravenna: ". . . played with my mastiff – gave him
his supper. . . . The crow is lame of a leg – wonder how it
happened – some fool trod upon his toe, I suppose. The falcon
pretty brisk – the cats large and noisy – the monkeys I have not
looked to since the cold weather, as they suffer from being
brought up."[42] But his chief favourites were his dogs and, among
them, none was so much loved as the Newfoundland Boatswain,
the faithful friend of his youth, who was tragically seized by a fit
of madness and died at Newstead before his master's eyes. He
never forgot Boatswain, "the dearest and, alas! the maddest of
dogs."

The freedom which the Byronic hero found in nature he
demanded also in his personal life. It included freedom of feeling
and, above all, freedom to love where he chose. His exaltation of
passionate love was, for temperaments as ardent as those of the
young Brontës, an essential part of his attraction. Here his verse
tales had more to offer than *Childe Harold's Pilgrimage*, for in them
it is love that motivates the action. The natural setting has still,
however, an important part to play. Most frequently the destiny
of the lovers is played out against a southern background,
cypress groves beside the Hellespont or the cliffs of a Greek
island.

For the Brontës, as for most of their generation, it was Byron's
overtly romantic works that had the strongest appeal. They read
Don Juan, in spite of Charlotte's cautionary advice to Ellen
Nussey, and she herself appreciated his satirical vein. But it was
no doubt the episode of Juan and Haidée which principally

appealed to them, where nature and passionate feeling are predominant, though interwoven with satire and a deeper because a more resigned disillusionment. Haidée, like Zuleika at Abydos, is "Nature's bride" and "Passion's child" and, like her, dies of grief when her lover is torn from her. Byron was in fact both "the pilgrim of Eternity" and the disillusioned man of the world that Juan finally becomes. Moore's *Life* revealed to the Brontës the development of his complex character, and one cannot wonder at the great and lasting influence he exercised on them, an influence due both to his work and to the magnetic personality of which it was the reflection.

Byron's influence, however, made itself felt in a more diffused manner than that of Scott. Direct allusions are fewer, though none the less significant. In *The Professor* one of the pupils at the pensionnat is described as possessing the Latin type of beauty, at once classic and sensual, which Byron would have admired. Phrases from *Childe Harold* and *Parisina* are quoted in *Jane Eyre*,[43] from *Childe Harold* and *The Giaour* in *Shirley*,[44] and from the "Stanzas to Augusta" in *Agnes Grey*.[45] In *Wuthering Heights* there is an evident resemblance between the agonised appeals of Heathcliff to the dead Catherine and Manfred's supplication to the phantom of Astarte.[46] There is also a link with Byron's *Ode to Napoleon Buonaparte* in the image employed by Catherine when she says that those who attempt to separate her from Heathcliff will suffer "the fate of Milo".[47] In his Journal, quoted in Moore's *Life*, Byron had already used this mythological allusion as a metaphor for Napoleon's plight at the time of his abdication: "Like Milo, he would rend the oak; but it closed again, wedged his hands, and now the beasts – lion, bear, down to the dirtiest jackal – may all tear him."[48]

More significant than any specific allusion, however, is the Byronic colouring in the delineation of the heroes of the two most romantic of the Brontë novels, *Jane Eyre* and *Wuthering Heights*. Rochester owes much to the aspect of Byron which had visibly attracted Charlotte most in her juvenilia, the travelled man of the world who is at the same time a passionate lover. In the charades at Thornfield he seems to fit naturally into an exotic setting: "His dark eyes and swarth skin and Paynim features suited the costume exactly; he looked the very model of an eastern emir, an agent or a victim of the bowstring." Heathcliff also carries on the Byronic tradition, but in a different manner. He is nearer to the outlaws of the verse tales, and even to the Byron of so intimately personal a poem as *The Dream*, which has been suggested as one of the possible sources of *Wuthering Heights*.[19] When separated from Catherine he becomes a rebel, as enigmatic as Lara, as implacable in revenge as the Giaour, as doomed as the Corsair after the death of Medora. But he does not forsake Wuthering Heights as the Corsair did his island, because he is convinced that to leave the farm on the moors would be to renounce all possibility of that reunion with her spirit which has become the goal of his blighted existence.

It is a measure of the intrinsically poetic character of the Brontë novels that a poet should have such a far-reaching influence on them. Only Anne does not seem, as a novelist, to have felt it to the same extent as her sisters. Where their actual verse is concerned, the impact of Byron is also evident, though in varying degrees. Charlotte, a competent versifier from an early age, responded instinctively to his rhetoric, as well as to his exoticism, in her early poems. In her later ones, Byronic echoes are less persistent than in her novels. Anne is indebted to his exoticism in an early poem "Alexander and Zenobia", where the action begins in Arabia's "distant land". She comes nearest to Byron, however, in the vitality and excitement of one of the later poems, "Song", where the spokesman, formerly a "wandering Outlaw" but now outlawed no longer, looks back with intense regret to the freedom of his former life.

But it is in the poetry of Emily that the Byronic influence is most marked. Sometimes she shows exotic landscapes, characterised by such features as "Palm trees and cedars towering high". But she prefers the northern scene and, though her chief model for this is her native moorland, she adds characteristics reminiscent of Byron, as also of Scott: loftier mountains, broad lakes with rocky shores and sometimes the near presence of the sea. She uses far less detail than Byron in painting landscape, but at times a verbal resemblance suggests her intimate knowledge of his poetry. Helen Brown points out, among other examples, how the line

The blue ice curdling on the stream

recalls Byron's

The blue flames curdle o'er the hearth[50]

A deeper affinity is shown in the relationship between the natural scene and the emotions of the writer. In a poem written when she was eighteen she combines the theme of nature's freedom and man's desire for freedom in stanzas whose fullness and vigour recall Byron, though the tone is already unmistakably her own:

High waving heather, 'neath stormy blasts bending,
Midnight and moonlight and bright shining stars;
Darkness and glory rejoicingly blending,
Earth rising to heaven and heaven descending,
Man's spirit away from its drear dungeon sending,
Bursting the fetters and breaking the bars.[51]

The example of Byron, like that of Scott, did much to encourage the literary vocation of the Brontës, above all by showing how that contact with nature which was a vital part of their own experience was a potential source of inspiration, full of rich and varied possibilities. It was, however, the poet Wordsworth, familiar to them since their childhood, whose allegiance to nature was most complete and in whose work the Romantic concept of nature was most fully realised. Nearly twenty years older than Byron, but a contemporary of Scott, he gained recognition as a poet earlier than the author of *The Lay of the Last Minstrel*, though he never enjoyed the same meteoric rise to fame as Scott with the Waverley novels. His works had an honoured place in Haworth parsonage, and must have been particularly congenial to Mr. Brontë, who would find in many of the *Lyrical Ballads* the simplicity of language he had himself tried to achieve in his *Cottage Poems*, and the power to give full expression to that admiration of nature and the countryman which he himself so deeply felt.

Such poems must have seemed to him especially suited to appeal to the imagination and interests of his children, and they came increasingly to appreciate him. He is one of the poets recommended by Charlotte when, in 1834, she writes to advise Ellen Nussey on her reading. It was to Wordsworth himself that her brother Branwell wrote, two years later, asking for advice on the possibility of a literary career for himself. The terms he uses, though characteristically inflated, show that at the parsonage Wordsworth's importance was recognised both as poet and thinker:

> "Do pardon me, sir, that I have ventured to come before one whose works I have most loved in our literature and who most has been with me a divinity of the mind . . . I must come before one from whose sentence there is no appeal; and such a one is he who has developed the theory of poetry as well as its practice, and both in such a way as to claim a place in the memory of a thousand years to come."[52]

The sample of his verse which Branwell enclosed was, in his own words, "the description of an imaginative child", a theme he no doubt hoped would appeal to the author of the Ode, "Intimations of Immortality from Recollections of Early Childhood". Unfortunately neither the style of his letter nor his verse pleased Wordsworth, who returned no answer. His sisters may not have been surprised at this result, if they were aware of Branwell's remark to the ageing poet that the field must be open for new talent "in this day, when there is not a *writing* poet worth a sixpence". Certainly their own interest in Wordsworth was an enduring one. When Charlotte found a publisher for the poems of her sisters and herself in 1846, it was her express wish that the format of the book should resemble that of "Moxon's last edition of Wordsworth", which had appeared the previous year.

There was indeed much in Wordsworth to appeal to the Brontës. He found his chief inspiration in his native region, and the Lake District, like Scott's Border country, had a good deal in common with their own moors and hills. He could appreciate the grandeur of the landscapes he saw on the Continent, but, like Scott and unlike Byron, found that no landscapes satisfied him like those familiar to him since childhood. The Lakeland was and remained his true home, and the few years he spent away from it only intensified his admiration of its intrinsic beauty.

His knowledge of the country went hand in hand with a natural understanding of its inhabitants. No one was more keenly alive than he to the value and dignity of the simple life. In the Preface to *Lyrical Ballads* he affirmed his conscious belief that, in "low and rustic life", the "essential passions of the heart" had a better soil in which to mature, and the "elementary feelings" existed in a state of greater simplicity and could thus be more accurately contemplated. In the poems the place of honour is given to characters like an ageing shepherd, a "little cottage girl", an old Cumberland beggar. They were followed in later poems by similar figures, a leech-gatherer, a widow living on alone in her ruined cottage, the pedlar who is "the Sage" of *The Excursion*. But Wordsworth's pastorals are never sentimentalised. Life can be as hard for his country-dwellers as for Scott's clansmen, though the threat to their survival does not come from the feuds of rival chieftains but from factors in which they often have no personal involvement: the calamities which war brings in its train, the exploitation of the poor by the rich, the system of parish relief which penalised the man who retained any property of his own, however small. Wordsworth understood the sturdy independence of his countrymen and knew what it meant for them when, as in "The Female Vagrant", they were torn from an existence rooted in their native soil.

In such an environment freedom was in the air which the poet breathed from childhood, and he grew up believing in it as a necessity for human growth and dignity. None of the Romantics cared for freedom more deeply than he, and when, as a young man, he visited revolutionary France, he sympathised ardently with a cause where liberty was associated, as in his native dales, with equality and fraternity. Only when the Jacobin excesses convinced him of its dangers did he become disillusioned with the revolutionary cause in France, though never with the ideal of liberty in itself. When the emergence of Bonapartism was followed by the despotism of the Empire, his sympathies were with England in her struggle against Napoleon. The "Sonnets on Liberty", which struck a responsive chord in the Brontës, are a protest against tyranny in all its forms.

There is no doubt that Wordsworth's disillusionment with the aftermath of the French Revolution played a decisive part in the reorientation of his genius from political preoccupations to that all-embracing love of nature which had characterised his childhood and youth and inspired his first poems. After an intermediate stage when he sought satisfaction in the rationalism of Godwin, he returned, helped by the friendship of Coleridge and the companionship of his sister Dorothy, to the true source of his inspiration.

Nature for him is clearly a vaster conception than for either

Scott or Byron. It implies nothing less than the universe, but there is a bond between the universe and the mind of man. They are indeed interdependent, and it is this reciprocity which makes it possible for him to blend, in his descriptions, subject and object, imagination and sense impressions. They are not, as often with Scott, primarily a background to the action. Nor does he, like Byron, allow his feelings to determine the tonality of the scene. The nature he evokes is a reality which can be clearly sensed, but one senses as keenly the imaginative response of the poet to the natural phenomena:

> . . . Once again
> Do I behold these steep and lofty cliffs,
> That on a wild secluded scene impress
> Thoughts of more deep seclusion; and connect
> The landscape with the quiet of the sky.[53]

Wordsworth's nature is thus a living universe, where nothing exists in isolation or can fail to find a response in the mind of man. The poet who can evoke the majesty of Helvellyn can also appreciate the modest charm of the lesser celandine. Beauty allied with grandeur the Brontës could find in the descriptions of Scott or Byron. The humbler beauty of the myriad living things, down to the smallest flowers and plants, which are also part of nature, was something, in Wordsworth's belief, equally worthy of expression. The Brontës, who delighted in the rare flowers that spring brought to their moorlands, and the changing colours of heath and grass throughout the seasons, must have appreciated his deep awareness of this aspect of nature.

The poet who could enter into the life of the humblest flower was also the inspired interpreter of animal life. Just as he habitually chose the more familiar birds for his subject – though he could sympathise passionately with the plight of a captive eagle – so he made himself, as a rule, the interpreter of the humbler animals, the dog, the kitten, the mountain lamb. Even the deer in "Hart-Leap Well" is no proud "monarch of the waste"; he is an "unoffending creature" who, at the price of cruel physical effort, manages to outstrip the hunter just long enough to reach the spot where he wishes to die, the mountain stream near which he had been born. The hart's death is not a triumph for the hunter, it is a violation of nature's harmony:

This Beast not unobserved by Nature fell;
His death was mourned by sympathy divine.

When, on the contrary, there is affection between man and animal, nature's harmony is reaffirmed, in spite of tragedy, as in "The White Doe of Rylstone". But the apotheosis of the humble animal comes in "Peter Bell" when, like Hugo in a moving poem of *La Légende des Siècles*, Wordsworth takes for hero a brutalised ass who, at the cost of much suffering, averts disaster for others and changes, through his generosity, the whole course of a human life.

For it is human life that is, in the last analysis, Wordsworth's chief concern. Though he loved nature as he did, he would not have consecrated so much of his poetic genius to becoming its interpreter had he not become convinced that in this way, rather than by advocating political revolution or the cold consolation of a mechanistic universe, he could best help to solve the problems of modern man. This was his true vocation as a poet, and the fervour with which he accepted it is reflected in the poems "Expostulation and Reply" and the sequel in *Lyrical Ballads*:

One impulse from a vernal wood
May teach you more of man,
Of moral evil and of good,
Than all the sages can . . .[54]

It was logical that Wordsworth, in this belief, should attach particular importance to that period of human life which is most receptive to natural impressions, when there is a freshness of sensation, a joy and a confidence which can never afterwards be recaptured. This conviction of the peculiar significance of childhood, confirmed by the memory of his own early years in the Lake District, is most fully expressed in the first books of *The Prelude*, not published till after his death. But it also found expression in many of his poems, some inspired by his sympathetic understanding of his own young children, and supremely in the Ode "Intimations of Immortality from Recollections of Early Childhood". Such an attitude had its own relevance for the Brontës, for whom their childhood – in spite of some traumatic experiences – was a time on which they all afterwards looked back with nostalgic affection.

What Wordsworth found most valuable in such recollections, however, was the state of mystic awareness in the child which they implied, a state accepted unconsciously and only to be fully appreciated, though never fully recaptured, in later years. This visionary element is an essential part of his work. The culminating experience in "Tintern Abbey" is of a force which vivifies both the mind of man and nature:

> A motion and a spirit that impels
> All thinking things, all objects of all thought,
> And rolls through all things.[55]

This visionary power was, for Wordsworth himself, something felt only in moments of mystic illumination and fully appreciated only when he had begun to attain maturity.

Some degree of maturity was also needed in the reader before this aspect of the poet's genius could be adequately comprehended, and such comprehension could only have come gradually to the young Brontës. The sense of as yet imperfect understanding, blended with deep and rather awe-struck admiration, is interestingly reflected in a passage of Charlotte's first novel, *The Professor*. When Crimsworth, carrying the master-pupil relationship into marriage, makes his Swiss-born wife, prone to talk French, read English to him by way of penance and instruction combined, it is often Wordsworth's poetry that he chooses:

> I frequently dosed her with Wordsworth in this way, and Wordsworth steadied her soon; she had a difficulty in comprehending his deep, serene and sober mind; his language, too, was not facile to her; she had to ask questions, to sue for explanations. . . . Her instinct instantly penetrated and possessed the meaning of more ardent and imaginative writers. Byron excited her, Scott she loved; Wordsworth only she puzzled at, wondered over, and hesitated to pronounce an opinion upon. (ch. 25).

That she should experience such difficulties is comprehensible. For Byron poetry was "the expression of excited passion". Scott's best verse had the immediacy and the dramatic intensity of the Border ballads. For Wordsworth poetry was not, as in the ballad, feeling objectified in action; in his verse "the feeling therein developed gives importance to the action and situation and not the action and situation to the feeling". The emotions themselves are no less intense than with Byron: ". . . all good poetry is the spontaneous overflow of powerful feelings". But a reservation is added: "and though this be true, Poems to which any value can be attached were never produced . . . but by a man who, being possessed of more than usual organic sensibility, had also thought long and deeply".[56]

It is evident that, for youthful readers, such poetry might at first sight be difficult to evaluate at its true depth. It has also to be remembered that, by holding back the publication of *The Prelude* during his lifetime, Wordsworth withheld at the same time the full revelation of a personality as ardent and imaginative in its own way as that of Scott or Byron. *The Prelude* was the crowning achievement of the career inaugurated by *Lyrical Ballads*, but it did not appear till 1850, after the poet's death, when, of the Brontë family, only Charlotte and her father were alive to read it.

Direct quotations from Wordsworth sometimes occur in the Brontë novels, though less frequently than those from Scott or Byron. The schoolmaster narrator of *The Professor* quotes, or adapts, a famous line from "The Rainbow": "The boy is father to the man." The striking visual image in Wordsworth's "A Night-Piece", evoking the emergence of the moon from behind clouds:

> There in a black-blue vault she sails along

seems to have fascinated the Brontës. It recurs in *Shirley*, where reference is made to "the 'black-blue' serenity of the air-ocean", in *Villette* where a stormy evening sky is said to be "settling into a mass of black-blue metal, heated at the rim, and inflaming slowly to a heavy red", and in *The Tenant of Wildfell Hall*, where the moon is described as floating in the "black-blue vault of heaven".[57] In *Shirley* the courage of Moore and Helstone during the attack on Hollow's Mill is characterised by a phrase from one of Wordsworth's "Sonnets on Liberty": they are "of 'earth's first blood' "[58] Not a direct quotation but an allusion to his poem, "Yes, it was the mountain echo" is seen by F. B. Pinion in the episode of Rochester's call to Jane Eyre, uttered at Ferndean but mysteriously heard and answered by her when she is among hills many miles away. Rochester senses that her reply "seemed spoken amongst mountains; for I heard a hill-sent echo repeat the words".[59] There seems to be a reminiscence of the opening line of Wordsworth's sonnet "Nuns fret not at their convent's narrow room" in the impatience of the younger Catherine when forbidden to move out of the garden at Wuthering Heights: ". . . it fretted her sadly to be confined to its narrow bounds".[60]

More significant, however, are affinities of mood and situation. Charlotte Brontë's most Wordsworthian heroine is Frances Henri of *The Professor*, half Swiss, half English, with her love of liberty, her impatience with Hunsden's dogmatising rationalism, her combination of vivacity and seriousness. *Jane Eyre*, though its narrator looks back over a distance of ten years, is essentially the novel of youth, and also of childhood, so well understood by Wordsworth. The doleful ballad of "the poor orphan child", sung by the servant Bessie to comfort the ten-year-old Jane, has echoes of "Lucy Gray". And Jane, in her passion for her "miniature scarecrow" of a doll, recalls the orphan Alice Fell, heartbroken because her tattered cloak has become entangled in a carriage wheel and reduced to

A weather-beaten rag as e'er
From any garden scare-crow dangled.

Shirley, where the action is directly concerned with the problems of the Industrial Revolution, is further from the world of Wordsworth than *Jane Eyre*. Charlotte Brontë, in a digression which she cannot resist, herself emphasises the chasm which yawns between the world of the counting-house or the Piece Hall and that of the "true poet" who, "quiet externally though he may be, has often a truculent spirit under his placidity, and is full of shrewdness in his meekness", and who "can have his own bliss, his own society with his great friend and goddess, Nature . . ." (ch. 4). The description seems most pertinent when applied to Wordsworth and, in spite of counting-house and cloth exchange, there are passages in *Shirley* which recall his view of life. Both Shirley and Caroline love nature, whether wild or rural. They love birds and animals, down to the humblest, and do not hesitate to judge a man's character by his treatment of such defenceless creatures. On a more philosophic level, Shirley expresses in the opening of her essay written for Louis Moore the belief expressed by Wordsworth in his poem "Three years she grew" in nature's power to educate certain favoured beings who grow up in solitude, directly exposed to the formative influence of the elements. In her last novel *Villette*, where the narrator looks back over a gap of many years at her distant youth, Charlotte Brontë realises finally, in her own way, Wordsworth's ideal of "emotion recollected in tranquillity".

Anne Brontë, in her novels, manifests the same preference for country life and the moral qualities it breeds which her father had shown in his *Cottage Poems*, and to which the genius of Wordsworth had given both practical and theoretical expression. One of the most sympathetic characters in *Agnes Grey* is the widow Nancy Brown, a cottager with "a serious, thoughtful turn of mind". Helen Huntingdon much prefers a quiet domestic life at Grassdale to the "throng and bustle, the restless hurry and ceaseless change" of the London life which is a necessity to her husband. After the break-up of her marriage, it is in her family home, Wildfell Hall, an isolated house near moorland country, that she takes refuge.

Even more isolated is the scene of *Wuthering Heights*, and some aspects of Emily's novel show a marked affinity with Wordsworth. The childhood of Heathcliff and Catherine has much in common with childhood as Wordsworth felt it should be, a happy state of which wildness is an essential feature. It is the state which the older Catherine describes in retrospect as "half savage and hardy, and free . . .". Wordsworth is indulgent to the irresponsibility of the two young shepherds in "The Idle Shepherd-Boys" because they are performing the chief function of their age, which is to share in the natural joy of spring, even though he is not indifferent to the fate of the lamb which they should have been watching. Similarly Heathcliff and Catherine find one of their chief amusements in running away to the moors and remaining there all day. It is exile from the bliss enjoyed in childhood and from nature, as well as from Heathcliff, that later shakes the balance of Catherine's mind. In her delirium she expresses, like the unhappy Ruth of the *Lyrical Ballads*, "the essential passions of the heart", her love of Heathcliff, her craving for the freedom of her girlhood and the freedom of the moors. When she slowly regains a semblance of health, the sight of a few crocuses, "the earliest flowers at the Heights", rouses in her momentarily a flash of the same delight with which the poet greeted the primrose or the celandine. The younger Catherine participates in the movement, the melodies and the brightness of returning spring and summer in an ecstasy of pleasure which recalls Wordsworth's similar delight in the song of the green linnet or the fluttering and dancing of the daffodils. For her, too, the whole world is, in her own words, "awake and wild with joy" and she wants everything to "sparkle and dance in a glorious jubilee". The city dweller Lockwood, the narrator of the opening chapters of the novel, finds himself, when he first arrives among these northern hills, in an alien world. But although he himself could never live permanently anywhere but in "the stirring atmosphere of the town", even a short experience of life in this region brings him to a grudging admission that its inhabitants do seem to be distinguished by sincerity, depth and durability of feeling, qualities which Wordsworth had claimed in the Preface to *Lyrical Ballads* for those who live close to nature. He has to concede that "people in these regions . . . *do* live more in earnest, more in themselves, and less in surface change, and frivolous external things. I could fancy a love for life here almost possible . . ." (ch. 7).

Resemblances with Wordsworth are found also in the verse of the Brontës. Miss Ratchford has indicated the links between one of Charlotte's early poems, "Lines on seeing the portrait of – (Marian Hume)", and "She was a Phantom of delight."[61] But it is in her prose rather than in her verse that her affinities with Wordsworth emerge. Anne Brontë's poetry, on the contrary, has qualities resembling certain essential features of Wordsworth. The retrospective interpretation of the growth of her own personality which forms the theme of her most revealing poems like "Self-Communion" is, in its own way and on a far more modest scale, a product, as Derek Stanford has said, of the same "reflective imagination" which is at work in *The Prelude*.[62] Memory is in general a favourite theme of hers, sometimes associated with the joys of childhood and frequently with nature:

> As in the days of infancy,
> An opening primrose seemed to me
> A source of strange delight.[63]

Emily Brontë, in her poems as in her novel, sometimes shows an affinity with Wordsworth. Her precision in noting some half-hidden wild flower recalls his close observation and like him she can afterwards recall the sight with no loss of visual clarity:

> I could think in the withered grass
> Spring's budding wreaths we might discern;
> The violet's eye might shyly flash
> And young leaves shoot among the fern.[64]

But her affinities with Wordsworth go deeper than this. Her belief in the innocence of early childhood, and its close link with the divine, resembles that expressed in the Ode "Intimations of Immortality":

> I love thee, boy; for all divine,
> All full of God thy features shine.[65]

Like Wordsworth she is profoundly conscious that "shades of the prison-house" will inevitably darken what she describes as "the pure light of childhood's morn". For her indeed the process is more rapid and more destructive:

> . . . the poison-tainted air
> From this world's plague-fen rises there.[66]

But, like Wordsworth, she cannot renounce the consolation that still exists in these "shadowy recollections" of a clearer vision, nor the joy that still comes from nature, from

> . . . the sunshine and the wind . . . .
> And all the joyous music breathing by,
> And all the splendour of that cloudless sky . . .[67]

Above all, like him she is in her most inspired moments a true visionary, expressing in her greatest poems the kind of experience for which Jonathan Wordsworth finds parallels in "that serene and blessed mood" evoked by the poet in Tintern Abbey or in his apostrophe to Imagination in *The Prelude*, "the experience of "the human power to reach out beyond the limitations of self".[68]

Through their closeness to three of the greatest masters among the Romantics, the Brontës acquired a deeper insight into what

nature could mean for the creative artist. Inevitably they came
to know something of other writers belonging to the same circles
and sharing to some extent the same sympathies. Thomas Moore's
Lalla Rookh, a paler version of Byron's orientalism, had its appeal
for them and so, it need hardly be said, had his *Irish Melodies*.
Southey, admired especially by Charlotte, who wrote to consult
him about her own work in 1836, also subscribed to the oriental
mode dear to the Romantics in his epic poems *Thalaba* and *The
Curse of Kehama*, though he, too, could not rival the authentic
orientalism of Byron.

Coleridge, who collaborated with Wordsworth in *Lyrical Ballads*, could not fail to appeal to the Brontës, though his chosen
subject matter in the collection was different from that of his
friend. Wordsworth chose in the main everyday situations and,
at the same time, aimed "to throw over them a certain colouring
of imagination, whereby ordinary things should be presented to
the mind in an unusual way".[69] Coleridge chose the supernatural, but was none the less committed to "the truth of nature",
as well as to "the modifying colours of imagination". His "Ancient Mariner" has a supernatural subject, but he, too, shows
the essential unity of creation. The killing of the albatross, the
friendly and harmless bird, is an infringement of the divine order
which has to be atoned for by an odyssey of spiritual suffering,
until the guilty mariner recognises that, as Coleridge himself
phrased it, "every Thing has a life of it's own, and . . . we are all
one Life". His unfinished "Christabel" is also concerned with the
supernatural, in the guise of a mysterious stranger, met in the
woods, who is invited by an innocent girl, unaware of her evil
magic, into her father's castle. The maleficent spell of the sor-
ceress affects all nature as well:

> . . . By tairn and rill
> The night-birds all that hour were still.

There is a striking similarity, as has been remarked, between the
use of the supernatural here and in Emily Brontë's poem "And
now the house-dog stretched once more"[70] In the latter case it is
into a shepherd's home that the mysterious stranger is received,
but their "hospitable joy" is frozen, like Christabel's, by

> something in his face,
> Some nameless thing they could not trace . . .

The Brontës could hardly have read Moore's *Life* without interest in the account of the poet's friendship with Shelley, and recent enquiry has increasingly pointed to the probability that his work became known to them in the decade that followed. In 1839 Charlotte quoted in one of her juvenilia, "Caroline Vernon", his description of the hours as "wild-eyed charioteers", and the quotation from *Prometheus Unbound* suggests, as Edward Chitham has said, that they had had access to the new edition of Shelley's poems published by his widow earlier the same year. It seems likely that it was above all Emily who was attracted by the work and the personality of the poet who celebrated Prometheus and wrote the "Ode to the West Wind". The question has been studied by Chitham who, as earlier F. B. Pinion, sees most affinity with Shelley in her later metaphysical poems.[71]

Tennyson, who belonged to a younger generation, seems also to have appealed chiefly to Emily. There is a possible reminiscence of "Locksley Hall" in a speech of Heathcliff's in *Wuthering Heights*,[72] and it was for Emily that Charlotte bought a copy of Tennyson's latest poem *The Princess* during her visit to London in 1848. She herself preferred Wordsworth and later, after Emily's death, disagreed with Mrs Gaskell as to the relative merits of *The Prelude* and *In Memoriam*. Of the latter she wrote: "It is beautiful, it is mournful, it is monotonous." Perhaps she sensed in the melancholy of Tennyson a new quality, lacking in the melancholy of the Romantics, a sense of struggle and uncertainty closely allied to a different evaluation of nature, less optimistic than the equation of nature with cosmic harmony which characterised the Lakeland poet.

Any consideration of the literary affinities which fostered the Brontës' concern with nature would be incomplete without a final mention of their early contact with French Romanticism. It was probably the references to him in *Childe Harold* and Moore's *Life of Byron* which first made them aware of the fame of Rousseau. Through Moore's *Life* they also became acquainted with the forceful personality of the author of *Corinne*, which was to have repercussions on their juvenilia. The library of Ponden House gave them the opportunity to read the actual text of another great ancestor of French Romanticism, Chateaubriand's *Itinéraire de Paris à Jérusalem*, in translation. His descriptive orientalism could rival in prose the magic of Byron's in verse. But translation cannot give the full flavour of the original, and it was only when Charlotte acquired a sound knowledge of written if not of spoken French that a truly fertile contact with French Romanticism became possible. It was through the medium of the French novels sent to her in 1840 by her friends the Taylors that she came to know contemporary novelists across the Channel. It was most probably at this time that she first came into contact with the work of George Sand. Emily and Anne, though not so proficient in French as their sister, were able to read the language and, as avid readers, no doubt shared her interest in the woman novelist already well known in England, and now beginning to be considered with less hostility by English critics.

In her early novels George Sand was concerned primarily with the situation of the woman who could not find happiness in marriage or understanding in society. But it was as a writer of pastoral novels that she was ultimately to excel, and her early work is already rich in landscape description. She possessed at the same time, as Patricia Thomson has said, the ability, fostered by her admiration of Rousseau, Chateaubriand and Senancour, "to use natural description as a counterpart of the emotions of her characters".[73] Such an amalgam of natural description with feeling was already familiar to the Brontës from the poetry of the English Romantics, but they had not yet encountered it as a salient aspect of the novel. With Scott landscape was indeed an essential feature, and an ethnic influence of great importance, but it was linked with the action rather than seen through the prism of the emotions of the individual characters.

Of all George Sand's early novels it was *Mauprat*, published in 1837, which was most calculated to appeal to the young Brontës. As often in the novels of Scott, whom George Sand admired, this historical novel, set in the Berry country in the years prior to the Revolution, depends for its structure on the opposition between the primitive and the sophisticated. The cousins Bernard and Edmée de Mauprat both belong to the same race, but Bernard has been reared in the semi-barbaric traditions of the elder branch, who live in a fortress on the edge of the moors, while Edmée belongs to the more civilised younger branch, who live in a manor on the plain. They love each other, but Bernard, when transplanted to his uncle's luxurious mansion, longs passionately for the freedom of his native forests, and only his devotion to Edmée makes him submit to the civilising process of education, without which she could not have married him with any hope of happiness. The stormy course of their love owes much of its drama and poetry to the natural setting in which some of the crucial scenes take place, and whose influence becomes inextricably interwoven with their own feelings. It is evident that there are striking similarities between *Mauprat* and *Wuthering Heights*,[74] though the happy denouement of *Mauprat* finds a parallel only in the second generation in Emily Brontë's novel.

In February 1842 Charlotte and Emily left England for the first time and crossed the Channel to study languages in Brussels, with a view to adding to their qualifications as future teachers. Anne remained in her employment as governess at Thorp Green, near York, where she was later joined by Branwell, who became a tutor in the same family. As a consequence the family ceased, for the time being, to share a common background. But for Charlotte and Emily the result of the stay in Brussels was in no sense to diminish their admiration of the English Romantics. It was rather to reinforce it by a clearer realisation that Romanticism was not only an English but a European phenomenon. They found that, inevitably, nature occupied as prominent a place with the European Romantics as with their own countrymen. Their personal reactions to this encounter with another culture were, however, very different. It meant more to Charlotte than to Emily, and it was she who returned to Brussels for a second year. It was she, too, who learned to appreciate the place given to nature in the work of Chateaubriand and Bernardin de Saint-Pierre, and further developed by Hugo and Lamartine. But she retained, no less than Emily or Anne, that lasting allegiance to Scott, Byron and Wordsworth which contributed so much to their understanding of what nature could mean for the artist. They continued to share also that love of their native moorlands which made Haworth home for them all.

The common background thus remained fundamentally unchanged. Inevitably, as they matured, their genius demanded individual expression. Each was to develop her own art and, in the art of each, nature was to play an important role. But that role owed much to the nature tradition of the English Romantics, and to the northern moors that had encircled their childhood, as well as something to their own father's lasting love of nature. The common heritage was always to unite them in a bond as strong as life itself.

2   Nature in the Juvenilia

It is evidently in the Brontës' published works that the treatment of nature presents the greatest interest. But any study of the subject must involve some preliminary concern with the juvenilia, that "web of sunny air" which the parsonage family began to weave in childhood and whose folds ultimately encompassed so wide an area. Into their juvenilia the Brontës poured all the preoccupations and the passions of their imaginative childhood and their ardent youth.

Among these an important place belonged to the stirring events which were still recent history in the period in which they grew up. Their father had come to England at the time when the war with France was entering its most dramatic phase. He had followed the careers of Nelson and Wellington with passionate interest and he had communicated that interest to his children. Not surprisingly the playthings which he gave to his young son included toy soldiers, and it was the present of a box of a dozen wooden soldiers in 1826 which inspired the series of games which ultimately led to the creation of the children's dream world. Branwell's sisters were each invited to appropriate one of the puppets for their own use, and Charlotte instantly named hers Wellington, while Branwell's allegiance to a rival leader was reflected in his choice of Bonaparte for the name of his favourite. In the course of the children's various "plays" the soldiers, with the exception of Charlotte's, changed their names, but they remained the herioc "Twelves", whose ultimate destiny was to found a new and magnificent kingdom overseas. By 1829 the history of these adventurers had reached the stage when their owners, constantly enlarging the sphere of the childhood games, imagined for them the voyage to Africa which was to have momentous consequences for their own future as writers.

The choice of an exotic setting reflected the fascination exercised on the children, from an early age, by their reading of *The Arabian Nights*.[1] and of the Rev. James Ridley's *Tales of the Genii*

48

published in 1764.[2] But it also reflected, like the campaigns of the wooden soldiers, their interest in recent events, fostered by their reading of *Blackwood's*. Contemporary hostilities between the Ashantis and the British no doubt helped to decide the selection of the Guinea coast as the landing-place for the enterprising "Twelves". This region of Africa was at the same time associated in their minds with the records of recent explorations, especially Mungo Park's account of his travels in tracing the course of the Niger. Explorers featured prominently among their heroes, particularly in the case of Emily and Anne, whose chosen representatives among the original "Twelve Adventurers" who disembarked on the Guinea coast were named after the Arctic explorers Parry and Ross. In establishing the topography of their new kingdom the young Brontës drew also on another source, their father's copy of the Rev. J. Goldsmith's *Grammar of General Geography*, whose African section provided its salient outlines.

It was a matter of course that "the Twelves", supernaturally aided by their supporting genii – in fact, the four Brontë children – should rapidly conquer the Ashantis and establish their own dominion. This ultimately developed into a confederacy of four kingdoms, presided over by the most outstanding of the original adventurers, with the Duke of Wellington as their acknowledged leader. The federal capital was Glass Town, a magnificent city, erected in a few months with the help of the genii, which took its name from the mirror-like harbour in which its impressive buildings were reflected. Once established the Confederacy rapidly developed its own political, social and artistic life. It was now that Charlotte and Branwell, both of whom had already begun to write stories as well as to act them, began to record, in microscopic printing, the day to day history of Glass Town, a subject which was to occupy them for years to come.

They began with a magazine on the model of a miniature *Blackwood's*, which continued to the end of 1830. In addition both wrote independently on the same absorbing theme, Charlotte showing herself more concerned with narration and poems and Branwell constituting himself historian of the new Confederacy. Charlotte's contributions to the Glass Town saga were temporarily interrupted by her schooldays at Roe Head, but her collaboration with Branwell was resumed on her return to Haworth in 1832. In 1834, however, Glass Town, which by now had acquired the more sophisticated title of Verdopolis, lost its central

importance when the original Confederacy was enlarged by the
creation of the new kingdom of Angria. The event marked the
end of the first period of the Brontë juvenilia.

In the writings of this period, the fruit of the transition from
childhood to adolescence, the physical background derived from
geographical text books and explorers' records is combined with
the supernatural background of the *Arabian Nights*. The new
territory discovered by the "twelve adventurers" is defined in its
broad outlines: "Far off to the east the long black line of gloomy
forests skirted the horizon. To the north the. . . . Mountains o
the Moon seemed a misty girdle to the plain of Dahomey; to the
south the ocean guarded the coasts of Africa; . . . to the west lay
the desert."[3] But an excursion into the desert leads to another
and a magic world: "Out of the barren desert arose a palace o
diamond, the pillars of which were ruby and emerald illuminated with lamps too bright to look upon. . . . In the midst o
the hall hung a lamp like the sun."[4]

Clearly for Charlotte and Branwell, as for most imaginative
children, the nature they saw every day had to be supplemented
by scenes more colourful and more novel. Even the exotic was
not sufficient without the added attractions of the *Arabian Nights*.
In Charlotte's earliest tales the *Arabian Nights* element is sometimes the dominant one. "The Search after Happiness", written
in the summer of 1829, when she was thirteen, has only tenuous
links with the history of Glass Town, though the Duke of
Wellington and his two young sons do play a subordinate part.
Yet paradoxically it is this fabulous setting which contains some
of the clearest indications as to what her future attitude to nature
will be. This apparently naïf tale shows a fascination with nature
at its most elemental, as the hero and his companion move from
one strange landscape to another:

> They were upon the top of a rock which was more than a
> thousand fathoms high. All beneath them was liquid Moun-
> tains tossed to and fro with horrible confusion roaring and
> raging with a tremendous noise and crowned with waves of
> foam. All above them was a mighty firmament in one part
> covered with black clouds from which darted huge and ter-
> rible sheets of Lightning. In another part an immense globe of
> Light like silver was hanging in the sky . . .[5]

The wild play of the elements obviously has its own appeal for the seekers after happiness, and later they are content to spend long years in a cave in a desolate region, simply watching the alternations of nature between storm and calm:

> Sometimes they would sit upon a high rock and listen to the hoarse thunder rolling through the sky . . . sometimes they would watch the lightning darting across black clouds and shivering huge fragments of rock in its terrible passage sometimes they would witness the great glorious orb of gold sink behind the far distant mountains which girded the horizon and . . . the silver moon arising in her splendour till the cold dews of night began to fall and then they would retire to their bed in the cave with hearts full of joy and thankfulness.[6]

Both these descriptions show the same fascination with the elemental, but there is a difference between them. The scene from the rock "more than a thousand fathoms high" has a supernatural quality stemming from the *Arabian Nights* and also, as Winifred Gérin has shown, from John Martin's painting "The Deluge", an engraving of which hung in the parsonage and strongly appealed, as did his art in general, to the young Brontës. But the stormy skies, the sunset and the rising moon of the second description could have been viewed from Haworth moor or from the windows of the hilltop parsonage. Even the dramatic displacement of huge boulders had actually happened, at the time of the Crow Hill eruption, and lived on in local legend, and perhaps the terrors of that unforgettable evening still survived in the memory of the younger children. There is a personal note in this second description, and an implicit homage to nature in the concluding words.

"The Search after Happiness" also contains an early poem by Charlotte, "The Song of the Fairies". It was followed, in the same fertile period, by a number of other poems, some of which likewise introduce the realm of gramarye. The elves of these verses have, like the "good folk" of Scottish legend and, no doubt, the "fairishes" of Tabby's tales, a potentially sinister quality. When they make their rare appearances to mortals, it is usually against a background of storm, and particularly of storm at sea. But the majority of these poems have as their main subject nature, as Charlotte herself knows it, and predominantly

nature in calmer mood. Titles like "Sunrise", "Sunset", "Morning" and "Evening Song" show her preoccupation with the ever-
changing beauty of the skies. Sunlight and moonlight, clouds
and the movement of the winds are favourite themes, and it
seems as if, for her, other aspects of nature are frequently seen in
relation to this dominant interest. It is the variations of sunlight
and shade on the foliage which gives the trees their greatest
attraction, it is the iridescent quality of raindrops or dew which
lends a magic lustre to grass and flowers:

> Behold, the valley glows with life and light:
>   Each rain-drop bears a glory in its cell . . .

Sound is a natural part of this airy universe, bird song, the rustle
of trees, a murmuring stream. Moonlight seems even more
congenial than sunlight to the youthful versifier, and the "Evening Song", composed by a harper in the darkening woods,
contains lines which hold promise of a geniune lyrical gift:

> And here I sit, until night's noon
>   Hath gemmed the heavens with many a star,
> And sing beneath the wandering moon
>   Who comes, high journeying, from afar.[7]

A further development of her verse is seen when she begins to
use the pseudonym "The Marquis of Douro". The Duke of
Wellington's elder son, who increasingly overshadowed his father
in the chronicles of Glass Town, began to acquire Byronic qualities
when Charlotte and Branwell first read *Childe Harold*, and became poet as well as soldier. His favourite themes are defined by
Charlotte in one of the Glass Town magazines: "The Meditations of a lonely traveller in the wilderness or the mournful song
of a solitary exile are the themes in which he most delights . . .
though often his songs consist of grand and vivid descriptions of
storms and tempests . . .".[8] With the advent of Byron, the descriptive range of Charlotte's poetry is enlarged. "The Evening
Walk" is a microcosm of the romantic landscape, varying from
chasms, cascades and frowning forests to flowery plains, haunted
dells and rivers bearing their tribute waters towards the boundless sea. At the same time, more variations of metre correspond
to the increased range of themes. Above all, there is a new

self-consciousness: the writer no longer responds to nature with the spontaneity of a child but sometimes stands wrapped in thought or finds a melancholic pleasure in listening to the "pensive strains" of the nightingale.

Byron's influence also enlarged the cultural range of Charlotte's verse. His hellenism, reinforced by the contemporary enthusiasm of her brother Branwell for his Greek and Latin studies, introduced a classical element into her poems. This was not without effect on her view of nature. Classical allusions now make their appearance: "Apollo's burnished car" climbs the heavens or "silver-robed Luna" appears with her train of stars. In the poem "The Violet", by "The Marquis of Douro", English poets are seen as heirs of the classical tradition. But, for Charlotte Brontë, the chief glory of Greece is obviously the power of her mythology to give visible form to the elemental splendours of nature. At fourteen, she creates her own myth in emulation, and it is nature itself that she attempts to evoke in "The Violet":

> A woman's form the vision wore:
>   Her lofty forehead touched the sky . . .[9]

In Charlotte's belief Nature alone can bestow the gift of poetry. The supplicant for poetic fame in these verses is promised no laurel wreath but, in a conclusion more suggestive of Wordsworth than of Byron, is directed by the "Mighty Mother" to pluck for a coronet the violets which grow "beside a stone, green moss amid" – modest flowers but ones which have an enduring perfume.

A new note is struck with "The Fairies' Farewell", written in 1831 when Charlotte had been nearly a year at school at Roe Head. The genii and the fairies who had collaborated in the construction of Glass Town meet at midnight in their aerial palace over the city, but their purpose now is to decree its destruction, and both metre and theme recall Byron's "Destruction of Sennacherib".[10] The farewell to Glass Town proved to be premature – it was fated to survive for years – but the fairies disappeared henceforward from Charlotte's work.

The increasing maturity of her approach to nature emerges from her "Lines on Bewick", written a year later. The 1804 edition of Bewick's *History of British Birds* was on her father's bookshelves and the illustrations had been one of the delights of her childhood, as of Jane Eyre's. But her praise of Bewick's engravings begins with the recognition that the scenes showing each bird in its native habitat are

> True to the common Nature that we see
>   In England's sunny fields, her hills and vales,
> On the wild bosom of her storm-dark sea . . .

At the same time this "common Nature" still speaks powerfully to the imagination. A phrase adapted from Byron's "The Dream" – "A change comes o'er the spirit of our dream" – operates the transition from the actual engravings to childhood memories of woodland scenes. Then comes a return to "Bewick's enchanted page", but now the writer's concern is no longer with landscape as the background of some ornithological species, but with Bewick's landscapes, or seascapes, in themselves, and also with the inimitable vignettes in which the artist's imagination is allowed freer play and does not necessarily exclude the supernatural.[11] It is interesting to find here the first explicit reference of any length to the moorland scene which was most familiar to her. But it is on the wide sky above the moor rather than on the heath itself that her gaze is principally focussed:

> O'er the far hills a purple veil seems flung,
>   Dim herald of the coming shades of night;
> E'en now Diana's lamp aloft is hung,
>
>   Drinking full radiance from the fount of light.
> Oh, when the solemn wind of midnight sighs,
>   Where will the lonely traveller lay his head?
> Beneath the tester of the star-bright skies
>   On the wild moor he'll find a dreary bed.[12]

But for the adolescent Charlotte the figures in the landscape were becoming increasingly important. From 1833 her poems are predominantly narrative and dramatic. Their subjects are often taken from the Glass Town saga. There is more vigour in these verses, but the authentic lyricism apparent in some of the early nature poems is less in evidence, though it was later to find unforgettable echoes in her prose.

Prose was indeed to be her principal means of expression and she contributed to the Glass Town saga, during the same prolific period, an abundance of stories and sketches. Her first love story, "Albion and Marina" was written in 1830. Though she took the name of her hero from her father's *Maid of Killarney*, Albion is in fact the Marquis of Douro and Marina his first love, the ethereal Marian Hume. They feature again in 1832 in the story "The Bridal". When writing these tales, Charlotte changed her pseudonym from "the Marquis of Douro" to "Lord Charles Wellesley" and, under cover of writing as Douro's younger brother, adopted a more critical attitude to her hero, though so far he remained an admirable character. In the second of these tales Glass Town has become Verdopolis, and the growing industrialisation of the maritime city, and the accompanying industrial unrest, strike a contemporary note and throw into relief the peaceful beauty of the valley in the hinterland, where the marquis has his country villa.

In "The Bridal" Charlotte's descriptive powers as a prose writer have evidently matured. They are still more apparent in "The Foundling", a much longer tale of the following year. A visitor from England, arriving in Verdopolis, pauses on the quay to admire the impressive scene: "Far above him the city walls and ramparts rose to a tremendous height, frowning terribly on the foam-white waves which rushed roaring to their feet . . .". One can recognise here, as in the early "Search after Happiness", the affinity, noted by Winifred Gérin, with the paintings of Martin, so familiar to the parsonage children.[13] But the harbour is only part of the wider perspective that finally opens out before the traveller as he proceeds on his way: "Verdopolis lay at the mouth of a wide valley which was embosomed in long, low hills, rich in hanging groves and gardens. . . . The background was closed by lofty, peaked mountains, whose azure tint almost melted into the serene horizon . . .".[14]

Charlotte's growing powers of description are paralleled by the increasing sophistication of her drawing of the social scene, no doubt influenced by her study of the fashionable Annuals.[15] The Marquis of Douro is now beginning to acquire the characteristics of a social leader. The supernatural reappears, however, in the episode of the "Philosophers' Island", where a secret society, said to have "dived deeply into the mysteries of nature", is presided over by one of the Glass Town patriarchs and "his wonderful brother Manfred". But there is little in common between the dialogue with the elemental forces in *Manfred* and the activities of the "Philosophical Association", which represent an excursion into the Gothic and the macabre. In spite of this, "The Foundling" as a whole foreshadows a more realistic era in the fortunes of the Brontës' exotic kingdom.

While Charlotte was describing its scenery and social life, her brother Branwell was compiling detailed accounts of its history. His "History of the Young Men from their first settlement to the present time" was largely a record of the military exploits of the colonists, and culminated in the supposed return of Wellington from Europe, where he had been summoned to defeat Napoleon, who subsequently established himself on an island adjacent to Glass Town, named in consequence Frenchland. Branwell's next contribution to Glass Town history, "Letters from an Englishman", traced the course of a rebellion in the Confederacy, led by the demagogue Alexander Rogue, who was to evolve into one of the leading personalities of the saga, becoming finally – thanks to Charlotte's discovering for him a romantic family background – Alexander Percy, Earl of Northangerland. Even after the crushing of the rebellion, Glass Town continued to be harassed by the wars which were Branwell's main interest. Napoleon invaded the territory to the east, but was repelled by the Marquis of Douro, who had become more prominent than his father in the affairs of the Confederacy. Douro, now better known as the Duke of Zamorna, demanded the cession to himself of his fields of battle, and this wide territory became the new kingdom of Angria, with Zamorna as its first king. This development was recorded by Branwell in 1834 and marked the end of the first period of the Brontë juvenilia.

During this first period the main contributors to the Glass Town saga were Charlotte and Branwell. Emily and Anne were involved, like their elders, in the original plays of the wooden soldiers, and their favourites, Parry and Ross, reigned over two of the kingdoms in the Confederacy. But an early account by "Lord Charles Wellesley", otherwise Charlotte, of a visit to "Parrysland" showed that the way of life there was very different from that of "Wellingtonsland". Parrysland was much nearer to contemporary Haworth, with cottages in rows, and factories; the royal palace itself was simply a modest stone house with a paddock behind, and their Majesties' only conveyance a one-horse gig, which also served to bring home provisions from the market.[16] There is a desire for greater independence implicit in this divergence from the splendours of the Wellesley domain. It is not surprising that, with Charlotte's departure for school in 1831, Emily and Anne, unresponsive to the politics and military details of Branwell's "History of the Young Men", created their own imaginary world of Gondal. This supposed island was like Haworth in climate and was a land of mountains, moors and lakes. It was a region much more in keeping with the characters of the Arctic explorers who were the early favourites of Emily and Anne than the eponymous kingdoms of Parrysland and Rossland in the African colony. Gondal possessed the same importance for its creators that Glass Town had for Charlotte and Branwell. It, too, soon acquired a literature of its own. But none of the prose chronicles of Gondal have survived. It is from the existing Gondal poems that this other dream world has had to be reconstructed by critics. Emily and Anne never said farewell to Gondal as Charlotte ultimately did to Angria. In consequence the Gondal poems, even the early ones, are best considered in the context of their work as a whole. The four Brontës continued to know of each other's inventions, but after the creation of Gondal Emily and Anne ceased to participate actively in the life of Glass Town. It was Charlotte and Branwell alone who were responsible for the foundation of Angria, which inaugurated the main period of the Brontë juvenilia.

The new kingdom was supposed to be situated in the region east of the Niger delta and included seven provinces. Its geography and population were carefully noted by Branwell, relief maps drawn, routes established and distances calculated. This meticulous accumulation of detail may sometimes have seemed excessive to Charlotte, more interested in story-telling than in statistics, but it proved to have its value for her as well, for it was thanks to this solid foundation that Angria so quickly became a territorial reality, of which each province had its own physical features. Angria did not, however, completely overshadow the four kingdoms originally founded by the first colonists. It became itself part of the Verdopolitan Confederacy, and although its new capital Adrianopolis (so called in compliment to Zamorna, one of whose forenames was Adrian) replaced Verdopolis as the seat of government, the original Glass Town did not cease to play an important role in political and social life.

With the foundation of Angria, an increasing realism pervaded

the juvenilia. The exploits of the first colonists, the "Twelve
Adventurers", were now relegated to the world of folklore. The
last echoes of gramarye are heard in "The Spell", written in
1834. It was evidently influenced by Scott's verse romances and
qualified by Charlotte herself as "an Extravaganza". But the
charm of "The Spell" does not lie in the ambiguous and circu-
itous plot but in the delightful rural scenes of the concluding
chapter. Although the building of Adrianopolis has already
begun, the denouement takes place in Zamorna's country villa in
the Vale of Verdopolis. Lord Charles Wellesley, the supposed
narrator, makes his way there on a spring morning, and there is
all the freshness of spring in the description of his walk across
fields to reach the boundary of the park:

> Having reached the second field, I sat down at a stile over
> which two lofty beeches hung their embowering branches. It
> was very delightful, being early morning, the air cool and
> fresh, the grass green and dewy, the flowers in the hedgerows
> exhaling their sweetest perfumes; a little rill wandered along
> down the sides of the pasture fields, a plenty of primroses, of
> wood-sorrel with their clustering leaves and faintly tinted
> blossoms, of vetches, wild hyacinths and geraniums, budded
> in blushing beauty on the borders . . .[17]

"My Angria and the Angrians", completed in October of the
same year, is an introduction to the new kingdom presided over
by Zamorna. The narrator is, as before, Lord Charles Wellesley
and he begins by a description of the exodus of the younger and
livelier members of Verdopolitan society, who forsake the original "Glass Town" for the new capital Adrianopolis a hundred
and fifty miles to the east. The contrast between east and west,
emphasised by him, is a contrast both between two climates and
two ways of life. Verdopolis and the older kingdoms to the west,
which include Wellingtonsland, evoke a peaceful landscape of
woods and valleys, of temperate sunlight and mellow moonlight.
Angria has a different climate; her eastern frontier is nearer to
the desert sands and her sun burns more fiercely. This "burning
clime" finds a parallel in the development of Zamorna, now her
king and both a Byronic and a Napoleonic figure, as avid for
conquest in love as in war. The association between changing
climates and changing attitudes is used again by Charlotte

Brontë in her poem of the same period, "We Wove a Web in Childhood", to explain the natural evolution of their dream world:

> Dream that stole o'er us in the time
> When life was in its vernal clime,
> Dream that still faster o'er us steals
>   As the mild star of spring declining
> The advent of that day reveals
>   That glows in Sirius' fiery shining . . .[18]

In the strong light of Angria, landscapes become more clearly defined. When, in "My Angria and the Angrians", Lord Charles Wellesley himself sets out on the journey to Adrianopolis, his route is charted by Charlotte with an assurance which shows her complete familiarity with the topography of the new kingdom. The way lies through the fertile province called Zamorna and its leading city of the same name, which lies on the banks of a swiftly flowing river, the Olympian. To the north are woods and hills, and further north, out of sight, is a wilder region of moor and mountain. The varying features of the different provinces constitute indeed an important part of the charm of Angria, and are enthusiastically celebrated by Charlotte in her "National Ode for the Angrians":

> The sun is on the Calabar, the dawn is quenched in day . . .
> The sandy plains of Etrei flash back arising light . . .
> Zamorna lifts her fruitful hills like Eden's to the sky,
> And fair as Enna's fields of flowers her golden prairies lie . . .[19]

Place names and physical features is Angria inevitably contain echoes of the cosmopolitan origins of the Brontës' dream world. The supposed West African location is recalled by the mention of the Calabar, and the "sandy plains" suggest the desert and jungle on the eastern frontier, domain of the dispossessed Ashanti chief Quashia. The name Zamorna is derived from the Spanish town Zamora on the Douro and thus a reminder of Wellington's triumphs in the Peninsula, while Enna's "fields of flowers" suggest the Mediterranean landscapes of Byron. Irish and Scottish names were already to be found in the older kingdoms of the west and the north, but in Angria English place names become more frequent – Arundel is one of the seven provinces, Northangerland, obviously reminiscent of North-umberland, another, and Evesham one of the main cities. In the "National Ode for the Angrians" landmarks well known to the Brontës appear:

> . . . from the crags of Pendlebrow the russet garb has gone;
> And Boulsworth off his giant sides rolls down the
>   vapours dim. . .[20]

Growing use of the Yorkshire landscape is evident in "My Angria and the Angrians". There is even a passing reference to Haworth in the satirical episode where the narrator, Lord Charles, on his way to the city of Zamorna, encounters "Patrick Benjamin Wiggins" – evidently Branwell – and deflates his exaggerated praise of his native place "Howard" by scornfully calling it "a miserable little village, buried in dreary moors and moss-hags and marshes". This description, which takes no account of the "royal purple" of the moors in summer, is obviously not meant to be taken too seriously. Soon afterwards, on arriving at Za-morna, Lord Charles shows that he is keenly appreciative of its fine setting, "the noble champaign of field and park and woodland . . ." Zamorna itself is obviously in origin a Yorkshire woollen town, which owes its place on the map of Angria to the fact that the leading millowner, as imagined by Charlotte and Bran-well, is Edward Percy, son of the redoubtable Northangerland.

However, it is the Duke of Zamorna who dominates the Angrian scene, and the Yorkshire countryside is left behind when Lord Charles arrives at his brother's majestic palace in Adrianopolis. The Duke is now married to Northangerland's daughter Mary Percy, to whom he had transferred his affections, thus causing his first wife, the unhappy Marian Hume, to die of a broken heart. The fortunes of Angria are at their zenith, and Charlotte's rambling narrative ends with the birth of twin sons to the royal pair.

This happy time in the history of Angria was also a period of enjoyment for its creators, still at liberty to revel in the freedom of their dream world. But in the summer of 1835 that freedom came to an end when Charlotte went as a teacher to Roe Head, where she had previously been a pupil. For the next three years her writing had to be confined to her holidays, a deprivation

which caused her keen suffering. Her collaboration with Branwell did not cease, however, for he embarked on a "History of
Angria" which was to run into nine parts: the kingdom suffered
invasion and civil war and Zamorna, betrayed by the jealous
Northangerland, had to endure defeat and exile before he finally
returned in triumph. Against this stormy background Charlotte,
in her vacations, imagined a series of episodes, usually dramatic,
sometimes satirical, and always firmly localised in Angrian
settings.

"Passing Events", written in the Eastern vacation of 1836,
and "Julia", written in the summer of 1837, are thus the product
of a disturbed period, both for the author and for Angria. Their
structure is episodic, betraying inner tensions, and Charlotte
alternates uneasily between straight narration and the continued
use of "Charles Townshend" – an older and more disillusioned
version of Lord Charles Wellesley – as chronicler. In these
circumstances the Angrian setting has a unifying effect on the
whole. The fundamental east–west opposition remains, and
Verdopolis still has an essential role, but the main action is
increasingly concentrated in the province of Zamorna and the
hilly region on its northern border. The episodic character of
these tales does not favour descriptions of any length, but a few
lines can suffice to give a vivid impression of physical reality.
Charlotte's constant awareness of the ever-changing beauty of
the sky is shared by the narrator "Charles Townshend" who,
after watching Zamorna's cavalrymen watering their horses in
the Guadima river, lifts his gaze to the scene above: "The
heavens were gathering their sombre blue, in the quarter where
the full & newly-risen moon hung over the Warner hills, that
blue was softened by a suffusion of mellow gold, the Zenith was
dark & little stars were kindling out of its gloom. 'Is any one man
amongst the scores that surround me thinking about that sky?',
said I, speaking unconsciously aloud."[21]

The sky was to be a constant in her work. Where setting was
concerned, she had already shown a liking for rural as well as for
wilder and more dramatic scenery. Even when she was un-
happiest at Roe Head, she was aware of its pleasant situation
and the wide view over its sloping lawns to Kirkleas Park and
the Calder Valley. Increasingly a liking for the park landscape,
with the country house at its centre, was beginning to emerge in
her stories. It had been evident in "The Spell". It is the inspira-

tion for a series of sketches in "Passing Events" and "Julia", where the country estates destined to become the focus of Angrian drama – the Lodge of Rivaulx, Girnington Hall, Hartford Hall – already have an individuality of their own. There is a more finished picture of such a landscape in the opening section of "Julia". As in "The Spell", a bypath known to the narrator leads to the "park-field" in the centre of which stands the house. Unlike the "fair Grecian villa" of "The Spell", this mansion is perfectly in keeping with its surroundings. Large and grey and grand, it needs neither shelter nor ornament, and instead of shrubbery or flowerbeds the daisied and undulating field which is the park stretches green as emerald to its very walls. The picture is convincing in its realism, but it is typical of the fragmentary nature of Charlotte's writing at this stage that this particular Angrian house remains without a name and plays no part in the subsequent action.

A great advance in technique is evident in "Mina Laury", written in the Christmas holidays of 1838. By this time the Angrian wars had ended with the reinstatement of Zamorna, and Charlotte was able to concentrate on what was now her deepest interest: the study of the passions and especially the passion of love. Mina Laury, Zamorna's mistress, who had already featured in earlier tales, is at the centre of this one. It represents a new level of achievement both in character analysis and skill of composition. What is equally evident is that the natural setting has now become an organic part of the whole. "Mina Laury" is, in its own way, a "Winter's Tale". The opening description, which contrasts a sheltered interior with the whirling snow without, sets the tone: "The cheerfulness within is enhanced by the dreary, wildered look of all without – the air is dimmed with snow careering through it in wild whirls – the sky is one mass of congealed tempest – heavy, wan & icy . . ."[22] One recognises already the sure touch that will paint Jane Eyre gazing at the dreary November garden from the precarious shelter of her window-seat at Gateshead. The Lodge at Rivaulx, on the edge of the forest of Hawkscliffe, is the scene of the main action. Its isolated situation, which harmonises with the life of Mina, is accentuated by the winter setting; the earth is "bound in frost, hard, mute & glittering" and the trees of the leafless forest cut off, "with a harsh serrated line", the wintry sky from the frozen countryside.

From "Mina Laury" onwards, Charlotte's tales can properly be classed as "juvenilia" only because they 'still belong to the Angrian saga. The growing maturity of her art is evident in "Captain Henry Hastings". When she wrote it in the spring of 1839, she was in her twenty-third year. She had left her teaching post and was at home again, but the family peace was increasingly disturbed by concern over Branwell. Hopes for a brilliant future for him as an artist had begun to decline with his abortive journey to London when he failed to enter the Academy schools. He tried to compensate for his failure partly by conforming to his own image of social rebel and partly by dramatising himself, in his continued Angrian writings, as Captain Henry Hastings, poet and soldier, who ruins a brilliant career through instability. Charlotte herself had already introduced the character of Henry Hastings in an episode of "Julia". The story of 1839 shows her deep concern over the decay of Branwell's brilliant promise. After shooting a superior officer whose provocative attitude has infuriated him, Hastings becomes a deserter and a fugitive from justice. His tragic fate is the main theme of a sombre tale.

In this story action and setting are once more indissolubly linked. Though the opening scenes are in Verdopolis, where Hastings is in hiding, his presence there is soon suspected and he decides to seek shelter in his native countryside, the hill and moorland region immediately to the north of the province of Zamorna. The actual home of the Hastings family is at Pendleton, whose situation offers evident analogies with the surroundings of Haworth. Their house, "Colne-Moss Tarn", combines manor and farm like other moorland homes belonging to yeomen farmers. But Henry's disgrace has disrupted the life of the family, and his sister Elizabeth, having quarrelled with their father on his account, has left home to become companion to the daughter of a local magnate. She is temporarily in charge of their isolated manor-house, Massinger Hall, nearer to the city of Zamorna, while the family are away, and it is with her that Hastings hopes to find refuge. After reaching the city, and crossing the river, he takes to the fields, threading, with rapid strides, "the broad far stretching Ings of the Olympian". It does not need the north-country term to show how familiar his route is to the author. He reaches the Hall in safety, but his pursuers soon hear of his presence there. The last stage of the pursuit, as described by one of the participants, is a headlong drive through

a wintry countryside lashed with rain and wind. The fierceness
of the elements contributes powerfully to the sombre effect of the
whole, conveying the sense of chaotic forces unleashed:

> . . . Evening was now setting in, & all the woods of the dale
> were bending under the gloom of heavy clouds & rushing to
> the impetus of the tremendous wind . . . on we thundered
> through rain & tempest & mist . . . I shall not soon forget that
> ride . . . woods & hills rolled by in dusky twilight – spangled
> with lights from the scattered houses of the valley – while rain
> drove slanting wildly over everything – & the swollen &
> roaring Olympian seemed running a mad race with ourselves.[23]

The hunt ends, in spite of his sister's desperate attempts to
save him, in Henry's discovery and arrest. A month later he
faces a court-martial in the city of Zamorna. His life is spared,
but the death sentence is commuted to service for life as a private
in an Angrian regiment notorious for its harsh discipline. Nevertheless his sister is thankful that he has left gaol with "the breath
of life in his body", and rather defiantly conscious that her
affection for him remains undiminished. But her involvement
with his misfortunes has lasting repercussions on her own destiny. Permanently exiled from home because of her sympathy
with him, she makes a life for herself as a teacher in the city of
Zamorna, but often longs passionately for her native moors and
hills:

> . . . So wild was her longing that when she looked out on the
> dusky sky – between the curtains of her bay-window – fancy
> seemed to trace on the horizon the blue outline of the moors –
> just as seen from the parlour at Colne-Moss – the evening star
> hung over the brow of Boulshill – the farm-fields stretched
> away between – & when reality returned, Houses, lamps &
> streets, she was phrenzied . . .[24]

It is in the vicinity of the moors that Elizabeth confronts a
further and unexpected crisis. Her courageous efforts to help her
brother had impressed the officer who had received the King's
commission to track him down, Sir William Percy. This fastidi-
ous aristocrat, who had begun by despising her, is now attracted
to her, and seeks her where he knows she is sure to go when she

has an afternoon's freedom, the solitary fields miles away from
the busy city, from which can be seen the landscape she loves, "a
line of hills darkly ridged with heath – now all empurpled with a
lovely sunset". In this setting he declares his love and asks her to
be his mistress. But though she adores him, and makes no
attempt to conceal the fact, she is no Mina Laury. She knows
that to yield would be to incur "the miseries of self-hatred", and
she forces herself to leave him, with the certainty that they will
never meet again.

"Captain Henry Hastings" is the most powerful of the juvenilia. It was followed the same year, 1839, by "Caroline Vernon",
begun after Charlotte's return from Stonegappe in Lothersdale,
where she had been a governess for a couple of months in the
Sidgwick family. There the difficulties of her uncongenial situation had prevented her from enjoying, but not from observing,
the beauty that surrounded her: "The country, the house, and
the grounds are, as I have said, divine . . . pleasant woods, white
paths, green lawns, and blue sunshiny sky . . .".[25] She had been
equally appreciative of the scenery, though equally unhappy in
her occupation, when she had accompanied the Sidgwicks, in the
course of the summer, on a visit to relatives at Swarcliffe, near
Harrogate, "a beautiful place in a beautiful country – rich and
agricultural". Her position had given her some opportunity to
observe, if from a distance, the life and occupations of a landed
proprietor as represented by Mr. Sidgwick who, when he strolled
through his fields, accompanied by his magnificent Newfoundland dog, "looked very like what a frank, wealthy Conservative
gentleman ought to be".

It is doubtless as a result of this experience that, in the first
chapters of "Caroline Vernon", Charlotte shows the Duke of
Zamorna, now peace has returned, enjoying a respite from his
not too arduous duties as monarch of Angria on his country
estate at Hawkscliffe. The growing emphasis on natural description is apparent in the highly visual presentation of the approach
to the manor:

Beyond these Gates there was no more forest, only de-
tatched clumps of trees & vast solitary specimens varying the
expanse of a large & wild Park which ascended . . . the long
aclivity of one of the Sydenhams. the remoter hills of the same
range rolled away clad in dusky woodland – till distance

softened them & the summer sky embued them with intense
violet. near the centre of the Park stood Hawkscliffe
House . . .[26]

At Hawkscliffe, visitors are soon made aware of the country
interests of the owner, who is generally out all day superintend-
ing the haymaking in his fields or fishing the river. Bound
volumes of the Agricultural Magazine are conspicuous in the
library, where neatly labelled packets containing samples of
wheat and oats lie on sidetables. Crops and planting trees are
topics of conversation. Dogs compete for their master's attention
and accompany him wherever they can: ". . . the door was
promptly opened & his Grace walked in – some Dogs walked in
too – the whole party equally heedless of who might or might not
be in the room . . .".[27]

The chief interest of the story, however, is centred on Zamorna's young ward Caroline Vernon, daughter of Northangerland
and the dancer Louisa Vernon, who is being educated at a house
in the vicinity. When, at the wish of her father, who has returned
from exile and been pardoned by Zamorna, she is removed from
this sheltered environment and sent to "Paris", capital of the
island of "Frenchland", to acquire the social graces, she gains
sophistication without maturity. Now aware that her much
admired guardian is a libertine, she also becomes aware that she
loves him. Her father tries to prevent their meeting by sending
her away to a remote part in the extreme north of the Verdopolitan territory, a region obviously corresponding, in Brontë topography, to the Highlands of the Waverley novels. She arrives
there "late on a wet & windy November night" and, obsessed by
romantic dreams of Zamorna, never feels anything but repulsion
for "that amphitheatre of Highlands towards which the cottage
looked". Escaping from her exile, she returns to Angria and
becomes Zamorna's mistress, doomed in future, like Mina Laury,
to live in luxurious isolation. The hothouse atmosphere of the later
chapters contrasts with the pastoral opening scenes and appears
out of harmony with their realism. "Caroline Vernon", though
acute as a psychological study, fails for this reason to convey the
sense of place as powerfully as "Captain Henry Hastings". But
here, too, the changes of physical environment are an essential
part of the whole.

By the end of 1839 Charlotte Brontë felt that the time had

come to bid a reluctant farewell to Angria, though her brother
continued for some years to make spasmodic additions to the
story of Alexander Percy, epitome of the spirit of revolt in the
cycle. Charlotte's farewell is addressed both to the country and
its inhabitants. The country comes first:

> I have shown my landscapes in every variety of shade and
> light which morning, noon and evening – the rising, the
> meridian and the setting sun can bestow upon them. Some-
> times I have filled the air with the whitened tempest of winter:
> snow has embossed the dark arms of the beech and oak and
> filled with drifts the parks of the lowlands or the mountain-
> pass of wilder districts. Again, the same mansion with its
> woods, the same moor with its glens, has been softly coloured
> with the tints of moonlight in summer, and in the warmest
> June night the trees have clustered their full-plumed heads
> over glades flushed with flowers.[28]

Charlotte Brontë herself here defines the nature of the landscapes of her juvenilia. She recognises that they are usually of
two types, the wooded park with the country house at its centre,
or the moorland with its glens and high passes. Variety comes
from variations in the light, the weather, the seasons. Her
lifelong interest in the play of the elements, evident from childhood, is reflected in her intense sensitivity to climatic conditions,
and this in turn is reflected in her landscapes. The timing of the
action in her stories often approximated more or less to the
actual period of their composition, with the result that they may
incorporate her own reactions to the warmth of a July afternoon
or the chill of a December evening. So deep was her involvement
with this aspect of her narration that she sometimes mentioned
the actual date of crucial events. It was in the early spring of
1839 that "Captain Henry Hastings" was written, and the
court-martial of Hastings takes place in March, on "the 19th day
of the month, & Tuesday by the week", both day and date being,
as Winifred Gérin has confirmed, "correct by the calendar for
1839".[29] The court-martial is held in the town of Zamorna, and
there is an arresting freshness in the description of the March
morning, and also in the charming coda: "One could tell that in
the country the grass was growing green, that the trees were
knotty with buds & the gardens golden with crocuses."[30]

But Charlotte's "Farewell to Angria" is also addressed to its inhabitants. And she claims that she has used the same method in her portraits as in her landscapes, studying one set of people, but in different moods and at different times. Certainly her sitters, like her landscapes, are recurrent subjects. Their physical appearance and their dress are often admirably rendered. But she has more to learn in character analysis than in her observation of nature. In Angria no one is old, and few are middle-aged. It is the land of youth, and especially of Byronic youth. Charlotte, naturally attracted to passionate temperaments, is at her best when painting them, as long as her sympathy with them does not prevent her from exercising at the same time the critical faculty which she undoubtedly possessed and, when her sympathy was not engaged, could carry to excess.

It is noticeable that, in this revealing valedictory, she makes no explicit reference to any relationship between her landscape painting and her portraits which goes deeper than a similarity of approach. It is clear, however, that the action of her stories is closely linked with the various settings, and that there is increasingly a correspondence between setting and general atmosphere. What is less clear is the relationship between the natural environment and the individual. But there is a recognition, in "Captain Henry Hastings", that there are temperaments which possess "that strong refinement of the senses" which makes them "thrill with undefined emotion at changes or chances in the skies or the earth, in a softness in the clouds, a trembling of moonlight in water – an old & vast tree – the tone of the passing wind at night . . .".[31] It is evident that such exceptional sensitivity is rare, and there is a suggestion that this conscious affinity with the elements is an indication of unusual imaginative power.

There is only one figure of the Angrian cycle who is throughout associated by the author with elemental forces and that is the Duke of Zamorna himself. His ancestral home is in the "woodland west" which, for the Brontës, corresponds to Ireland, the green isle of their father's nostalgic memories, and to the "vernal clime" of their own childhood. When he becomes King of Angria, however, he establishes his kingdom in the east, and the difference between east and west is also, in this context, the difference between the poetic dreams of his early youth and the "burning clime" of his young manhood. The description of a portrait of him at this time begins: "Fire! Light! . . . Zamorna's self blazing . . . like the sun on his own standard . . .".[32] The sun is his emblem, as fire is his element. As a man he is unconvincing, an unlikely combination of the majestic, the charming and the completely amoral. But in attempting to portray him, Charlotte took the first step towards that use of nature and the elements to convey emotions and passions which was to become one of the most original features of her art. Zamorna's changing moods can be described in terms of natural forces. His anger is the electric explosion of a thundercloud, but the outburst may be succeeded by a darkness like that of an extinct volcano. At such moments the art of Charlotte Brontë already approaches greatness, for what she is describing in terms of the elements is not Zamorna alone but the Romantic genius destroyed by the fierceness of its own fires:

> Long Zamorna lay awake . . . he saw his lamp expire – he saw the brilliant flame of the hearth settle into ruddy embers – then fade, decay & at last perish – he felt silence & total darkness close around him – but still the unslumbering eye wandered over images which the fiery imagination pourtrayed upon vacancy – thought yielded at last & sleep triumphed – Zamorna lay in dead repose amidst the hollow darkness of his chamber . . .[33]

Part II
Anne Brontë and Nature

3 Poems

It might seem unlikely that Anne, the youngest of the family, should prove, in her attitude to nature, the least of an innovator. But she was in reality nearer to the eighteenth century than either of her sisters, and for this reason it seems fitting to begin the study of their individual relationship to nature with her writings. This is not to say that her work was in any sense an anachronism. Like her sisters, she was of the nineteenth century, and was steeped in the poetry of Scott, Byron and Wordsworth. But her deepest affinities were with Wordsworth, not with his metaphysical ecstasies but with his use of what has been described as the "reflective imagination".[1] Feeling and reflection were Anne's salient qualities, and these were qualities much esteemed in the eighteenth century. But, with her, feeling was intense and, unlike sensibility, never degenerated into sentimentality, and reflection had to do not with philosophical abstractions but with personal experience. There was fire and steel in Anne, as in her sisters, but they were less evident on the surface and she strove more consciously for equilibrium. Such an attitude was not perhaps likely to produce an interpretation of nature as original as that of Charlotte or Emily. But, like them, she was not looking for originality but for truth.

Like Charlotte in her juvenilia, she and Emily began with the chronicles of a dream world, growing naturally out of the oral "plays" of childhood. But, unlike Charlotte, they retained their allegiance to their kingdom of Gondal throughout most of their adult life. It is consequently impossible to treat the Gondal literature otherwise than as an integral part of their work. The prose chronicles have disappeared, but the poems, the earliest dating from 1836, still survive.

Of Anne's poetic output about a third stems from this source. Such poems are usually identifiable by the use of Gondal signatures or the inclusion of characters with Gondal proper names.[2] In most of them a situation is evoked which presupposes the

73

influence of past events, but these remain largely unrevealed. They obviously belong to the legendary scenario, but whereas, in the case of Emily, attempts have been made to reconstruct the history of Gondal with the help of her poems, such attempts would clearly be doomed to failure in the case of Anne. She conveys atmosphere rather than action and treats themes rather than events. But her themes, inevitably, resemble those of Emily. And for her, as for her sister, nature plays an important part in the harmony of the whole.

In climate and physical features their imagined island in the North Pacific was very similar to their home surroundings, though on a grander scale, with hills elevated to mountains. Anne, unlike Emily, makes no mention of the southern colony of Gaaldine in her verse. If the characters in her early poem "Alexander and Zenobia" first meet "on Grecia's classic plain", and part from each other "in Araby", this intrusion of the Byronic exotic does not prevent them from being reunited ultimately beneath the skies of their native Gondal. Basically the landscape evoked by Anne in these poems is that familiar to her from childhood.

From that childhood she was not yet separated by many years when, between sixteen and eighteen, she wrote the first group of her Gondal poems. Her rambles on the moors with Emily, her "almost twin", had undoubtedly been the happiest feature of those early years. When she hears the north wind blowing, it seems to speak to her in a familiar language of that blissful time:

"I have passed over thy own mountains dear,
Thy northern mountains – and they still are free,
Still lonely, wild, majestic, bleak and drear,
And stern and lovely, as they used to be

When thou, a young enthusiast,
As wild and free as they,
O'er rocks and glens and snowy heights
Didst often love to stray.[3]

It is worth noting that "the gentle Anne" shared instinctively Emily's delight in the wilder aspects of nature. Like Emily also she delighted in the hidden valleys that broke the surface of the moors, the streams that flowed there, the birds that sang among the trees:

".. . do you remember
A little lonely spring
Among Exina's woody hills
Where blackbirds used to sing . . ."[4]

But nature can only be enjoyed where there is liberty. The poem "The North Wind" has a mournful resonance because it is from a prison cell that the listener replies to the wind's message. In Anne's Gondal poetry, as in Emily's, nature is not infrequently glimpsed through prison bars or remembered in the vaults of a dungeon. Imprisonment was a familiar feature of life both in Gondal and Angria, where the children of leading families were sent for their education to a "Palace of Instruction" which included subterranean prison cells as well as schoolrooms. But what had begun as a childhood fantasy, of a suitably gruesome kind, soon acquired deeper implications. Captivity was a favourite theme with the authors they knew best. Scott showed Highland chieftains in the power of their enemies, Roderick Dhu in Stirling Castle or Fergus Mac-Ivor in the tower at Carlisle, still thinking of the blue hills of his own country. Byron explored the whole gamut of the captive's sufferings from despair to apathy in *The Prisoner of Chillon*. In the more mundane sphere of their everyday life both Anne and Emily, when called on to exchange their freedom of their native hills for the schoolroom routine at Roe Head, must have viewed their new environment very much as a prison. Emily's health broke under the strain. Anne endured for two years what was certainly as pleasant a régime as any school could provide. But it is noticeable that her early Gondal poems were chiefly written in the holidays, or after finally returning to Haworth. "The North Wind" concludes with an appeal to the beloved element which is charged with an emotion obviously much less derivative than that of the first Gondal love poems:

Confined and hopeless as I am,
O speak of liberty,
O tell me of my mountain home,
And I will welcome thee.[5]

During her second and longer period of exile, when she was a governess at Thorp Green, Anne wrote only a few Gondal poems. It was after she had given up her post in June 1845 and returned home that most of the later group were written. At Haworth she and Emily resumed their collaboration, which still included oral improvisation. But their diary papers for 1845 reflect a marked difference in their attitude. For Emily, "The Gondals still flourish as bright as ever", but Anne shows much less enthusiasm: "The Gondals in general are not in first-rate playing condition." By this time the history of their imaginary world which, in its broad outline, showed an analogy with Angria, had reached a stage when open war had broken out between Royalists and Republicans.

In the poems of this period the theme of captivity still alternates at times with that of nature, like shadow with sunlight. From the vague indications given it appears that the cause of captivity is not usually war but family hostility, like that of the Montagues and the Capulets, to youthful lovers. With the idealism which characterises the portrayal of love in Anne's Gondal poems, each suffers most in the suffering of the other. In "Weep not too much, my darling", the prisoner consoles himself with the thought that at least his beloved Zerona is still free to look on "the charms of Nature", though he cannot do so himself. But he admits that he suffers keenly from the deprivation. When the moonbeams shine through the prison grating he longs wildly

> To see the orb divine
> Not crossed, deformed, and sullied
> By those relentless bars . . .[6]

As Joseph Le Guern has pointed out, the striking image is at the same time an unconscious reflection of Wordsworth's use of the words "deformed and sullied", in his poem "Nutting", to express, in different circumstances, a similar sense of the desecration of nature.[7]

In the Gondal poems of this period Anne is also obliged to come to terms with the theme of war. It was not a theme naturally congenial to her, and it is all the more surprising that it should have provided material for some of the best of her Gondal verse. In fact, it impelled her to reflect, as the Romantics who were contemporaries of the French Revolution had done, on the consequences when the ideals of nature and liberty were invoked to justify revolution by violent means, especially the conse-

quences for the revolutionaries themselves. The spokesman in
the poem entitled simply "Song" is one of the conquering
Republicans, but this is no song of triumph. In a vivid metaphor
he expresses his intense distaste for the task of hunting his
conquered foes as he had himself been hunted, declaring that he
would rather be the startled hare, forced to abandon cover and
seek the bare hillside, than the hunter's hound. This poem is
followed by a second "Song" still more ironic in tone. Here the
speaker again refuses, even more decisively than before, to rejoin
the chorus "in praise of deadly vengeance", and comes to the
conclusion that he had been closer to nature and to freedom
when he had had to seek shelter from his enemies in the wilds:

> Is *this* the end we struggled to obtain?
> O for the wandering Outlaw's life again![8]

A year later Anne returned to the same situation, but treated
it from a different angle, in the longer and more dramatic poem
"I dreamt last night . . .". The Gondal speaker, whose initials
are given as "E.Z.", is a political leader, presumably a Republican one, who in pursuance of his aims has killed the dearest
friend of his boyhood. The exact circumstances of the assassination and the political situation remain obscure. The main
emphasis is on the dream itself, an imaginary scene in the
boyhood of the two former friends, and on the awakening that
follows.

In the dream, and significantly here alone, nature has a vital
part. Two boys, of whom "E.Z." is the elder, have wandered far
away across the hills on a breezy sunny day. They are completely in harmony with their well-known and much loved
surroundings and with each other, even though the younger has
some difficulty in keeping pace with his more vigorous companion:

> He bade me pause and breathe a while,
> But spoke it with a happy smile.
>
> His lips were parted to inhale
> The breeze that swept the ferny dale,
> And chased the clouds across the sky,
> And waved his locks in passing by,
> And fanned my cheek; (so real did seem
> This strange, untrue, but truthlike dream;)[9]

The elder boy, out of high spirits, then initiates a trial of strength
between them, but he brings it to an end when he suspects that
the other is beginning to resent his physical superiority, and
perfect harmony is restored.

But the passing hint of discord is in reality the prelude to the
gradual and reluctant return of the dreamer to full consciousness
and to the horrified realisation that he has been the pitiless agent
of the cruel death of his former friend. For the first time he feels
remorse, but it proves to be an emotion in which he dare not
indulge without endangering the cause to whose furtherance he
has determined to devote his life:

> Time's current cannot backward run;
> And be the action wrong or right,
>   It is for ever done.[10]

He foresees that the course on which he has embarked will call
for more victims in the future, but feels he has no option but to
continue. His situation offers evident analogies with that of the
reluctant victor of the earlier "Songs", but is more tragic because of his personal involvement with one of the victims, and
because he considers himself inescapably committed to further
violence. Anne is not concerned primarily, in either case, with a
political but with a moral issue. The tragedy of "I dreamt last
night" is that, in the course of a fratricidal struggle, two close
friends have been turned into implacable enemies.

Anne's Gondal poems inevitably bear a family resemblance to
those of Emily. Both sisters were attracted by the same aspects of
nature: the moors in all seasons and the elements, especially the
wind. Both loved liberty and sympathised with the sufferings of
those who, for whatever reason, were deprived of it. Both were
influenced by Byron in their painting of the captive's plight. But
Anne's prisoners are more resigned, though they do occasionally
express themselves with a desperation that suggests the direct
influence of Emily. Her treatment of love, however, is, unlike her
sister's, unfailingly idyllic. Even in the rare cases where the lover
has to suffer not only from family hostility but from indifference
or even faithlessness on the part of the loved one, bitterness is
entirely absent. In their treatment of the Gondal wars neither
sister shows the Angrian admiration of military glory in itself.
But Emily does not hesitate to evoke, though briefly, scenes of

blood and carnage. Anne shows only one act of violence, in "I dreamt last night . . .". She puts the main emphasis on the moral tragedy, but the fact that the moorland setting has now been reduced to a dream suggests that the man who hates his brother is unlikely to remain in tune with nature.

Anne's Gondal poems thus express, to a recognisable degree, her own individuality. But it is doubtful if she would have retained her allegiance to the dream world as long as she did, had she not felt it to be a means of preserving her close links with Emily. In her personal verse, on the other hand, she expresses herself directly, without the interposition of a fictional screen. It is here that her feelings and thoughts manifest themselves most clearly and here, in consequence, that her attitude to nature is most fully revealed.

Her devotion to her native landscape remains one of her recurrent themes. Without the transparent disguise of Gondal its characteristic features stand out even more clearly. Not surprisingly it was during the years she spent near York, in the midst of lush, open country, that Anne first realised the full extent of her commitment to the moors and hills of her childhood. In a poem called "Home", written at Thorp Green, she deliberately contrasts the climate, milder even in winter, and the more sheltered situation of her present abode with the bleakness of the moors and round Haworth, but only in order to affirm her devotion to the latter:

> . . . That sun surveys a lovely scene
>> From softly smiling skies;
> And wildly through unnumbered trees
>> The wind of winter sighs:
>
> Now loud, it thunders o'er my head,
>> And now in distance dies.
> But give me back my barren hills,
>> Where colder breezes rise:
>
> Where scarce the scattered, stunted trees
>> Can yield an answering swell,
> But where a wilderness of heath
>> Returns the sound as well.[11]

In the circumstances any reminder of the moors was precious. Such was the unexpected sight of a bluebell in the first months of her exile, and the flower inspired a nostalgic poem. Later, shutting her eyes to the floral splendours of the gardens at Thorp Green, it was no longer any visible flower that she praised but the power to conjure up, irrespective of the present, all the flowers that had charmed her childhood and, by extension, its familiar setting:

> Sweet memory, ever smile on me;
> Nature's chief beauties spring from thee . . .
>
> Forever hang thy dreamy spell
> Round golden star and heatherbell,
>   And do not pass away
> From sparkling frost, or wreathed snow,
> And whisper when the wild winds blow
>   Or rippling waters play.[12]

The Wordsworthian echoes are evident, and become still more so in the concluding lines, where Anne recognises that it is only the memories of early childhood that have such peculiar power to charm, though, for her, even early childhood is not remembered as having been totally immune from grief and consequently not as "all divine".

It is certain, however, that is was in her early years that she enjoyed the most complete and blissful communion with nature, and she remained faithful to her memories of Haworth throughout her period of exile at Thorp Green, broken only by the twice-yearly holidays. But exile brought at least one compensation: it gave her her first opportunity to know the sea. Every summer her employers spent some time at Scarborough, where she accompanied them, and there, in sight and sound of the ocean, she experienced a sense of exhilaration comparable to that she had felt in listening to the voice of the mountain wind. It was the same elemental freedom, the same elemental strength which attracted her in both. Wild seas, like wild winds, became a treasured part of her experience; memories of both blended in her imagination and in "Lines Composed in a Wood on a Windy Day" the sound of the wind is enough to suggest the surge of the waves and induce a mood of exceptional gaiety:

> My soul is awakened, my spirit is soaring,
> And carried aloft on the wings of the breeze;

For, above and around me, the wild wind is roaring
Arousing to rapture the earth and the seas.[13]

It was rare, however, for Anne in her personal poems to be
transported into a state like this, where joy in nature precludes
reflection. More characteristic of her attitude is the poem "In
Memory of a Happy Day in February", written at Thorp Green
in the same year 1842. Here her considered attitude to nature is
made clear. She appreciates the sunshine and the breezes of
early spring, but they are not in themselves the chief cause of the
"rapture strong and deep" of which she is conscious. Nature is
beautiful above all because it is God's creation, and important as
it is to Anne, it is not of such vital importance as the inner world
of the spirit:

I knew there was a God on high
  By whom all things were made.
I saw his wisdom and his power
  In all his works displayed.

But most throughout the moral world
  I saw his glory shine . . .[14]

It was during the years at Thorp Green that Anne's personality
matured and nature, though always dear to her, both as inspiration and consolation, became increasingly associated with
other major themes concerning her personal life.
  It might have been expected to play an important role in her
love poems, since love and nature are closely associated in her
Gondal verse. But the opposite is the case, and the reason is that
Anne, when she writes not of the experience of an imagined
Zenobia but of her own, is obliged, in material terms, to speak
mainly of absence and death. After lamenting the absence of the
loved one, she expresses, in the key poem "To _____", written at
the end of 1842, her reaction to the news of his death. It is typical
of her attitude that she thinks more of him than of herself, and
finds her chief consolation in the knowledge that his life, though
short, has been a happy one. If the one spot on earth that
commemorates him is a tomb within church walls, she can still
see him in dreams, not in the higher state of being to which he
has attained, but as she remembers him. If, as the evidence

seems to indicate, the object of her love was her father's curate
William Weightman, who came to Haworth in 1839 and died
there in September 1842, she can only have seen him in her
holidays and there is little to show how he really felt towards
her.[15] Anne herself does not speak of his love but of his smile, his
"laughing eye" and his kindness, qualities which endeared him
to all the parsonage family. There is little trace of possessiveness
in her attitude, but there is no doubt about the strength of her
own feelings for the young man in whom she recognised

> The lightest heart that I have known,
> The kindest I shall ever know.[16]

The reflective power which, with her, accompanied depth of
feeling enabled her, however, at the same time, to ponder on the
general significance of her situation and to express it by means of
an archetypal image. "The Captive Dove", mostly written in the
spring of 1842 but bearing the date 31 October 1843, a year after
Weightman's death, says much within a narrow compass. Anne's
tenderness for the animal creation, as well as her own longing for a
less restricted existence, can be sensed in her initial description
of the imprisoned bird. Like any other in the same plight, it can
only flap its "useless wings" and gaze into the distant sky. But
the dove is particularly associated with love for its mate, and
their mutual devotion has been celebrated in song and fable by
many writers, including Cowper, whom she much admired.[17]
That it should be mateless is a dual frustration of its natural
destiny. The symbolic use of the captive bird is frequent in
poetry, and Edward Chitham has indicated the analogy with
Shelley's use of the nightingale in "Epipsychidion".[18] But there
is a peculiar fitness in Anne's choice of the dove. Her symbolism
combines classic generality with personal emotion, and never
more so than in the transparent depth of the concluding lines:

> But thou, poor solitary dove,
> Must make unheard thy joyless moan;
> The heart that nature formed to love
> Must pine neglected and alone.[19]

Until she came to Thorp Green Anne does not appear to have
written any religious poetry. But as one of her last poems

"Self-Communion" shows, she had from an early age felt the need of a personal religion. Temperamentally she was probably nearer, in this respect, to her mother and her eldest sister Maria than any of the other Brontë children. She was very conscious of her own shortcomings and was comforted, even as a child, by finding in her much admired Cowper the reflection of many of her own hopes and fears, though, as she afterwards recognised, she never plumbed the same depths of despair and was to reject emphatically, in her poem "A Word to the 'Elect'", the Calvinistic doctrines that caused him such suffering. But at Thorp Green, during the difficult years when her hopes of love, her hopes of a better future for her brother Branwell and her efforts to make the best of her uncongenial employment were all frustrated, she came increasingly to depend on her religion for the inner strength she so much needed. At the outset of this period she could still attain the happiness and assurance of "In Memory of a Happy Day in February", where the sense of spiritual elevation does not exclude an awareness of the beauty of the physical universe. But the growing pressure of despondency and at times of doubt drove her sometimes to withdraw even from nature for meditation and prayer.

Such moments are recorded in a series of poems which have much in common with the evangelical hymns of the eighteenth century, including those of Cowper. Written between 1840 and 1845 they trace the oscillations of her spiritual life, in the Thorp Green years, between despondency and confidence. Basically her faith was assured, but she found it hard, in her difficult circumstances, to achieve the serenity for which she craved. Nature is normally absent from this series of poems but reappears, used symbolically, in the curiously enigmatic "Fluctuations". The title suggests Anne's spiritual dilemma, but there is no explicit reference to religion, until the closing lines. The speaker mourns the disappearance of the sun, but is cheered by the slow rising of the moon out of a haze of mist. Soon, however, thick vapours obliterate the moonlight and plunge the scene again into darkness. This retrogression from light to darkness is twice repeated; a star appears, only to vanish, and is followed by a meteor, which disappears in its turn. Finally a faint light struggling through the clouds suggests the possible re-emergence of the moon. Unlike "The Captive Dove" this poem admits of no general interpretation. The symbolism is elusive, but suggests a

reference to the speaker's own experience both on the spiritual
and the emotional level. In fact the two are indissolubly blended
and only the last verse makes it clear that the ultimate hope of
returning light rests not with the natural but with the super
natural.

> Kind Heaven, increase that silvery gleam
> And bid these clouds depart . . .[20]

When she finally returned to Haworth in June 1845 Anne
resumed, as has already been said, her collaboration with Emily
in the Gondal saga, where, as before, nature had its part. Her
personal poems, however, show an evolution during which the
theme of nature, like her other themes, undergoes significant
modification. Her starting-point is, as always, her individual
experience, but she now felt the need, and the capacity, to relate
it to life in general. In this final period of her poetic creation
Anne emerges as a moralist, and the increased scope of her work
is reflected in the more ample treatment she accords her subjects
in these few but significant poems. It is now her evident desire to
make her terms of reference as wide as possible and nature
considered in general terms, frequently provides an analogical
framework for her argument.

In "Vanitas Vanitatis" the ceaseless movement of the waves is
paralleled by the unending succession of the generations:

> While yet the rolling earth abides,
> Men come and go like Ocean tides;[21]

In "Views of Life" the gradual fading of the colours from the
sunset sky is a symbol of the slow process of disillusionment that
lies in store for all. It forms the prelude to a dialogue between
hope and experience, both personified, in the presence of youth
Here the traditional comparison between the seasons and the
successive stages of human life is treated in a way that allows it
to become a cogent part of the argument. Experience tells of
having been promised by hope, when young, the joys of spring
when instead the sky was overcast, hope held out the promise of
a glorious summer, but instead came scorching days of utter
languor; hope then predicted a golden autumn, but this proved
to be a season of chilling mists, and was followed by winds that

unmistakably heralded the winter. As a result experience warns youth that no confidence can ever be placed in the promises of hope. But Anne Brontë, while admitting that there is much truth in the words of experience, comes none the less to the defence of hope as a necessity of human life:

> . . . hope itself a brightness throws
> O'er all our labours and our woes . . .[22]

If there is no necessary correspondence between the harmonious rhythm of the seasons and the often difficult course of human life, there is an undoubted correspondence between hope and courageous living, and ultimately between hope and confident dying.

"The Three Guides", like "Views of Life", uses the dialogue form, particularly suited to rational argument. The poet, faced with three possible attitudes to life, considers the claims of each in turn and makes her own response. The first is personified by the "Spirit of Earth", but it at once becomes clear that "earth", in this context, means not nature as part of the divine creation but nature as interpreted by rationalist thought. The "Spirit of Earth" is the spokesman of positivism. Here Anne's didacticism has an obvious relevance to the contemporary climate of ideas. That rationalism did represent a temptation, though never an attraction, to her reflective temperament, is evident from the vehemence with which she reacts against it. She rejects it primarily and explicitly on the grounds of her faith, but her whole soul is revolted by a philosophy which, in her eyes, reduces nature to its bleakest aspect, symbolised by such elements as miry clay and flinty stone, and shuts out all the glories of "hill and dale and sky". Very different to this earth-bound attitude is that of the "Spirit of Pride". Its appeal is to exceptional natures, who feel themselves above their fellow-men. Its votaries are summoned not to keep their eyes fixed on earth but to climb the mountain-side, pitting their strength triumphantly against the fury of the elements. Theirs appears to be an enviable position when they are finally seen standing against the sky, dominating immense vistas. But their triumph is temporary, for the Spirit of Pride makes no attempt to save them from falling to their death in the abyss or perishing among the snows. Both the landscape and the attitude of the Spirit are reminiscent of Byron's *Manfred*, and of Byronic Romanticism at its most defiant.[23] In rejecting the Spirit of Pride, while acknowledging that it possesses an almost supernatural fascination, Anne is at the same time recognising the dangers of the Byronic cult carried to extremes. This is not to say that she has ceased to love either mountain scenery or liberty as Byron did, but that she has grown aware of the dangers of elevating genius to the status of divinity. The only sure guide proves to be the third and last, the Spirit of Faith. It does not offer an easy journey through life. Indeed those who follow its guidance must often turn aside from "pleasant meads" and "running waters" to deserts and rocky uplands. But it alone can reveal

Secrets concealed from Nature's ken . . .

Unlike the others, it offers the certainty of divine protection throughout the rough journey and of safe arrival at the ultimate goal.

"Self-Communion", Anne Brontë's longest poem, is personal rather than didactic, and frankly autobiographical. But it once more takes the form of a dialogue, in which the speakers are herself and "Reason, with conscience by her side". Reason is personified as a mentor who brings back memories of the past and reveals its true meaning. The autumnal background is in perfect harmony with the theme and, as the poem was begun in the late autumn, is likely not to have been purely symbolic in origin but a reflection, such as often occurs in the work of her sisters and herself, of the weather conditions at the time of writing:

The mist is resting on the hill;
The smoke is hanging in the air;
The very clouds are standing still;
A breathless calm broods everywhere.[24]

But the function of this autumnal setting, with its sense of arrested life, is to induce a mood in which the poet can pause, in the company of reason, to reflect on the past. She sees herself first, far back, as a child, "more timid than the wild wood-dove", affectionate by nature and intensely vulnerable. It is noticeable that the particular incident chosen to illustrate this vulnerability, and its implications for the future, is the child's overwhelming grief at the death of a bird:

That heart so prone to overflow
E'en at the *thought* of other's woe,
  How will it bear its own?

How, if a sparrow's death can wring
Such bitter tearfloods from the eye,
Will it behold the suffering
Of struggling, lost humanity?

In the succeeding verses, Anne retraces first the stages of her religious experience and then, in revealing lines, the process by which she gradually acquired, under the pressures of life, a stoicism which was, for her, more of an unwelcome necessity than a consolation. The allegorical use of nature reappears with the comparison of her entire past to the gradually fading colours of an initially brilliant sky. The beginning is Wordsworthian:

My life has been a morning sky
Where Hope her rainbow glories cast
O'er kindling vapours far and nigh . . .

But the colours gradually fade not into "the light of common day" but into what promises shortly to become a cheerless monochrome, "a rayless arch of sombre grey", evidently intended as a memento mori by the poet, who from the outset has known time to be her enemy. Reason makes no attempt to contradict the truth of her forebodings, but emphasises the need for urgent action, while time still allows it, to ease the suffering of others, and encourages her with the assurance of finally attaining lasting rest beyond the grave. In the concluding lines there is the same confidence as that of Wordsworth

In the soothing thoughts that spring
Out of human suffering;
In the faith that looks through death,
In years that bring the philosophic mind.[25]

In "The Narrow Way", written a year before her death, Anne Brontë returns to the hymn tradition and to the archetypal pilgrim image of the Christian life. The toils of the journey, and the hope that lies ahead, are her theme, and nature in itself has no place here, but can still provide a fitting symbol for beauty of a higher order:

> . . . there amid the sternest heights,
> The sweetest flowerets gleam; –

> On all her breezes borne
> Earth yields no scents like those;
> But he, that dares not grasp the thorn
> Should never crave the rose.[26]

Ann Brontë's last poem, written in January 1849, shows her coming to terms with approaching death. Darkness and mist, both so intense as almost to supersede thought, are at first the natural symbols of her bewildered state. But she finds strength where she has always found it, in faith and in reason clarified by faith, and her last poem becomes the final and finest illustration of the same process which has always characterised her religious poetry, the sure ascent from initial faltering to a renewed capacity for a fuller life, either here or hereafter.

Her poetic work is small in volume but not in significance. It was, as she explains in *Agnes Grey*, in poetry that she found a means of expression for those intensely personal thoughts and feelings which she was obliged to keep to herself, knowing they would not be understood by others, but which were too precious to her to be entirely suppressed. The poems offer the most direct access to the inner life of Anne Brontë.

But their value is not only autobiographical. She had qualities as a poet in her own right. She did not aspire to romantic richness of imagery, and the style of her didactic poems is reminiscent of eighteenth century poetic diction in its clarity and its allegorical use of abstractions, as the style of her religious poems is reminiscent of the evangelical hymn-writers. But her utter sincerity and her resolute rejection of inessentials give a compelling quality to her lucid verse. And she frequently showed a sensitivity and a perceptiveness which recall Wordsworth rather than the eighteenth century. This is particularly evident when she speaks of nature. If she personifies memory, she knows there is no need to personify a flower:

> A fine and subtle spirit dwells
> In every little flower,

Each one its own sweet feeling breathes
With more or less of power.

There is a silent eloquence
In every wild bluebell
That fills my softened heart with bliss
That words could never tell.[27]

Where the verse form is concerned, Anne Brontë was at her
ease from the first. Even in her earliest Gondal poems the
stanzas flow smoothly and effortlessly, and she is already sufficiently master of her art to introduce variations in rhyme
scheme and length of stanza, and occasional changes of metre
where they suggest themselves. Derek Stanford has pointed out
her debt, in this respect, to Scott and to the Border Ballads
whose verse represents "the greatest variety of rhythmical effects
within a simple verbal structure".[28] As in the ballads themselves
the rhythm may be associated with that of nature:

The flowerets twice on hill and dale
Have bloomed and died away,
And twice the rustling forest leaves
Have fallen to decay . . .[29]

Here the regular pace of the iambics perfectly corresponds to the
recurrent rhythm of the seasons. But Anne Brontë's verse can
also echo the exhilaration of nature's most rapid movements, as
in the joyous cadence of the anapaests in "Lines composed in a
Wood on a Windy Day":

I wish I could see how the ocean is lashing
The foam of its billows to whirlwinds of spray,
I wish I could see how its proud waves are dashing
And hear the wild roar of their thunder today![30]

4 Agnes Grey

Anne Brontë's first novel *Agnes Grey* is basically similar in outlook to her personal poems. In the opinion of a number of critics, it may have been begun during the Thorp Green period. The evidence for this is usually considered to be Anne's mention, in her birthday note of 1845, of having begun the third volume of "Passages in the Life of an Individual", which is held to suggest a work of the same type as *Agnes Grey*. But the identification is not certain, for the same birthday note alludes to the Gondal Chronicles, and the "individual" could be a Gondal character.[1] But whether Anne preceded her sisters in beginning the first Brontë novel intended for publication or not, it is certain that *Agnes Grey*, like *Wuthering Heights* and *The Professor*, was completed by July 1846, a year after her final return from Thorp Green.

The material she used in it was drawn largely from her experience in her two situations as governess. This is not to say that the Bloomfields of Wellwood House were replicas of the Inghams of Blake Hall, or that the life of the Murrays at Horton Lodge offered an exact parallel to that of the Robinsons of Thorp Green. When Anne Brontë claimed, in her opening chapter, that her tale was a "true history", she made it clear that, like any artist, she had introduced modifications, while remaining true to the basic reality of experience. She also showed, by alluding to the "lapse of years", that Agnes Grey, in reviewing her trials as a governess, now sees them in a broader perspective. Nor can even the more mature Agnes be completely identified with her creator. But the deliberate choice of the autobiographical form, maintained throughout, permits a certain sense of intimacy with the writer's personality. When Charlotte Brontë said that *Agnes Grey* was "the mirror of the mind of the writer",[2] her verdict contained a good deal of truth.

In *Agnes Grey* Anne Brontë shows the same virtues of lucidity, concision and sincerity which were evident in her poems. To readers who look for the brilliance of *Wuthering Heights* or *Jane Eyre* the work is inevitably disappointing. Her originality is of another sort. As in her poetry there are affinities with the eighteenth century. Winifred Gérin has suggested Goldsmith and Maria Edgeworth as her literary progenitors. But it is the vibrations of a nineteenth-century sensibility, as well as the reflective processes of a thoughtful and logical mind, which Anne has succeeded in capturing in her spare and unadorned prose. It should be remembered that in moments of extreme tension it is to poetry that Agnes Grey turns as a secret source of consolation, either to her own efforts or to Byron:

> They may crush, but they shall not subdue me!
> 'Tis of thee that I think, not of them.

But normally her prose is in itself able to convey both emotional tension and logical thought with what appears to be effortless simplicity. George Moore claimed that *Agnes Grey* was "the one story in English literature in which style, characters and subject are in perfect keeping".[3] If he claimed too much in restricting such functional harmony to *Agnes Grey* alone, he did not err in discerning its existence in Anne Brontë's first novel.

It is this functional quality which determines the treatment of nature in *Agnes Grey*. The subject of the book is essentially the development of personality through hard but fruitful experience. Since Anne's chief experience of life had been as a governess, it was her years spent away from home which provided her main material. In these laborious years she was largely exiled from the landscape she loved best and debarred, in any case, from that daily contact with nature which had been one of her chief pleasures. The theme of nature is introduced in *Agnes Grey* only when it is felt by the author to have direct relevance to the development of the main subject.

It follows that it has a place in the introductory chapter, "The Parsonage", though not the leading one that would certainly have been indicated, had Anne Brontë's aim been to give a complete picture of her own childhood. She is concerned here principally to explain the motives that decide Agnes to leave home. Her father, a parson with modest private means, loses his small capital through an unlucky investment. Agnes and her sister have till then led a happy if secluded life, which included "wandering on the heath-clad hills" among its chief pleasures. But she now resolves to obtain a post as governess in order to help the family's fallen fortunes. The prospect is not without attraction for her, as she genuinely welcomes the idea of teaching young children, and she finally wins the family's consent and secures a post in a region not far away, which can be reached in the course of a long morning's drive. When it comes to the last day at the parsonage, an important part of the leave-taking consists of farewells to the animals who are obviously part of the family, the kitten, the pet pigeons and especially Agnes's "own peculiar favourites, the pair of snow-white fantails".

Next morning she departs in the hired gig. Her last view of home provides the only descriptive passage in the chapter. It is obviously not a set-piece but a real landscape whose pale sunshine, falling on the familiar landmarks, suggests to her the possibility of a brighter future for her family:

> We crossed the valley, and began to ascend the opposite hill. As we were toiling up, I looked back again; there was the village spire, and the old grey parsonage beyond it, basking in a slanting beam of sunshine – it was but a sickly ray, but the village and the surrounding hills were all in sombre shade, and I hailed the wandering beam as a propitious omen to my home. With clasped hands I fervently implored a blessing on its inhabitants, and hastily turned away; for I saw the sunshine was departing; and I carefully avoided another glance, lest I should see it in gloomy shadow, like the rest of the landscape. (ch. 1).

It is noticeable that Agnes makes no attempt to mould the reality to correspond to her wishes; she sees that the shadow of the clouds is bound shortly to engulf the whole scene, and deliberately averts her gaze so that she can retain in her memory the brighter picture, with its faint promise.

Once she has arrived at Wellwood, the home of the Bloomfield family, she has little leisure for admiring the beauties of nature. The children, whom she has innocently pictured as sharing her own tastes at the same age, prove to be, on the contrary, noisy, turbulent and unmanageable, and the governess's position is made impossible by the parents' refusal to support her in any attempt to enforce discipline, while at the same time they blame

her for being ineffective. The children are as difficult to manage
out of doors as in the schoolroom, and the sinister implications of
the name "Wellwood" become apparent when Agnes finds that
the chief attraction of the large garden, for her pupils, is the well
at the bottom of the lawn where they persist in dabbling with
sticks and pebbles, getting thoroughly wet and dirty in the
process. When winter comes, it is not the well but the snow-
covered lawn – a sight which would formerly have delighted her
– which spells disaster for the governess, as she is obliged to
watch her rebellious charges "rioting, hatless, bonnetless, glove-
less and bootless, in the deep soft snow" till they are seen and
shouted at by their irascible father, whom they obey, as he points
out to her, at the first word.

Unfortunately for Agnes, she has more to endure at Wellwood
than the misdemeanours common to spoiled children. The eldest
child Tom, a boy of seven, encouraged by his father and uncle,
finds a perverse pleasure in deliberate cruelty to animals. Having been presented, by the uncle, with a brood of little callow
nestlings, found in a neighbouring plantation, he is preparing to
make them undergo various forms of torture before killing them
when Agnes, after vainly remonstrating with him, picks up a
heavy stone and, at a cost known only to herself, crushes his
intended victims to death. She does not go unrebuked by Tom's
indignant mother:

> "I am sorry, Miss Grey, you should think it necessary to
> interfere with Master Bloomfield's amusements; he was *very*
> much distressed about your destroying the birds."
> "When Master Bloomfield's amusements consist in injuring
> sentient creatures," I answered, "I think it my duty to interfere."
> "You seemed to have forgotten," said she, calmly, "that the
> creatures were all created for our convenience."
> I thought that doctrine admitted some doubt, but merely
> replied – "If they were, we have no right to torment them for
> our amusement."
> "I think," said she, "a child's amusement is scarcely to be
> weighed against the welfare of a soulless brute."
> "But, for the child's own sake, it ought not to be encouraged
> to have such amusements," answered I, as meekly as I could,
> to make up for such unusual pertinacity. "'Blessed are the
> merciful, for they shall obtain mercy'."

"Oh! of course; but that refers to our conduct towards each other."

" 'The merciful man shows mercy to his beast'," I ventured to add.

"I think *you* have not shown much mercy," replied she, with a short, bitter laugh; "killing the poor birds by wholesale in that shocking manner, and putting the dear boy to such misery for a mere whim."

I judged it prudent to say no more. This was the nearest approach to a quarrel I ever had with Mrs. Bloomfield; as well as the greatest number of words I ever exchanged with her at one time, since the day of my first arrival. (ch. 5).

It is no accident that the one confrontation recorded between Agnes Grey and her employer should be on this subject. Undoubtedly, as has been noted by Inga-Stina Ewbank, Mrs. Bloomfield included governesses as well as animals in her category of "inferior creatures", and her treatment of Agnes is an integral part of the significance of the episode.[4] But what rouses Agnes to unwonted protest is not self-defence but her employer's callous attitude to the birds who are nature's children, who have been dear to her heart since infancy and who cannot plead their own cause. Love of animals is obviously one of the criteria by which Agnes judges character, and it is evident that she does not accept, any more than Cowper in *The Task*, the doctrine that they were created uniquely for man's convenience. Needless to say, she fails to convince Mrs. Bloomfield, who becomes sufficiently heated to blame not her son but the governess for cruelty to the "poor birds" whom she had shortly before dismissed as "soulless brutes".

Clearly Agnes's stay in her first post was not destined to be a long one. She is dismissed after a few months, but she finds another situation with the Murrays of Horton Lodge, a family living at a much greater distance from her native village. Horton Lodge, when she finally arrives there after a long journey on a bitter winter's day, proves to be a more imposing mansion than that of the nouveau riche Bloomfields. It has its own deer-park, whose fine old trees contrast with the saplings and "mushroom poplar-groves" of Wellwood House. The house and its environment were evidently suggested by Thorp Green Hall, the home of Anne Brontë's second employers, the Robinsons, near the

village of Little Ousebourn in the Vale of York. The open
country, with its acres of cultivated land, was very different from
the moors, and Agnes Grey's brief description of her new environment, made after she has had time to form some idea of it,
shows her acute awareness of the contrast:

> The surrounding country itself was pleasant, as far as fertile
> fields, flourishing trees, quiet green lanes, and smiling hedges
> with wild-flowers scattered along their banks, could make it;
> but it was depressingly flat to one born and nurtured among
> the rugged hills of ____. (ch. 7)

The Horton Lodge section is longer than the previous one and
covers a crucial stage in Agnes's apprenticeship to life. For a
considerable time she is mainly concerned, as in her previous
post, in adjusting to her circumstances and her pupils, in this
case two boys and two girls. The boys are eventually despatched
to school but the governess continues to be responsible for the
education of the girls. The younger, Matilda, is a "veritable
hoyden", preferring the stableyard to the schoolroom, while the
elder, Rosalie, is a beauty who, encouraged by her mother,
thinks only of social success.

At eighteen the elder girl makes her début, and realises her
ambition of becoming the belle of the neighbourhood. Her
emancipation from the schoolroom means that Agnes, with only
one pupil, has a little time at her own disposal, part of which she
spends in walking in the grounds of Horton Lodge and the
adjacent fields. It is natural that, at this stage, there should
occur in passing one of those brief descriptions where Anne
Brontë shows herself capable, like Emily, of catching the essence
of a landscape in a few lines. The time is early spring, for, as
usual with the Brontës, events are firmly located in a seasonal
framework. It is in the sunlight of a February morning that
Agnes has leisure to observe the charm of the pleasant scene
before her:

> . . . the park with its glorious canopy of bright blue sky, the
> west wind sounding through its yet leafless branches, the
> snow-wreaths still lingering in its hollows, but melting fast
> beneath the sun, and the graceful deer browsing on its moist
> herbage already assuming the freshness and verdure of
> spring . . . (ch. 11)

With the artist's eye she unerringly selects the significant details that combine to evoke the landscape as a whole and at the same time conveys, as Wordsworth might have done, the sense of the freshness of spring just emerging from winter – a spiritual experience but one primarily derived from the natural scene.

But it is rare, even at this stage, for Agnes to have leisure to enjoy the beauty of nature undisturbed. She is now frequently required to act as escort to Rosalie who, on her walks abroad, finds the opportunity to flirt with ineligible admirers, to the alarm of her mother, though she has no intention of marrying any of them. Having had the satisfaction of refusing the handsome rector, Hatfield, she decides to subjugate the new curate, Edward Weston, who had already impressed Agnes by the sincerity of his preaching and his kindness to the cottagers. Suspecting a mutual attraction between Weston and Agnes, Rosalie takes steps to prevent their meeting and continues her efforts to fascinate the curate, without much success, until her marriage to the wealthiest landowner in the neighbourhood.

Weston, the evangelical curate, is in all respects the antithesis of his rector, whose affectations recall the "theatrical clerical coxcomb" described by Cowper in Book II of *The Task*. As might be expected, Hatfield ignores the existence of the governess, while showing himself (until his rejection by Rosalie) obsequiously polite to the squire and his family. Towards the poor among his parishioners his attitude varies from the patronising to the bullying. Agnes does not fail to note also his treatment of animals, so important a criterion of character in her eyes. When an old cottager's favourite cat, with surprising lack of insight, jumps on his knee, he promptly knocks her off, and a terrier who gets in his way receives a resounding thwack on the skull from his cane. Weston, on the contrary, treats the cat with kindness, and ultimately intervenes to save the terrier, who belongs to the younger Murray girl, from a worse fate than the parson's cane when his mistress, jealous of his preference for the kind governess, gives him away to the village rat-catcher, "a man notorious for his brutal treatment of his canine slaves". At this crisis in the animal's precarious existence it is Weston who buys him back and gives him a home. When one of Matilda Murray's dogs chases and kills a leveret, he and Agnes are equally repelled by her evident enjoyment of "the fun". Called on by Matilda to agree that it has been "a noble chase", he replies in a tone of

quiet sarcasm that leaves no doubt as to his real opinion.
Matilda then turns to Agnes, and their brief subsequent dialogue
is in its way as eloquent an indictment as Cowper's attack on
hare coursing in Book III of *The Task*:

> "Didn't you see how it doubled – just like an old hare?
> and didn't you hear it scream?"
> "I'm happy to say I did not."
> "It cried out just like a child." (ch. 18)

Weston is not only kind to animals, he is a good friend and
counsellor to the poor who constitute the majority among his
parishioners. He also notices on his visits their material needs,
and does his best to supply them out of his own limited resources. But in spite of the care which is taken to describe him,
he remains rather a shadowy figure. If Anne Brontë is thinking
of her own feelings for Weightman when she describes Agnes's
dawning love for Edward Weston, she seems to have used her
freedom as a novelist to modify the actual circumstances as
much as possible. The brusque and dark-browed curate of
Horton is very different in manner and appearance from the
lively curate of Haworth.

But he has the insight to notice the isolation of the governess
and to realise that it is more than a physical one. Their few
meetings usually occur when she is escorting her pupils on their
walks. At such times Agnes finds herself longing intensely for
"some familiar flower that might recall the woody dales or green
hill-sides of home". On a mild March afternoon she sees some
primroses on a bank out of her reach and Weston, noticing her
desire, gathers them for her. On another occasion he gives her
some bluebells. There is no sentimentality about his manner on
either occasion, but the incidents unobtrusively link the theme of
dawning love with the flowers of her native dales, as they had
been linked years before in Anne Brontë's early Gondal verse.[5]

In the Horton Lodge section of *Agnes Grey* there is, inevitably,
more portrayal of country life than in the opening chapters. The
nouveau riche Bloomfields were only on the fringe of the squirearchy, to which the Murrays belong by birth. Unlike the omni-
present Mr Bloomfield, the squire is rarely seen by Agnes, but
her brief sketch of him adequately conveys his dominant interest:
"Mr. Murray was, by all accounts, a blustering, roystering,

country squire: a devoted fox-hunter, a skilful horse-jockey and
farrier, an active, practical farmer, and a hearty *bon vivant*." His
younger daughter who, in her father's opinion, "would have
made a good lad", looks eagerly forward to the time when she
will be allowed to hunt, and meanwhile finds her chief pleasure
in the companionship of "the coachman, grooms, horses, grey-
hounds and pointers". The major role played by hunting and
shooting at Horton Lodge is evidently accepted by Agnes as part
of country life, though the account of the death of the levered
shows how uncongenial she personally finds sports that involve
the killing of animals. Here, as so often, her role has to be one of
stoic acceptance. Anne Brontë probably experienced similar
feelings when her brother found one of his pleasures in going out
with the guns on Haworth moors with the Heaton family. But
unlike Branwell, Matilda Murray seems to have no interests
apart from these activities.

In taking a post with a family of what her mother described as
"genuine thoroughbred gentry", Agnes had hoped for wider
horizons than could be looked for with the Bloomfields. But
sport is the paramount interest of the squire and Matilda, while
his wife and Rosalie care only for social brilliance. The sole
society available to the governess, apart from that of her pupils,
is to be found among the cottagers on the estate. The attitude of
Rosalie and Matilda, when they visit their father's tenants, is
that of "grand ladies" to beings of an inferior order, and while
Agnes recognises that this defect is chiefly due to their upbringing, she sees the embarrassment it causes to the cottagers, often
old and infirm, and much prefers, when possible, to visit them by
herself. It is in the course of these visits that she meets the widow
Nancy Brown, whose idiomatic turns of speech reflect the rusticity of her milieu, but whose "serious, thoughtful turn of mind"
gives her something of the dignity of Wordsworth's country
dwellers. Nancy proves to be, apart from the curate Weston, the
only person who can offer Agnes friendship and understanding
in the Horton milieu. It is significant that it is among the
labouring poor that Anne Brontë, like her father in his *Cottage
Poems*, finds the moral strength conspicuously lacking among
many of those who are supposedly their betters.

Agnes Grey's period of employment in the squire's family is
brought abruptly to an end by the death of her father. Her elder
sister is now married, and her mother decides to set up a small

chool which she and Agnes can run together. The best place for
uch a project seems to be a seaside town, which means leaving
1ot only the parsonage but the heath-clad hills which had
1itherto always been associated with home for Agnes. First,
1owever, there is a brief interlude involving another change of
cene, since her former pupil Rosalie, now Lady Ashby, invites
1er to come on a visit. Ashby Park is Horton Lodge on a grander
cale. Sir Thomas belongs not to the local squirearchy but to the
anded aristocracy. But Rosalie has won her social elevation at
he cost of an unhappy marriage, which she already bitterly
egrets. It is the measure of her unhappiness that the company of
1er former governess now appears to her as a boon to be desired.

Agnes herself is in a desponding frame of mind, still uncertain
vhether Weston returns her love and no longer certain of seeing
1im again, since he has now left Horton. She finds her forlorn
ituation mirrored in the restricted view from the window of her
·oom, a side window which can only show "a corner of the park,
1 clump of trees whose topmost branches had been colonized by
1n innumerable company of noisy rooks, and a high wall . . . no
loubt communicating with the stableyard . . . (ch. 22). As the
lay draws to a close, the whole scene is gradually engulfed in
·hadow. The sunlight lingers last in the tree-tops, imparting a
inge of deep red gold to the sable plumage of the rooks, but
inally even the rookery is reduced, in Agnes's words, "to the
·ombre, work-a-day hue of the lower world, or of my own world
vithin". Here, as in the opening chapter, Anne Brontë paints the
·ffects of lighting on a particular landscape with obvious fidelity
1nd at the same time realises the fusion of her own feelings with
he landscape, not only with the slowly engulfing shadow but
vith the dominant characteristics of the scene in itself: its
·eclusion, its high wall, the sombre colony of rooks with their
liscordant cries. The whole description is, in the words of F.B.
Pinion, "one of those scenes which reveal a writer capable of
·ombining feeling and imagination with high artistry".[6]

The denouement of *Agnes Grey* is brief and unexpected. While
valking on the sands of the seaside town where her mother and
·he have their school, she is astonished to meet Weston again.
He is now in fact vicar of a neighbouring parish, and is anxious
:o discover in what part of the town they are living. His obvious
ntention in seeking them out is to ask Agnes to marry him, and
1e has no difficulty in obtaining her consent. Marriage with

Weston means for her not only the fulfilment of her natural
hopes and desires but the end of the spiritual isolation against
which she had been struggling for so long. It is not the social but
the moral world which means most to her, and it was Weston's
example that had reassured her at a time when she felt all her
moral values threatened in an alien milieu.

In describing the reunion of the lovers, Anne Brontë gives
considerable importance to the setting. Her choice of the seaside
reflects her own intense love of the sea, which she had learnt to
know when she accompanied the Robinsons to Scarborough and
which filled her with a sense of exhilaration she had not experienced since early youth. There are no overtones of melancholy in
her description of this landscape:

> ... No language can describe the effect of the deep, clear
> azure of the sky and ocean, the bright morning sunshine or
> the semicircular barrier of craggy cliffs, surmounted by green
> swelling hills, and on the smooth, wide sands, and the low
> rocks out at sea – looking, with their clothing of weeds and
> moss, like little grass-grown islands – and above all, on the
> brilliant, sparkling waves. (ch. 24)

But there seems to be a deeper significance in the sunset which
is watched the same evening by Agnes and Weston from the
summit of the Castle Hill, when he has just asked her to marry
him. Years before, when she had not actually seen the sea, Anne
Brontë had drawn an imaginary scene, in which a young girl
looks down from precipitous cliffs at the dazzling light spreading
over the water.[7] There is a suggestion of almost supernatural
revelation about this drawing, entitled "Sunrise over the Sea",
and there is a similar quality in the description of the sunset
watched by the lovers:

> I shall never forget that glorious summer evening, and always
> remember with delight that steep hill, and the edge of the
> precipice where we stood together, watching the splendid
> sunset mirrored in the restless world of waters at our feet –
> with hearts filled with gratitude to heaven, and happiness, and
> love – almost too full for speech. (ch. 25)

The quality of such happiness transcends, as Inga-Stina Ewbank has indicated, the limits of the conventional "happy end-

ing", and represents Anne Brontë's own belief in the ultimate happiness of all who, like her heroine, persist, "upright and firm, through good and ill".[8] But, characteristically, she chooses to express her feelings through the medium of a landscape known and loved. "External nature and internal emotion meet and fuse into one experience for Agnes Grey, much as they do for Wordsworth on the top of Snowdon in *The Prelude*."[9]

5 *The Tenant of Wildfell Hall*

It was probably soon after completing *Agnes Grey* in June 1846 that Anne Brontë began to write *The Tenant of Wildfell Hall*, published in June 1848. The title, as has often been remarked, resembles that of Emily's *Wuthering Heights*, whose composition belongs to the preceding period, when the sisters had resumed their former habit of discussing their work together, and there is no doubt that *Wuthering Heights* played its part in the inception of Anne's second novel. Sir Linton Andrews has indicated the obvious resemblances between the two works in setting, structure and some aspects of the subject matter. Of these resemblances the first to strike the reader is undoubtedly that of the initial setting – "lonely remote houses, with names that sound alike and have even the same initials; the arrival of a new tenant in the district . . .".[1] From this it would seem natural to deduce that the essential action of Anne's novel, as of Emily's, would take place in a wild and lonely region, even if she, too, introduced a more civilised milieu by way of contrast. Anne does indeed contrast the bleakness of Wildfell Hall, on its steep hillside, with the amenities of the farm of Linden-Car in the valley below. But the most memorable part of the action is centred in neither, but in the more imposing surroundings of distant Grassdale Manor, which, as her diary later reveals, had been the home of the mysterious "tenant" till she left her libertine husband to take refuge at Wildfell.

When Helen Huntingdon, as the new tenant, first arrives at Wildfell Hall, under an assumed name, her initially happy marriage belongs therefore to the past, just as, when Lockwood arrives to call on his landlord at Wuthering Heights, the early happiness of Heathcliff, the lover of Catherine, belongs to the past, though in his case a past much more remote. But there is still a spiritual link between Heathcliff and the old house on the moors, forged by his devotion to the dead Catherine, whose home it had been. No such link exists between Helen Huntingdon and Wildfell Hall. She had, it is true, been born there, but had left it as an infant, and only returns to it because it now belongs to her brother Frederick Lawrence, the local squire who, though he no longer lives at the Hall, can make it available to her as a refuge. But the house, by this time, has been uninhabited for years and is partially derelict. One wing is restored to some kind of order, on Helen's behalf, but it remains at best a bleak and grim abode. The blazing fires and the comfort that continue to characterise the interior of Wuthering Heights, even in the days of its decline, are completely absent here. Superficially Wildfell Hall has an almost Gothic air, with its broken windows and dilapidated roofs, and this is accentuated by the fantastic appearance of the garden in front, whose trees and shrubs, once clipped into decorative shapes, have now sprouted into strange forms that have a "goblinish appearance". In spite of this, however, Wildfell Hall proves to be simply what it at first appears, "a superannuated mansion of the Elizabethan era, built of dark grey stone", obviously described largely from first-hand observation[2] and entirely lacking the authentic haunted atmosphere of Wuthering Heights, just as its new tenant's past history lacks the strange and shadowed romance of Heathcliff's.

But if Wildfell Hall lacks the personal associations and the mysterious aura of Wuthering Heights, it certainly resembles the Earnshaw home in situation. Built on a hillside and adjoining a moor, it is "only shielded from the war of wind and weather by a group of Scotch firs, themselves half blighted with storms, and looking as stern and gloomy as the hall itself". Its isolated position is emphasised by the preceding description given by Gilbert Markham, the narrator of the opening section of the novel, of the long climb from his own sheltered farm to the summit of Wildfell:

> . . . I left the more frequented regions, the wooded valleys, the corn-fields, and the meadow-lands, and proceeded to mount the steep acclivity of Wildfell . . . where, as you ascend, the hedges, as well as the trees, become scanty and stunted, the former, at length, giving place to rough stone fences, partly greened over with ivy and moss, the latter to larches and Scotch fir trees, or isolated blackthorns. The fields, being rough and stony and wholly unfit for the plough, were mostly devoted to the pasturing of sheep and cattle; the soil was thin

and poor; bits of grey rock here and there peeped out from the
grassy hillocks; bilberry plants and heather – relics of more
savage wildness – grew under the walls; and in many of the
enclosures, ragweeds and rushes usurped supremacy over the
scanty herbage; – but these were not my property. (ch. 2)

This passage is already characteristic, in its length and realistic detail, of the increased fullness of the descriptions in Anne
Brontë's second novel, a development which corresponds to the
greatly increased scope of the work as a whole. But it is at once
evident that Gilbert Markham does not share the love of the
moorland that was inborn in the Earnshaws. What he notices
most is the poorness of the land, and his chief reaction is a
comfortable sense of complacency at the difference between this
inhospitable soil and his own rich farm lands at Linden-Car. His
attitude is very different from that of Agnes Grey, who found the
pastoral beauty of Thorp Green no substitute for the "heath-clad
hills" of her childhood. But it is an attitude explained by his
different circumstances, for he has recently succeeded his father
as the master of a prosperous farm.

However, the principal character, the tenant of Wildfell herself, might be expected to show more appreciation of the wilder
side of nature. Helen Huntingdon, even if, unlike Agnes Grey,
she has no childhood associations with her birthplace, is imaginative by temperament, and the old house and the moors around
would seem to offer a setting with its own type of romantic
appeal. Moreover, she is gifted as an artist and, since the
break-up of her marriage, her pictures have become her only
means of financial support and her constant occupation. She
does indeed paint several pictures of the Hall, "faithfully drawn
and coloured, and very elegantly and artistically handled". But
to Markham, who admires her art, she complains of "a sad
dearth of subjects": "I took the old hall once on a moonlight
night, and I suppose I must take it again on a snowy winter's
day, and then again on a dark cloudy evening; for I really have
nothing else to paint." It does not apparently occur to her that
the adjoining moor might also supply her with a subject, and one
as full of potential to an artist's eye as the valley of the Stour to
Constable. On the contrary, she feels that a change of theme is
imperative and, since Wildfell Hall, unlike Wuthering Heights,
is not above four miles from the coast,[3] eagerly looks forward to

renewing her inspiration by "a fine view of the sea". The visit to the coast, when it does take place, amply fulfills her expectation, providing a magnificent view from a cliff top, which she later transfers with great success to her canvas. It is this view, not of the ruinous hall or the moors but of the sea, which provides what is far the most attractive description in the first section of the novel:

> ... on gaining the summit of a steep acclivity, and looking downward, an opening lay before us – and the blue sea burst upon our sight! – deep violet blue – not deadly calm, but covered with glinting breakers – diminutive white specks twinkling on its bosom, and scarcely to be distinguished, by the keenest vision, from the little seamews that sported above, their white wings glittering in the sunshine: only one or two vessels were visible, and those were far away. (ch.7)

The chief function of Wildfell Hall and its moorland background, shown as persistently grim and bleak, seems to be its aptness to suggest the total disarray of Helen's life. There is no trace in her of that instinctive emotional response to a wild and stern environment which had breathed in Anne Brontë's early Gondal poems, and which still survived in the heroine of her first novel. This unenthusiastic treatment of the moorland setting in *The Tenant of Wildfell Hall* becomes more understandable when viewed in the context of Anne Brontë's work as a whole. Her first Gondal poems were full of her love of the moors, but her life changed radically when she left home to begin her career as governess, and Haworth increasingly became for her, as for Agnes Grey, a lost paradise. She returned to it on leaving her post with the Robinsons, but a lost paradise is never entirely regained. In her later Gondal poems, written after her return, Anne could still sometimes recapture the spirit of the moors. But by the spring of 1846, in the poem ironically entitled "Domestic Peace", she was lamenting the changed climate at the parsonage. Branwell had been there since his summary dismissal from his post as tutor at Thorp Green in July 1845, trying to forget his misery in drink and drugs. But it was not till May 1846 that his final decline began. It was in the two years between the onset of that irreversible decline and his death in September 1848 that *The Tenant of Wildfell Hall* was written and published. The composition of a work on this scale could have left Anne with little time to spare, when she had taken her share in the work of the unhappy household, and Charlotte no doubt had grounds for saying that she led "far too sedentary a life". But the moors may not have meant as much to her as formerly. A change in her attitude to nature is evident, as has been seen, in her poems of the same period.[4] Though she still loves it, it is increasingly subordinated to "the moral world", and used as an analogical framework as well as for its own sake. The moors round Wildfell are most significant, in the context, because they are barren. For Helen Huntingdon, their only positive quality is that they represent a refuge, but she would have felt more secure if, in her own words, "the broad sea (had) rolled between my present and my former homes".

It is no accident that the sea itself provides Helen, as an artist, with a more inspiring subject than the moors. For Anne Brontë it had come to have, at this stage, a peculiar value, as the conclusion of *Agnes Grey* made clear. There, like the moors, it had suggested freedom and, like the hill winds, breathed exhilaration, and she needed both. But it possessed, to a greater degree than the moorland, another quality for which she increasingly longed. Charlotte recalls how "the distant prospects were Anne's delight . . .".[5] But even the widest horizons of the hill-country could not rival the unending expanse of the sea. Like the sky, at a later moment of crisis in the novel, the sea represents the idea of infinity, something essential to the conception of *The Tenant of Wildfell Hall*, though the action is realistically rooted in place and time.

Although the actual setting of the first part of the action repeats the contrast between a house on a hillside and a house in a valley so vital to *Wuthering Heights*, the social content, as Terry Eagleton has noted, is inverted: it is the yeomanry who live in the valley.[6] But life at Linden-Car is less primitive than life at Wuthering Heights. Gilbert Markham is a gentleman farmer but, as Eagleton says, he is more gentleman than farmer. He is proud of his fertile acres for the credit they reflect on him rather than for themselves. He appears more really at home when involved in the gossip and small festivities of local society, which has, at least on the surface, something of the gentility of Cranford. The Markham house is the most hospitable in the neighbourhood and Gilbert's mother, who is renowned for her home-brewed ale, and always looks after "the brewing, as well as the cheese and the butter" herself, is not without some of the comfortable rusticity of Ellen Dean. But family life centres round the immaculate parlour, a "haven of bliss" but one where even Gilbert, the favourite son, dare not intrude with miry boots, and guests habitually include the vicar and his family, and, on occasion, the squire himself. An exception to all this gentility, however, is the younger Markham son, Fergus, who, debarred by his fond mother from going to sea or entering the army, expends his energy on such sports as badger-baiting. Gilbert himself is indifferent to the fate of the badgers, but he does at least feel that it is time his brother had more profitable occupations.

Gilbert is a more complex character than his mother or Fergus. The task of delineating him was not an easy one, since Anne had chosen, for the purposes of her story, a masculine narrator, who has to reveal himself by the way he recounts his tale. But she has succeeded in showing that, if he is not too enthusiastic a farmer, he is at least a competent one, and that he has sufficient sensitivity to mature ultimately from a spoiled and irritatingly complacent youth into a man who can be companion as well as lover for Helen Huntingdon. The process begins when he falls in love with the mysterious tenant of Wildfell Hall and is gradually admitted to her friendship. But it is all the more disconcerting to find him capable of almost sadistic violence when his jealousy at her apparent intimacy with Squire Lawrence drives him to a savage and unprovoked assault on his supposed rival. In the climate of Wuthering Heights this incident might not have appeared strange; in a milieu where domesticity is preferred to wildness it strikes a discordant note, and all the more so since Gilbert's jealousy was completely unjustified, as he realises when Helen gives him her diary to read. Now at length convinced that he genuinely loves her, and herself in love with him, she acknowledges his right to know the truth of her situation, and the diary contains the history of her marriage to Arthur Huntingdon.

It is this journal, extending over a period of six years, which constitutes the most absorbing section of the novel. They meet in London, to which Helen has come for her first season, in June 1821, marry in December and, after their honeymoon abroad, return to Grassdale Manor, Huntingdon's country estate, some hundred miles from London. The pastoral environment is obviously reminiscent of Thorp Green, and the description of country-house life, most animated during the autumn shooting season, clearly owes something to Anne Brontë's stay with the Robinsons. It was during the latter part of her stay that she had those "very unpleasant and undreamt-of experiences of human nature" to which she referred after her return,[7] and Branwell's fatal infatuation with his employer's wife must have played its part in the creation of the heated atmosphere of intrigue which surrounds the break-up of the Huntingdon marriage, and which is in such ironic contrast with the peace of the pastoral setting.

But Anne Brontë is at pains to show, through the opening pages of Helen's diary, written during the courtship period, that a similar contrast had existed in the first place between her lover's background and her own, and that this was one of the factors that made the success of a union between them hazardous. Helen is country-bred, having been brought up by her aunt and uncle on their estate of Staningley. Arthur Huntingdon, older than she by ten years, is the product of Regency society. He finds the country intolerably boring, unless he is hunting or shooting. He is a man of dissolute life, leader of a set with whom he has already enjoyed years of riotous living in Regency London. Still handsome and with all the charm of a naturally jovial temperament, he attracts Helen largely because his merriment and easy manners form such a contrast to the formality insisted on by her serious-minded aunt. He, on his side, is attracted by her youth and freshness, seeing in her "a sweet, wild rosebud". He is far from suspecting how strong-willed she is, or how passionately attached to the moral principles in which she believes.

An incident during the courtship highlights the difference between the superficial though glibly expressed feelings of the man about town and the ardent idealism of the country-bred Helen, unsophisticated but not undemanding. Like Jane Eyre, she sometimes uses her talent as an artist to draw sketches from memory of the man she loves, and Huntingdon is flattered to discover his portrait among her drawings. But he is even more interested in a more ambitious picture on which she is working, which shows a girl intently watching "an amorous pair of turtle doves" upon the bough of a tree in spring. The description of the picture is in itself much inferior to the evocation of the caged and mateless bird in Anne's poem "The Captive Dove", but it shows her preference for the dove as archetypal symbol and its relevance to her own feelings. Huntingdon is quick to identify the watching girl with Helen, and her youthful and feminine dreams of what love should be, but, in a significant exchange, she promptly counters with a defence of her idealistic view of love as the true one, and one equally applicable to both sexes:

> "Very pretty, i' faith," said he, " . . . Sweet innocent! She's thinking there will come a time when she will be wooed and won like that pretty hen-dove by as fond and fervent a lover; and she's thinking how pleasant it will be, and how tender and faithful he will find her".
>
> "And perhaps," suggested I, "how tender and faithful she shall find him."
>
> "Perhaps, for there is no limit to the wild extravagance of Hope's imaginings at such an age."
>
> "Do you call that, then, one of her wild, extravagant delusions?"
>
> "No; my heart tells me that it is not. I might have thought so once, but now, I say, give me the girl I love, and I will swear eternal constancy to her and to her alone . . ." (ch. 18)

Such promises cost Huntingdon nothing, since his only object in making them is to please the innocent Helen. He loves her enough to scandalise his dissolute companions by marrying her – an act they consider little short of treachery on his part. But it soon becomes clear that he has no intention of changing his way of life to please her. It is not long before he becomes bored with existence at Grassdale and she accompanies him on the visit to London which he desires. But the social round is not really congenial to her, and Huntingdon, on his side, says he does not wish their stay to be prolonged, since he has no desire for her to be "Londonized" and to lose her "country freshness and originality through too much intercourse with the ladies of the world". After a few weeks he discovers that the London air does not suit her and expresses his concern for the effect on her health, since she is pregnant. She agrees to return home and he promises to follow shortly, when the business which requires his presence is finished. But it is three months before he finally comes back to Grassdale, worn out by drink and debauchery.

This sets the pattern for their future life. Helen is left alone in the country, for ever increasing periods, and comes gradually to lose all faith in her husband's promises to return at the time he had specified. It is only during the shooting season that she can be sure of his presence at home. But the members of his dissolute London set are then invariably invited as guests, with the result that the house-party is frequently reduced, in the evenings, to the level of a drunken brawl. The main subject of this central section of *The Tenant of Wildfell Hall* is the study, remarkable for its realism and its lucidity, of the inevitable and often dramatic decline of a marriage between incompatibles, in which the profligate husband and the idealistic wife become antagonists in a prolonged duel which embitters both.

With such a conflict at the centre of the action, the natural beauty of Grassdale can only be a minor theme. Huntingdon is as indifferent to it as he is to the management of his estate or the welfare of his tenants. Helen does not lose her love of the pastoral scene, but its peace only serves now to emphasise the turmoil of her personal life. Grassdale Park, with its wide vistas, its lake and the ancient woods beyond, is the framework of her new existence. But she had hoped to enjoy it in her husband's company, and to persuade him to cultivate an appreciation of "the salutary and pure delights of nature". When such hopes prove completely illusory, she looks on it with different eyes. Landscape descriptions, when they occur, tend to be set-pieces, carefully planned but lacking vitality. It is only when Helen, unexpectedly confronted with indisputable proof of her husband's infidelity, tries to come to terms with her situation, alone in the moonlight, that the natural setting suddenly becomes transfused with supernatural meaning. The stellar spaces are filled with a strengthening influence:

> . . . Then, while I lifted up my soul in speechless, earnest supplication, some heavenly influence seemed to strengthen me within: I breathed more freely; my vision cleared; I saw distinctly the pure moon shining on, and the light clouds skimming the clear, dark sky; and then I saw the eternal stars twinkling down upon me; I knew their God was mine, and He was strong to save and swift to hear. "I will never leave thee, nor forsake thee," seemed whispered from above their myriad orbs. (ch. 33)

Anne Brontë was keenly conscious of the contrast between the beauty of nature and the havoc which men make of their lives. Nature for her meant harmony and a divine order, and she believed that the same qualities were attainable in the moral world, though at the cost of personal effort as well as supernatural aid. Such, too, is the belief of Helen Huntingdon, but her husband is, as she comes to realise, a sensualist for whom his desires are his only law: ". . . he has no more idea of exerting himself to overcome obstacles than he has of restraining his natural appetites; and these two things are the ruin of him". The turbulence, sometimes amounting to physical brutality, of Huntingdon and his associates differs in origin and kind from the wildness which prevails at Wuthering Heights. There wildness was closely allied to a primitive environment and elemental passions, and if Anne Brontë was aware of its dangers, as she had not been in the days when she wrote her early Gondal poems, she makes it clear that the debauchery of Huntingdon and his set stems from very different causes. They are aristocrats, for whom life is too easy, instead of too hard, and who seek to give it a purpose, and to kill the boredom which otherwise menaces them, by a febrile pursuit of pleasure among the splendours, and the squalor, of London society.

Gambling and drinking rank high among their sources of enjoyment and although Huntingdon assures Helen, before their marriage, that she need not fear he will ever be a heavy drinker, it is the insidious hold the habit gains on him which, more than any other physical cause, explains the deterioration of his health and his temper. With a clinical precision comparable to that of Zola tracing the decline of Coupeau in *L'Assommoir*, Anne Brontë charts the process by which Huntingdon, at first distinguished by the "joyous, playful spirit" Helen so admires, becomes as dependent on drink as on dissolute company for his enjoyments. In the study of his addiction, and his physical deterioration, she was evidently influenced by what she saw of the tragic decline of her brother in the grip of drugs and drink.

It has been rightly stressed, however, that temperamentally Huntingdon, a profligate without intellectual interests or ambitions, is very different from the unstable but highly imaginative Branwell. The only one of Huntingdon's set who shows any temperamental resemblance to Branwell is, as has been pointed out, the tormented figure of Lord Lowborough.[8] Unable to break free from his dissolute companions, yet haunted by his awareness of their folly, Lowborough, like Branwell, is far from being a careless hedonist. The hope of a happy marriage finally gives him the strength to reform, and when he meets Arabella Wilmot he believes he has found his ideal. But his idolisation of her, like Branwell's of Lydia Robinson, leads to disaster. Unlike Branwell, Lowborough does marry his idol, but only to discover, within a few years, that she has become Huntingdon's mistress. Anne Brontë's painting of the intrigues of Grassdale Manor suggests her mature awareness of the dangers inherent in the Byronic "grand passion".

With Helen's discovery of the relationship between Lady Lowborough, her guest, and her husband, her marriage breaks down irretrievably. She remains under his roof only because he refuses to let her leave with her son, and because she is determined to combat his influence on the child, whom he encourages to drink and swear and despise his mother. During his long absences she does her best to undo the effects of such lessons. But when he finally instals his mistress in the house in the guise of a governess, she escapes with her son to find refuge in Wildfell Hall.

In the final section of *The Tenant of Wildfell Hall* Gilbert Markham resumes the role of narrator. But the reconciliation which takes place between himself and Helen, after the reading of her diary has shown him the injustice of his suspicions of the intimacy between herself and Squire Lawrence, does not possess, for most readers, the compelling interest of the story of her marriage. The shadow of Huntingdon still falls between them, and when news comes of his illness after a hunting accident and Helen returns to nurse him, since he is now alone, her letters from Grassdale seem to restore the true focus of the action. Her horizon is now narrowed to a sick room, and since she is, in the end, the only one on whom her husband can depend for careful nursing, he finally comes to tolerate, and even to desire, her constant presence. But he cannot accept the fact that his life is drawing to a close, even though he lacks the control to abstain from the alcoholic stimulants which ruin his chances of recovery. Still less can he share his wife's certainty of a future life.

The fundamental issues which Anne Brontë had at heart in writing *The Tenant of Wildfell Hall* become clear in the closing scenes of Huntingdon's life. They lie deeper than the conscious intention, stated in her preface to the second edition, to show the pitfalls that lie in the way of over-indulged and heedless youth, for they are concerned with life as a whole, and nature as a part of it. She believed in nature as a divine creation, but not in the permanence of its individual physical manifestations, and she showed the approach of material dissolution with the same realism with which she showed the approach of spring. There was no morbidity in her attitude. She had seen death in her own family, and in the England of her day, especially where conditions prevailed such as those her father fought against in Haworth, mortality was a fact with which even the young were early familiar. Helen is being truthful, as well as humane, when she assures her dying husband, tortured by the thought that, when he has gone, his companions will still be enjoying a kind of earthly immortality, that they will all follow him soon enough. But she cannot impart to him her own assurance of a future life, though she herself, like Helen Burns, thinks of eternity as "a mighty home – not a terror and an abyss" and cherishes the hope, expressed years before in her poem "A Word to the 'Elect'", that even the least deserving will ultimately be fitted for such a destiny.

In the closing chapters of the novel Gilbert Markham resumes the role of narrator. For more than a year after her husband's death he forbears to write to Helen out of pride, believing that Squire Lawrence, her brother, considers him her social inferior. But the rumour that she is about to marry again sends him rushing south to Grassdale to learn the truth. He discovers that it is the squire himself who has just married a friend of Helen's, living in the neighbourhood, and that Helen is at present staying at Staningley, some distance away. Before he pursues his journey, he pauses to consider the mansion and the park of Grassdale, now in their winter beauty after a fall of snow. It is an enchanting sight, though one that makes him reflect again on the social distance between himself and the mistress of such a domain:

> My heart sank within me to behold that stately mansion in the midst of its expansive grounds. The park as beautiful now, in its wintry garb, as it could be in its summer glory: the majestic sweep, the undulating swell and fall, displayed to full

advantage in that robe of dazzling purity, stainless and print-
less – save one long, winding track left by the trooping deer –
the stately timber-trees with their heavy-laden branches gleam-
ing white against the dull, grey sky; the deep, encircling woods;
the broad expanse of water sleeping in frozen quiet; and the
weeping ash and willow drooping their snow-clad boughs
above it – all presented a picture, striking indeed, and
pleasing to an unencumbered mind, but by no means encouraging to me. (ch. 52).

This is a charming landscape and one which, in all but the
characteristic yet somehow regrettable touch of Markham prac-
ticality at the end, seems to epitomise the art of Anne Brontë at
its most delicate. The greys and whites, the leafless branches, the
sense of stillness and frozen calm convey, by the very absence of
colour, sound and warmth, the impression of a new life, an as yet
invisible springtime, waiting to be born from the matrix of the
snow.

It is the purpose of the final scene to implement this promise,
at least as far as the destiny of Gilbert and Helen is concerned. A
final obstacle has, however, to be surmounted first: Helen proves
to be heiress to her aunt's estate at Staningley and for Gilbert
Markham this increases the distance between them. But there is
no ambivalence about Helen's belief that social considerations
matter far less than moral ones. She knows that her love for
Gilbert, unlike her passion for Huntingdon, is based on genuine
knowledge of his character, and persuades him to abandon the
false pride which had made him think a marriage between them
too unequal to be possible. In the process of overcoming his
scruples, she picks a Christmas rose, just emerging from the
snow outside the window, and gives it to him as the emblem of
her heart. The flower is too explicit an emblem to have the same
power of suggestion as the snow-covered landscape at Grassdale,
but it brings the freshness of nature into the enclosed atmosphere
in which she has been immured for so long. The story ends with
the triumph of true love following on the moral triumph already
won by Helen over bitterness and despair. It must be admitted
that Huntingdon remains to the end a more convincing character than Gilbert Markham. But if the intended hero is something
of an anti-hero, Helen Huntingdon is not miscast in the role of
heroine.

It is significant that the married life of Gilbert and Helen is spent, as they themselves wish, in the country. In the closing lines of Gilbert's narrative, supposed to be written twenty years after their marriage, he records how he bequeathed the family farm to his brother and how he and Helen made their permanent home at Staningley, which shortly became her own on the death of her aunt. The theme of the superiority – for Anne Brontë essentially the moral superiority – of country life over town life is interwoven with the conception of the novel as a whole. Though principally illustrated in the lives of the three protagonists it also finds support elsewhere, notably in the eventual fate of Ralph Hattersley, one of Huntingdon's London companions. Hattersley, as much of a libertine as the others, and the most ferocious in his bouts of drunkenness, is none the less the most likeable. He is fond of his wife, one of Helen's close friends, and prepared to listen to Helen's protests at his sometimes brutal treatment of her. He is the only one of the London set who comes to visit Huntingdon in his illness and, as a result of this experience, he decides to implement his already half-formed resolution to forsake London for life in the provinces with his wife and children, "immersed in the usual pursuits of a hearty, active country gentleman". It remains to be added that, as at least one critic has noticed, it is with a eulogy of country life that the novel ends.[9] Gilbert Markham, in finishing the narrative of his courtship, which he has written down for the benefit of his brother-in-law Jack Halford, reminds him that he and his wife Rose are shortly expected on their annual visit to Staningley. The Halfords evidently live in a city, though in their case, it seems, for business reasons and not on account of town pleasures. And it is with a complete conviction of the superior joys of rural peace and the beauties of nature that Gilbert reminds his correspondent that the time is drawing near when he and Rose must leave their "dusty, smoky, noisy, toiling, striving city for a season of invigorating relaxation and social retirement with us".

Part III
Charlotte Brontë and Nature

6   Poems and *The Professor*

POEMS

When, in 1839, Charlotte Brontë took a reluctant farewell of
Angria, she had actually written a greater quantity of prose than
that contained in her published novels. But she had also written
a certain quantity of verse, and it was in the hope that she might
have a future as a poet that she wrote in 1836 to ask Southey,
then Poet Laureate, for his opinion. His response, though cour-
teous, was hardly encouraging. He admitted that she did "possess, and in no inconsiderable degree, what Wordsworth calls
'the faculty of verse' ". But he deprecated "the day dreams in
which you habitually indulge", and warned her against cultivat-
ing poetry with a view to celebrity, rather than for its own sake.

It is evident that, from the start, Charlotte never seems to
have felt the same compulsion to express herself in verse as in
prose. The majority of her verse juvenilia appeared in the
context of the literature of Glass Town, and later of Angria. Yet,
when this lack of an independent origin has been recognised, it
remains clear that they did have, for the young author, a certain
value of their own. Like the lyrics in Shakespeare's plays, with
which she was early familiar, they were intended, in a humbler
way, to represent emotional and imaginative highlights.

As has been seen, the earliest verse juvenilia were concerned
with a fairy world. But the supernatural was closely allied, in the
young Brontës' imagination, with the world of nature, and it was
nature, especially the effects of season, weather and time of day,
that provided Charlotte increasingly with her main themes.
"The Fairies' Farewell", of 1831, confirmed the final disappearance of the fairy legions from the skies of Glasstown, though the
supernatural in the form of the Gothic and the macabre continued to have a role in Charlotte's verse.

The influence of Byron had by now, however, become a major
factor in her development, showing itself, as has been indicated,

in the wider range of her landscape description, as well as in the growing sophistication of vocabulary and metre. At the same time, the narrative interest became increasingly important. In succeeding poems it is the fate of mortals, their loves and sorrows, which rapidly develops into the central theme. Nature continues to provide the indispensable background. But the freshness and originality of the earlier nature poetry, those touches of genuine lyricism, seem to have disappeared.

The stereotyped character of the descriptions in the later poems is all the more noticeable when it is compared with the increasing vigour and realism of Charlotte's descriptions in her prose juvenilia, now as superior to her verse in quality as they had always been in quantity. Since Glasstown and subsequently Angria continued to provide the chief scene of both, there was clearly nothing in the Angrian convention to preclude a similar development in both media. In works like "Mina Laury" the natural background is already, as has been seen, an integral part of the whole. But the verse narratives which Charlotte wrote between the ages of fifteen and twenty owe little of their artistic effect to natural description. Whether the action takes place, as most frequently, in Angria or, as in "Richard Coeur de Lion and Blondel", on the banks of the Danube, or, as in "Death of Darius Codomannus", in a valley of Asia Minor, the landscape painting is invariably littered with clichés. A "soft zephyr" passes among the trees, while "Dian is leading the hosts of the night" and moonlit groves are "all sparkling with dew". It would be easy to extend the list, and if these poems are less tedious reading than might be supposed, the explanation lies in their narrative interest, and the connection most of them have with the Angrian saga, rather than in any intrinsically poetic quality.

If there is little to single out as original in the style of these verses, the metrical form is handled with competence. At fifteen, Charlotte was echoing the anapaests of Byron. She learned to use the Spenserian stanza, the metre of *Childe Harold*, and the Ottava Rima, the metre of *Don Juan*, as well as the simpler form of the quatrain. But the technical competence which she soon acquired, thanks to a natural fluency, seems actually to have impeded her development as a poet. Provided the metrical form was correct, she does not appear to have felt it necessary to strive for a style which, avoiding the clichés still characteristic of much current poetic diction, should echo her thought with the same force and freshness she was increasingly revealing in her prose.

By the time she was twenty, she had lost much of the enthusiasm for writing verse which she had shown in her earlier years. A few poems scattered through the later juvenilia can momentarily recapture some of the lyric promise of her beginnings:

Lanes were sweet at summer midnight;
Flower & moss were cool with dew . . .[1]

But their significance is slight compared to that of the prose context in which they occur. Charlotte herself recognised the change in her attitude to verse writing. By the time she was twenty-four, it had apparently become for her something definitely associated with the past: "I have not written poetry for a long while."[2]

This statement was made in a letter of 1841. But when, in 1846, at Charlotte's instigation, the three Brontë sisters published their joint collection *Poems by Currer, Ellis and Acton Bell*, her own contribution constituted approximately a third of the whole, and the most interesting of these verses were works of recent date. The rebirth of her interest in writing poetry was largely the result of her stay in Brussels in the crucial years 1842 and 1843. The study of French poetry, and of poetic form, was part of the teaching of Constantin Heger, and it undoubtedly helped to rekindle in her an ambition to distinguish herself in this medium. At the same time the emotional crisis she experienced renewed her desire to find in verse an immediate outlet for her feelings. Her reawakened ambition is reflected in the ample scope of "Pilate's Wife's Dream" or "The Missionary", the turbulence of her feeling in the unresolved conflict suggested in "Frances" or "Mementos".

However, as Southey had long before warned her, ambition cannot of itself make a versifier into a poet, and no more can turbulent feelings in themselves. The poems of 1846 are psychologically revealing, sometimes moving, but they do not constitute major poetry. The language is rarely original, and this defect is not remedied by the general competence of the metre, whose very regularity no doubt contributed, as F. B. Pinion has remarked, to curb the free development of the style.[3] Verse was not in fact to be her medium, and one cannot but admit the justice of her own verdict on her share in the 1846 collection, which she judged much inferior to that of her sisters.

Yet there is one of these poems that remains in the memory. *Gilbert* uses ballad material in a bourgeois setting. The action begins in a city garden, obviously reminiscent of that of the Brussels pensionnat. Gilbert, a prosperous citizen, recalls, while walking there, the memory of Elinor, a love of his youth, whom he appears to have deserted. In the second part of the poem, the action shifts to the comfortable family parlour, which Gilbert re-enters, only to find himself gradually engulfed in the vision of a stormy sea, though it remains unseen and unsuspected by his wife and children. The hallucination culminates in the appearance of the corpse of a drowned woman, borne along on the water; then gradually the tumult subsides, leaving Gilbert no longer in doubt of Elinor's fate. He manages, however, to conceal his traumatic experience from his family, and to dismiss it himself as a dream. An interval of ten years elapses before the final part of the poem. Returning home late at night after a journey, the still prosperous Gilbert, well content with his life, discovers that the house-door is bolted against him. The woman who finally opens it to him proves to be the dead Elinor. This time he cannot defy the menace of the drowned corpse and, terror-stricken, rushes into the house and cuts his own throat.

The action is deliberately sensational, but it is redeemed from the worst crudities of its type by the power and originality of the sea imagery. The hallucination of the faithless lover, pursued by subconscious guilt, reproduces with nightmarish intensity the sense of greenish and undulating gloom associated with marine depths, and the mounting roar of the tempest. The final emergence of the corpse of the drowned woman, borne on the crest of a wave, has something of the quality of shock which Wordsworth communicates in the description of the sudden appearance of the drowned man who is raised by boatmen from the depths of a lake. But the latter sight can be looked on, even by a child, without "soul-debasing fear". It is a different matter when the mind, as well as the sea, gives up its dead:

No effort from the haunted air
　　The ghastly scene could banish;
That hovering wave, arrested there,
　　Rolled – throbbed – but did not vanish.
If Gilbert upward turned his gaze,
　　He saw the ocean-shadow;

   If he looked down, the endless seas
      Lay green as summer meadow.[4]

   As a poem "Gilbert" impresses, but does not satisfy. It has
tragedy without dignity and the stiffness of the metre is ill suited
to the changing rhythms of the action. But it possesses genuine
power, of a kind not found elsewhere in Charlotte's contributions
to the collection, and this power stems essentially from the
original use of nature imagery, in which there is a blending of the
elemental with the supernatural. Such a fusion is essentially a
poetic achievement, but Charlotte Brontë was to realise it most
completely in the lyric splendours of her novels.

THE PROFESSOR

It became evident, after the failure of the *Poems by Currer, Ellis and
Acton Bell* to attract any attention, that the sisters were more
likely to succeed with works of fiction. Since they had in fact all
been writing fiction for years, this was not a prospect to daunt
them. Indeed, before the actual appearance of the poems, they
were already engaged on three separate tales nearing comple-
tion. It might have been expected that Charlotte's story would
have been the first to find a publisher, since she had always
taken the lead in literary projects. But when *Wuthering Heights*
and *Agnes Grey* were at length accepted, rejection remained the
fate of *The Professor*. Even after the instant success of her second
novel *Jane Eyre*, which was, after all, the first Brontë novel to
appear in print, Charlotte never managed to persuade publishers to reconsider their verdict, and it was not till after her
death that *The Professor* finally appeared.
   The reason for its continued rejection was defined by Charlotte herself. There was not enough of "the wild, wonderful and
thrilling – the strange, startling and harrowing",[5] not enough
indeed of the very qualities which had abounded in the literature
of Angria. But in 1839, in her "Farewell to Angria", she had
announced her intention of quitting for a time "that burning
clime" for "a cooler region where the dawn breaks grey and
sober . . .". This is what she had attempted to do, without much
success, in "many a crude effort" destroyed before she went to
Brussels, and the lessons of Brussels intensified her awareness of

the need to exercise greater control over her imagination. *The Professor* was the result of a determined reaction which, like most reactions, went too far.

She did not, of course, succeed in eliminating all traces of Angria. That would have been impossible, for it was in that highly imaginative climate, which owed so much to English Romanticism, that the lasting foundations of her art had been laid. *The Professor* still shows its Angrian filiation, but also the conscious determination to emphasise the virtues of reason, and to explore the artistic possibilities of what is "plain and homely".

The Angrian filiation is most immediately obvious in the opening chapters. Clearly William Crimsworth, the narrator, and his elder brother Edward derive from the two sons of Northangerland, William Percy and his elder brother Edward Percy, the millowner. But they live in a much more restricted society. Gone are the hosts of inter-related characters, the intrigues, the sub-plots, the excitement and the splendour which activated Angrian society and even gave it, as Laura Hinkley claimed, an affinity with Balzac's *Comédie Humaine*.[6] The introductory section of *The Professor* presents a drab and restricted milieu, in which only three characters have a role of any importance, Crimsworth, his millowner brother and the manufacturer Yorke Hunsden.

The same drabness is reflected in the setting. As in the Angrian tales this is an essential part of the whole, but it, too, lacks the colour and the variety to which readers of the juvenilia are accustomed. The north-country manufacturing town of X— is, in situation and character, similar to that of Zamorna (itself obviously based on a Yorkshire wool town). It, too, stands on the banks of a river, and factory chimneys are a feature of the landscape. But the sombre mill of Edward Crimsworth, "vomiting smoke from its long chimney", lacks the impressiveness of the mill belonging to his Angrian sibling Edward Percy, with its colossal chimney which "towered nobly from the sloping banks of the Olympia". Similarly Crimsworth Hall, pleasantly situated in the countryside near X— but only one of the various millowners' houses in the district, cannot compare in grandeur with Edwardston Hall. It might be supposed that what the Crimsworth mill and mansion lost in splendour they would gain in realism. But paradoxically one is more convinced of the physical reality of the Angrian scene, where the buildings possess a convincing material presence, where the streets are thronged with life and where the countryside gives an authentic sense of space and changing scenery. By contrast the picture given in *The Professor* of X— and its surroundings is unnaturally circumscribed. And Charlotte Brontë has deliberately accentuated the limitations of her initial setting by choosing as first-person narrator William Crimsworth, who spends most of his time as a junior clerk immured in the dreary counting-house of his despotic brother.

Within such a circumscribed milieu, however, such descriptive details as are given stand out with a prominence they would not otherwise have had, and this is all the more noticeable when they recur at frequent intervals. The fireside, as Cynthia Linder has shown, is a feature of considerable importance.[7] This is, of course, in harmony with the north-country setting. One is not surprised to find, in Yorke Hunsden's sitting-room, "a genuine –shire fire, red, clear, and generous, no penurious South-of-England embers heaped in the corner of a grate". The fire is at the same time a status symbol; while his brother Edward basks in its warmth at Crimsworth Hall, William cannot be sure that he will find anything better than a grate "full of sparkless cinders" when he returns to his modest lodging. But the fireside is also, as Cynthia Linder indicates, a means of suggesting figuratively the emotions felt by Crimsworth himself at this initial stage of his career. He resents being doomed by his heartless brother to forego the warmth both of firelight and of natural affection. When Yorke Hunsden, who hates seeing anyone tyrannised over, persuades him to rebel against his brother's unjust treatment, the conversation takes place beside Hunsden's glowing hearth. This allusive use of fire makes it possible for Charlotte to include in her imagery not only its genial and re-vitalising effect but the potential power of the element when it is unleashed. When the inevitable confrontation between the brothers finally takes place, William, at first numbed with cold, feels "a warm excited thrill" run through his veins, while Edward's eye "shot a spark of sinister fire".

The links with Angria are obvious, but here is an attempt, though admittedly still a crude one, to suggest an affinity not only between natural forces and the general emotional atmosphere but between the same forces and the psychology of the individual. In the Angrian stories there had been no consistent

attempt to do so except, as has been seen, in the case of
Zamorna. But Zamorna was partly myth, an Apollo-like figure
possessing a natural affinity with "passion and fire unquench-
able". The position is very different when the character concerned has as drab an existence as Crimsworth. Yet this fire
imagery undoubtedly helps to illuminate the inner recesses of his
outwardly colourless life.

Fire, literal or metaphorical, seems indeed the one humanising
feature of his existence at this stage. When he begins work at his
brother's mill, his entrance into the gloomy counting-house is
virtually an entrance into prison. Henceforth his horizon is
limited by the high black wall of the mill. Crimsworth himself
indicates his consciousness of his situation in a telling image: "I
began to feel like a plant growing in humid darkness out of the
slimy walls of a well."

As might be expected, his first reaction, on the day when he
has flung off his servitude and regained his freedom, is to leave
the mill behind him. He follows the river that flows through the
town until it approaches the open country. At last he can enjoy
again the world of nature that has been lost to him. It is a wintry
world, for the month is January. The melting snows have swollen the river, and he looks down at the rushing waves and then
up at the "clear icy blue of the January sky" till "ear, eye and
feeling" are satisfied. Both visually and psychologically this is
the fitting prelude to a new stage in his life.

The main action of the story takes place in Brussels, since
Crimsworth, on the advice of the cosmopolitan Hunsden, determines to seek a new career as a teacher of English on the
Continent. It is introduced by a description of the Low Country
landscape as seen by him on his way from Ostend to the Belgian
capital. The belts of pollarded trees, the lines of the canals, the
rectangular precision of the patches of market garden present a
picture which appeals to him because it is foreign and therefore
novel, not because he admires such a controlled and regulated
nature in itself: " . . . not a beautiful, scarcely a picturesque
object met my eye along the whole route; yet to me, all was
beautiful, all was more than picturesque" (ch.7).

The realism evident in this initial description is sustained in
those that follow, and confirmed by Charlotte's deliberate use of
actual place names. When Crimsworth arrives in Brussels and
obtains a teaching post, the school proves to be adjacent to a

girls' pensionnat which occupies exactly the same site as the Heger pensionnat in the Rue d'Isabelle. Here, thanks to his success in teaching English at the boys' school, he shortly obtains further work as a visiting master. And for the next few months the action is concentrated in this secluded area in the heart of a capital, so well known to Charlotte Brontë. Secluded as it is, and essentially urban, Crimsworth does not feel the same sense of confinement here as he had done in his brother's counting-house, for the centre of interest soon shifts from the boys' school to the neighbouring pensionnat, and the pensionnat possesses a garden, enclosed, it is true, between high walls but sufficiently attractive to assume for a time a peculiar importance in Crimsworth's life.

It, too, is realistically described. As one would expect, it is symmetrically designed, a long strip of ground, with an alley bordered with fruit-trees down the middle, but the presence of flowers, "a sort of lawn", and "on the far side, a thickly planted copse of lilacs, laburnums and acacias" prevents this city garden from appearing too rigidly planned. Such surroundings had been associated in the later Angrian tales with the theme of sexual awakening. It had been in the garden at Hawkescliffe that Caroline Vernon had first revealed her as yet half unconscious love of Zamorna. William Crimsworth, no longer uniquely preoccupied with the problem of earning a living, first associates the garden with romantic dreams of Mlle Reuter's girl pupils. Such dreams are dissipated by closer acquaintance with them in the schoolroom, but he soon becomes attracted by the young directress herself. It is while talking with her in the garden on a bright May afternoon that he realises he is on the brink of falling in love. But his dreams are abruptly shattered when, the same evening, from his window which overlooks the adjacent Eden, he sees her walking in the moonlight with her neighbour, his own employer, and hears them discussing the date of their approaching marriage.

Crimsworth's true affinity is not with Mlle Reuter but with Frances Henri, the sensitive young Anglo-Swiss who teaches lace-mending at the pensionnat and shares the pupils' English lessons. When she is dismissed by the directress, who is jealous of his evident interest in her and refuses to disclose her address, his search for the lost Frances leads to the most impressive landscape description in the novel. When he has almost given up hope of finding her, his aimless wandering takes him, on a sultry afternoon, to the wide expanse of tilled fields beyond the city boundary, and finally to a walled space among them, planted with yew and cypress, which proves to be the Protestant Cemetery outside the Porte de Louvain.

There is no question of the realism of this landscape, well known to Charlotte Brontë since it was there that her friend Martha Taylor was buried. But it is also astonishingly atmospheric. A thunderstorm is imminent, and its approach is foretold by the livid sky, and even more by the unnatural stillness:

> Not only the winds, but the very fitful, wandering airs, were that afternoon, as by common consent, all fallen asleep in their various quarters; the north was hushed, the south silent, the east sobbed not, nor did the west whisper. The clouds in heaven were condensed and dull, but apparently quite motionless. (ch. 19)

Clearly there is an analogy between this landscape and the crisis in Crimsworth's life. The apparent loss of Frances meant the loss of his hopes of happiness, without which security in itself would now mean little to him. But the reader is conscious of a disproportion between the sombre power of the description and the actual position of Crimsworth. In choosing a masculine narrator, Charlotte Brontë was following her recognised practice in many of her Angrian writings, but it was difficult to convey through this medium the full force of feeling associated with the Brussels experience. In this passage all nature seems to be in mourning for some irretrievable loss, while Crimsworth is only mourning a lost love whom at heart he still hopes to find.

His hopes are realised when he sees a figure moving among the tombs and discovers it to be Frances. Her only remaining relative had recently died, and she had come to visit the grave. He leads her out of the cemetery and back to her lodgings, reaching them just as the threatened thunderstorm breaks. But these simple facts express at the same time the complete reversal of the until now unpropitious course of their love. On leaving the cemetery, they leave the world of death behind them.[8] In France's lodgings they are sheltered from what is dangerous in the play of the elements – the thunder, the "shattered cataract of lightning", "the rushing, flashing, whitening storm". And when

Frances, in honour of her guest, kindles a fire on the hearth, whose "peaceful glow" forms a cheering contrast with "the darkness, the wild tumult of the tempest without", the action marks the beginning of a new life for both of them.

The glow of the fire becomes henceforth a recurrent indication of the mutual happiness of the lovers. In accordance with his stoical determination to follow the dictates of reason and common sense, Crimsworth does not ask Frances to be his wife until he is in possession of a salary which can ensure their living in moderate comfort. Once he is assured of this, he returns to her lodgings, and it is by the fireside that he finds her. When he tells her of his love, and is confirmed in his belief that it is reciprocated, the hearth stands for the certainty of their happiness: "My gaze was on the red fire; my heart was measuring its own content; it sounded and sounded, and found the depth fathomless." (ch. 23). When they return from their wedding, on a cold January day, it is the warmth of a brightly burning fire that makes their little house in the Faubourg into a home. And it is the firelit evenings they passed together after their day's work was done that Crimsworth remembers with most emotion when he looks back on the first years of their marriage: "Looking down the vista of memory, I see the evenings passed in that little parlour like a long string of rubies circling the dusk brow of the past" (ch. 25).

Associated with fire is the warmth of the sun, and Crimsworth has an evident fondness for metaphors taken from this source when describing the response of Frances to his encouragement and later to his love. When he praises her *devoir*, he sees that "the sun had dissevered its screening cloud, her countenance was transfigured . . .". When he finds her again, after their long separation, and she recognises him, he compares the change in her face to "the summer sun flashing out after the heavy summer storm . . . burning almost like fire in its ardour".

In such imagery, as in her landscapes, Charlotte Brontë keeps close to nature. But she does introduce into the realistic framework of *The Professor* two episodes which seem to belong to a different dimension. The first is presented explicitly as a dream, but a dream suggested by a natural phenomenon. As Crimsworth returns from Frances Henri's lodgings after the storm, he has the sunset behind him as he walks, and before him a bank of clouds and the arch of a perfect rainbow. When he falls asleep that night, the setting sun, the clouds and the rainbow are reproduced in his dream. But the resultant picture has a complexity not found in the other descriptive passages in the novel.[9] As so frequently in visionary poetry and painting, the dreamer looks down from a height: "I leaned over a parapeted wall; there was space below me, depth I could not fathom . . ." (ch. 19). This prelude leads unexpectedly to the introduction of the element absent from the original experience: ". . . hearing an endless dash of waves, I believed it to be the sea; sea spread to the horizon; sea of changeful green and intense blue: all was soft in the distance; all vapour-veiled". Yet this sea is curiously unlike the element usually associated in Charlotte's poems with storm, danger and death. It almost suggests an ocean of air in its lightness and ethereal quality. And it is with an upward movement from sea to sky that the dream culminates. Above the horizon reappears the "mighty rainbow" so recently seen by Crimsworth. But beneath its arch, against a background of cloud, appears a visionary figure resplendent with the opalescent colours of the sunset, whose significance is explained by the inner voice which whispers to the dreamer: "Hope smiles on Effort!"

The other episode in *The Professor* which has a dream-like dimension is the account of the strange melancholia which suddenly attacks Crimsworth at the very moment when he has graduated from hope to certainty, and can look forward both to a happy marriage and a secure future. The effect of this depression is that, as once before, in his unhappy adolescence, he is tempted to find a sinister attraction in the thought of death. The episode in itself is difficult to defend. Crimsworth accounts for it as the result of physical reaction after extreme emotional tension, but this seems inadequate in view of the restraint he habitually imposes on himself, even in the scene where he declares his love to Frances. However there is indubitable power in the figurative presentation of this crisis, suggestive of subsconscious tensions. Crimsworth's disturbed state is translated into a vision, in which the dread spectre hypochondria tries to lure him with tales of "her own country – the grave". There is neither sea nor sky here, but a "black, sullen river", on whose further side the monuments of a vast necropolis are visible, "standing up in a glimmer more hoary than moonlight" (ch. 23). Such a vision anticipates the darkest moods of Lucy Snowe, but in her case it would have had the motivation which it lacks in *The Professor*.

The marriage of Crimsworth and Frances introduces the closing section of the novel. The marriage proves a happy one, and their financial position is assured when they achieve success as proprietors of a flourishing school. But their goal is to retire to England, as soon as they can afford to do so. This is the desire of Frances, no less than of Crimsworth, for she has long thought of England, her mother's country, as a sort of "Promised Land".

Their ambition is realised, after ten years of unremitting work, and they settle, with their only child, in Crimsworth's native shire. As was to be expected, they avoid the vicinity of the industrial town of X—, establishing themselves in "a sequestered and rather hilly region . . . whose verdure the smoke of mills has not yet sullied, whose water still run pure, whose swells of moorland preserve in some ferny glens that lie between them the very primal wildness of nature, her moss, her bracken, her bluebells, her scents of reed and heather, her free and fresh breezes" (ch. 25). Their house is in an idyllic situation, with a sloping garden which consists chiefly of a lawn "formed of the sod of the hills, with herbage short and soft as moss, full of its own peculiar flowers, tiny and starlike, imbedded in the minute embroidery of their fine foliage". The contrast between this unspoilt Eden and the city garden of Mlle Reuter, with its illusory air of peace and pastoral simplicity, could not be more complete.

However, even this Eden is not without its discords. Victor, the only child, shows signs of a passionate temperament, and he has not yet learnt the self-control which is so essential a part of the ethos of *The Professor*. The death of a favourite dog, given to him by Yorke Hunsden, now the near neighbour and close friend of his parents, is the cause of a violent outburst on his part. The unfortunate animal has been bitten by another dog in a rabid state, and Crimsworth shoots him to avoid worse consequences. The incident anticipates that of the mad dog in *Shirley* and recalls the grief of Byron, described in Moore's *Life*, at the death of his Newfoundland Boatswain. Its inclusion in the closing pages of *The Professor* shows that Charlotte Brontë, like her sisters, considered sympathy with animals as one of the surest indications of character. Victor remains inconsolable until finally convinced that his father had acted out of mercy, to spare the animal terrible and protracted suffering.

In *The Professor* Charlotte Brontë largely achieves what she set out to do: to show the efforts of an ordinary mortal towards modest success, a more mundane *Pilgrim's Progress* in which the leading character finds satisfaction first in earning a living and then in marriage to a wife who shares his moral outlook. Settings are usually realistic, sometimes to the point of drabness. But there are signs that herald the originality of *Jane Eyre*, and these include some that promise a more original treatment of nature, notably the elemental power of the catalytic thunderstorm, and the attempted correspondence of nature imagery, especially where fire is concerned, with the emotions of individual characters. Unfortunately the characters themselves are not sufficiently realised to sustain such correspondences in any depth. Crimsworth, the first-person narrator, is not always consistently portrayed; in Brussels he develops traits reminiscent of M. Heger, and he all too frequently recalls Charlotte herself. Yorke Hunsden, who promised to be the most original figure, is never completely convincing. The most lifelike portrait is that of Frances, and one feels that a feminine narrator would in fact have been more effective than a masculine one. In her next novel Charlotte Brontë was to widen her horizon, and nature, partially sacrificed in *The Professor* to a too rigid conception of realism, was to return in all its fulness and its mystery, seen through the eyes and the imagination of a heroine fitted by temperament and situation to do justice to both.

7 Jane Eyre

With *Jane Eyre* Charlotte Brontë found her true means of expression, the poetic novel. It was the form ideally suited to her. It was not in her power to express herself fully in verse, for metre seemed to shackle rather than to liberate her inspiration. In the flexible prose of the novel she could use that capacity for observation and often trenchant critical judgement which was part of her nature, and at the same time combine them with the imaginative genius which was her unique gift. *Jane Eyre*, the first of her works in which she fully succeeded in achieving this fusion, represented something new in the history of the English novel. But its very originality mitigated for long against a just critical assessment of all its qualities.

Its immediate success was no doubt partly due to the fact that Charlotte was a born story-teller, and, in *Jane Eyre*, no longer hesitated to include the "startling incident" and the "thrilling excitement" so notably absent from the *The Professor*, though this did not prevent her from being censored for "Gothic" melodrama and improbabilities in the plot. But there was little disagreement among critics as to what constituted the most remarkable feature of *Jane Eyre*: it was felt to be the power and the passion shown in the delineation of the character of Jane herself, "poor and obscure, and small and plain", who compels our attention, our sympathy and, increasingly, our admiration and ends by far outshining the conventional heroine of Romantic fiction.

The originality of Jane's personality made a strong appeal both to readers – and they included Thackeray – and to reviewers, glad to find such vigour and freshness, even if sometimes disconcerted by a frankness misleadingly described as "coarseness". But the same critics who were so aware of the novelty of Charlotte Brontë's heroine remained largely unaware of the novelty of the means used by the author to make her a figure of such compelling interest. Lewes was one of the few contemporary critics who, while recognising its melodramatic elements, found that the story as a whole evolved naturally, and that incidents and descriptions bore the same impress of reality as the character of Jane herself. But it was generally considered that the composition was the weak side of the work, and though Charlotte's descriptions were increasingly admired, they were seen as ornamental rather than functional. The inner relevance of the changing settings of Jane's life, the organic link between her experience and the landscapes, the interiors and the imagery in which the novel abounded, remained largely undiscovered. It was not till the mid-twentieth century that increasing emphasis on Charlotte Brontë as an artist began to reveal the full extent of her achievement in *Jane Eyre*. The claim was then made by one critic that the fictional conventions in the novel were essentially poetic and symbolic.[1] If this was an extreme view, it helped none the less to illuminate the true structural complexity of an apparently artless narrative. It is Jane's personality which, as had always been said, gives the book its unity, but that personality is echoed in her account of all she sees, feels and imagines in relation to the world about her. Since she is looking back on her past as well as reliving it, these echoes form not a succession of melodies but the constituent parts of a harmony: "The structure of the novel is symphonic, based upon an elaborate pattern of repetition of the major themes with variations."[2]

It goes without saying that one of the major themes in *Jane Eyre* is nature, already so important in the juvenilia, and, though muted, still the source of what was most original in *The Professor*. But Charlotte Brontë confirmed its vital significance in her own formulation of her artistic credo, made in a letter to her publishers: "The first duty of an author is, I conceive, a faithful allegiance to Truth and Nature; his second, such a conscientious study of Art as shall enable him to interpret eloquently and effectively the oracles delivered by these two great deities."[3] The "conscientious study of Art" was in fact almost completed when she returned from Brussels with an increased comprehension of the importance of form. *The Professor* was the last stage in her apprenticeship, and *Jane Eyre* the inspired performance of an artist sufficiently master of her form to be liberated from too close preoccupation with it. But her allegiance to "Truth and Nature" was a lifelong commitment and, in her view, they were complementary. She shared the belief of the Romantics that the poet possessed the power to discern the spiritual through the material, and to combine both in a new imaginative creation whose essential characteristic was, as G. H. Lewes had said of *Jane Eyre* on its first appearance, "reality – deep, significant reality".

It follows that the use of nature in *Jane Eyre* is intimately connected with the significance of the novel as a whole. From this point of view, as critics have increasingly recognised, the change of setting which accompanies each new stage in the action is essential to the portrayal of the heroine's development. In Angria the scene could shift from one province to another without following any clear overall pattern. In *The Professor* the Belgian setting dominated the whole. In *Jane Eyre* the five different settings represent no random selection but a planned and meaningful progression.

The action begins at Gateshead Hall, somewhere in the north midlands. The season and weather are carefully noted, for these are closely connected with the inner experience as well as the physical tribulations of the child Jane Eyre. It is on a dreary November day that the crisis occurs which leads to her being sent away in disgrace, in the course of the same winter, to Lowood charity school. Lowood is in a valley in fell country, some fifty miles distant. It is January when she arrives, and it is in bleak and wintry weather that she endures the initial trials of her life there. By the spring these have lessened, and the picturesque surroundings of the school, till now largely shrouded in fog, become a source of pleasure to the beauty-loving Jane. But the situation of Lowood is as unhealthy as it is picturesque, it breeds typhus, and contributes to the death of her friend Helen Burns. Jane herself survives to spend eight years – too monotonous to be chronicled in detail – within the school walls, first as pupil and then as teacher. At the age of eighteen she obtains a post as governess to a girl under ten years old at Thornfield Hall, near Millcote, seventy miles nearer London. Millcote is a manufacturing town, but Thornfield, though not far away, is in pastoral country. The manor-house and its grounds prove to be, as so often in Charlotte's juvenilia, the framework for romance. Arriving in the autumn, Jane does not meet the master of Thornfield till he returns home three months later. Spring and early summer witness their growing love, Midsummer-eve Jane's promise to marry him, and late July her flight after the

interrupted wedding ceremony and the discovery that Rochester
has a wife, alive but insane, concealed at Thornfield. She takes
refuge in "a north-midland shire", many miles distant, where
the Rivers family, later found to be her cousins, receive her into
their home. The Moor House period of Jane's life, like that of
Thornfield, occupies nearly a year. The following May she flees
from Moor House, and the loveless marriage proposed by her
cousin St John Rivers, and returns to Thornfield in response to a
supranormal experience in which she hears Rochester's voice
calling her. But she finds Thornfield has been burnt to the
ground in the fire started by Rochester's mad wife, who herself
perished in the disaster. It is Ferndean, another house belonging
to him about thirty miles away, buried in woods, that provides
the final setting. She arrives there on a wet June evening, and it
is at Ferndean that they are married. This last section is also the
shortest; it forms the conclusion of the action, but it does not
attempt to describe in any detail the happy married life of Jane
and Rochester.

Clearly, landscape, season and weather are an integral part of
the composition of the novel. Their presence was no new feature
in Charlotte Brontë's work. What is new is the ease with which
the correlation between the natural and the spiritual, often
suggested but never before completely realised, is established
and sustained throughout. And this is achieved through the
choice of a feminine narrator who, unlike Crimsworth, habitually uses her imagination as well as her reason to interpret the
world of the senses. As a consequence physical nature becomes,
in *Jane Eyre*, the surest means by which the heroine expresses her
emotional reactions to situations of widely differing kinds, rang-
ing from the prosaic to the poetic. It furnishes her with what
Baudelaire called "forests of symbols" and T. S. Eliot the
"objective correlatives" which he believed to be essential for the
expression of emotion in the form of art.

But physical nature, for Charlotte Brontë, consisted in essence
of the interaction of the elements. As David Lodge has said in his
important study, the four elements earth, water, air and fire were
at the core of her system of "objective correlatives".[4] As he also
stressed, there was no rigidity in her system: "She seeks in the
natural world, not order, but a reflection of the turbulent,
fluctuating inner life of her heroine. The elements have a constantly changing, and often ambivalent aspect in the novel,

sustained by its basic rhythms, the alternation of night and day, storm and calm."[5] Critics who have adopted this approach to *Jane Eyre* have sometimes chosen, in view of the richness of the material, to focus attention on one or more particular elements. David Lodge chose fire, feeling it to be of central importance in the novel, while at the same time recognising that references to fire derived their full meaning from the presence in some form of the conflicting element. The interaction of fire and water has been considered by another critic as indicating "the essential idea" of *Jane Eyre*.[6] The claims of the moon and of arboreal nature, individually or in conjunction, to possess exceptional significance have had more than one advocate.[7] But whatever view one takes of their relative importance, it is certain that each of the elements, however close their interaction, has its own individual part to play in the world of *Jane Eyre*.

Water, the Heraclitean element, appears in characteristically varying form. It features in the opening scene, both in the realistic aspect of ceaseless November rain, and as frozen into wastes of snow and ice in the Arctic landscapes which Jane pictures to herself, as she reads Bewick's *History of British Birds* in the shelter of her window-seat at Gateshead Hall. Both literal and figurative references are equally valid, since the nature imagery which provides the basic structure of *Jane Eyre* is inspired by the lasting sense of the intercommunication between the physical and the spiritual. What Jane, passionate by nature, clings to as an escape from the dreariness around her, is not the exotic world of the *Arabian Nights*, though she has read "some Arabian Tales", but a more extreme and dramatic version of her own wintry world. Such a choice shows both courage and fear. It is a mixture of fascination and fear which predominates when she turns from Bewick's introductory pages to his vignettes, and, with his description of the "death-white realms" of the Arctic Zone fresh in her mind, finds a deeper significance in "the rock standing up alone in a sea of billow and spray . . . the broken boat stranded on a desolate coast . . . the cold and ghastly moon glancing through bars of cloud at a wreck just sinking".(ch. 1)

Jane's fascinated but frightened contemplation of Bewick's vignettes is the first intimation of the peculiar significance of sea imagery in *Jane Eyre*. It is a visionary sea that is in question, and it is always connected with death or disaster. It reappears at the beginning of the Thornfield section, when Jane shows Rochester the water-colours she painted while still at Lowood. Of the three a seascape has pride of place:

> . . . The first represented clouds low and livid, rolling over a swollen sea: all the distance was in eclipse; so, too, was the foreground; or, rather, the nearest billows, for there was no land. One gleam of light lifted into relief a half-submerged mast, on which sat a cormorant, dark and large, with wings flecked with foam: its beak held a gold bracelet, set with gems. . . . Sinking below the bird and mast, a drowned corpse glanced through the green water; a fair arm was the only limb clearly visible, whence the bracelet had been washed or torn. (ch. 13)

The affinity with Bewick's shipwrecks is evident. The sea has obviously presented itself to the artist's mind as the most appropriate setting for disaster, but the emphasis has shifted from the wrecked boat to the human tragedy: the light is concentrated on the splendid ornament which has survived its owner. The symbolism of the picture has been variously interpreted.[8] Rochester considered that Jane had realised only "the shadow" of her thought. It seems more probable that she was trying to express by sea imagery fear rather than thought. Whatever the drowned corpse, the cormorant, bird of prey, and the bracelet may have corresponded to in Jane's mind, the origin of these symbols surely lay deeper, in the subconscious dread of being engulfed in unfathomable depths, in the vague hope that something of value might yet be saved from the wreck.

The second picture has a hill-top setting, but the background of the third recalls Bewick's Arctic wastes, "the pinnacle of an iceberg piercing a polar winter sky . . .". In the foreground is "a colossal head, inclined towards the iceberg, and resting against it". A veil conceals the lower part of the face, but above the temples gleams "the likeness of a Kingly Crown", emblem of the sovereignty of "the shape which shape had none". The quotations from *Paradise Lost* make it clear that the references are to Milton's figure of Death.[9] Sea imagery thus blends with death in these visionary scenes, which are the prelude to the drama of Thornfield, as the earlier dreams inspired by Bewick's vignettes had been the prelude to the drama of Gateshead. This sea imagery plumbs the depths of the unconscious and in doing so anticipates the creative discoveries of surrealism.

It is only in such imaginings, of sinister import, that Jane Eyre
looks on the sea. Rivers, like seas, enter her life in visionary form
and possess the same frightening quality. It is they who provide
her with the image to express the full horror of the hour when she
realises her separation from Rochester:

> ... I seemed to have laid me down in the dried-up bed of a
> great river; I heard a flood loosed in remote mountains, and
> felt the torrent come. ... It was near: and as I had lifted no
> petition to Heaven to avert it ... it came: in full, heavy swing
> the torrent poured over me ... in truth, 'the waters came into
> my soul; I sank in deep mire; I felt no standing; I came into
> deep waters; the floods overwhelmed me'. (ch. 26)

The quotation from the Psalms emphasises the profound significance of this passage.[10] Great expanses of water provide one of
the archetypal biblical symbols for the sort of menace in face of
which man, without divine aid, is utterly helpless and Jane,
faced with the supreme crisis of her life, is as yet too overwhelmed to implore such aid.

If sea and rivers belong to the realm of visions, there are also,
in *Jane Eyre*, descriptions of moorland becks and waterfalls as
real as any known to the Brontës. But these too are frequently
associated with physical or emotional discomfort, though of a
more definable kind. The "bright beck" of the Lowood summer
is also the "turbid torrent" of the long winter months. The hill
stream which rushes down the side of the glen at Morton is the
background to St John River's attempt to coerce Jane into a
loveless marriage, and becomes for her the symbol of her menacing situation: "I was tempted to cease struggling with him –
to rush down the torrent of his will into the gulf of his existence,
and there lose my own" (ch. 35).

In its everyday manifestations as part of the weather – rain,
ice or snow – the element of water rarely plays a favourable part,
whether the references to it are literal or figurative. At Gateshead penetrating rain and black frost suggest both the outer and
inner wretchedness of Jane's situation. At Lowood she is exposed
to the rigours of a northern winter in more acute form, rain,
snow and indoor temperatures that freeze the water in the
pitchers, and these are paralleled by the rigours of the Brocklehurst régime. At Thornfield the winter is more clement, but it is

a sheet of ice on the causeway that is responsible for Rochester's fall from his horse. Torrential rain accompanies the storm that disrupts the bliss of Midsummer eve for the lovers. It is rain which intensifies the sufferings of Jane when she is a destitute wanderer on the moors. And it is on an evening marked by "sad sky, cold gale, and continued small, penetrating rain," that she finds Rochester in the gloomy manor of Ferndean.

Figurative references to the ambivalent splendour of snow and ice, majestic but cold, are used with telling effect to evoke the fanatical asceticism of St John Rivers. Seeing in Jane a potential asset in his missionary career, he offers her marriage without love so that she can accompany him to India, and his sternly controlled anger at her refusal affects her like the rigours of an Arctic climate:

> Reader, do you know, as I do, what terror those cold people can put into the ice of their questions? How much of the fall of the avalanche is in their anger? Of the breaking up of the frozen sea in their displeasure? (ch. 35)

It seems on the whole that water is the least congenial of the elements in the world of *Jane Eyre*. It is only in the midnight crisis at Thornfield, when Jane extinguishes the flames surrounding the sleeping Rochester with a "shower-bath . . . liberally bestowed", that its action ensures safety rather than hardship or distress. On this occasion it temporarily averts catastrophe, but there is no water at hand to quell the conflagration which brings final disaster to Thornfield.

Earth, which the Elizabethans placed below water in their hierarchical order of the elements,[11] is more congenial to Jane Eyre, except in the aspect of rock or stone. This she clearly finds antipathetic. As a child, shut up in the red-room where her uncle had died, she thinks of the vault at Gateshead Church where he lies buried, and it is probable that the association of stone with tombstones, crypts and death – so vividly felt by Charlotte Brontë herself – lingered in her subconscious memory and accentuated her dislike of it. It is significant that the austere Rivers, her temperamental opposite, should choose to ask her to marry him in the rugged setting of a glen where "the mountain shook off turf and flowers . . . where it exaggerated the wild to the savage, and exchanged the fresh for the frowning" (ch. 34). But it is in the figurative references that her antipathy to stone becomes most clear. Mr Brocklehurst, the director of Lowood, is and remains "a black pillar"; Mrs Reed has to the last "a stony eye"; Rivers, a more complex character than either, can assume, when he judges it necessary, the frozen calm of a statue.

But earth, in its kinder aspects, speaks both to Jane's imagination and to her heart. Only at Gateshead does she find herself, when she attempts to seek solace outside its inhospitable walls, in a landscape which, if not actually of cliffs and crags, has much of their bareness and harshness: ". . . I leaned against a gate, and looked into an empty field where no sheep were feeding, where the short grass was nipped and blanched" (ch. 4). Yet even at this stage Jane feels there is another side to outdoor nature, and is fascinated by it, for the stories and ballads recounted or sung by Bessie, the nurse at Gateshead, have introduced her to the world of folklore. If, after looking for them in vain among foxgloves, under mushrooms and beneath ground-ivy, she can find no evidence of fairies in England, she pictures them as having taken flight to "some savage country where the woods were wilder and thicker . . .".

It is real woods that make the glory of the landscape round Lowood, once it has emerged from the frost and fogs of winter. Trees are restored to "majestic life", and in the woodland hollows the wild primrose plants make "a strange ground-sunshine". It is evident that this arboreal nature makes an instant appeal to Jane. But Lowood still bears the curse of its unhealthy situation, and it is not in that place of unhappy memories that her youth can flower. Its woods are only the pale foreshadowing of the Eden-like orchard and gardens at Thornfield.

This Eden is well guarded. The great meadow which borders the lawn and the grounds contains "an array of mighty old thorn trees, strong, knotty, and broad as oaks", which explain the name of the house and testify to its antiquity. This is still a feudal landscape, ordered and traditional, but there is a challenge about the thorn trees which corresponds to the unconventional personality of Rochester, with his physical vigour, his sardonic manner and his strength of will.

Jane first sees him on a January evening, and it is the firelit rooms of the old mansion which witness their first conversations, and the growing understanding between them. But when, in the course of the spring, liking has grown rapidly into mutual love, though as yet not openly acknowledged by either, it is the burgeoning beauty of the awakening earth that is the framework to their courtship. It is in the orchard, after the catastrophic visit of his brother-in-law has almost revealed the secret of his past, that Rochester begins more openly to plead his cause with Jane, and the blossoming fruit trees, the riot of spring flowers in the borders have a sensuous charm which is in perfect harmony with the amatory climate. Later, when she returns from her visit to Gateshead, the whole countryside in its summer richness seems to anticipate a happy issue to their love: "The hay was all got in; the fields round Thornfield were green and shorn; the trees were in their dark prime . . ." (ch. 23). All this is the prelude to the scene on Midsummer eve when Rochester finds Jane wandering in the orchard:

> No nook in the grounds more sheltered and more Eden-like; it was full of trees, it bloomed with flowers . . . a winding walk, bordered with laurels and terminating in a giant horse-chestnut, circled at the base by a seat, led down to the fence. Here one could wander unseen. While such honey-dew fell, such silence reigned . . . I felt as if I could haunt such shade for ever . . . (ch. 23)

It is in the shade of the chestnut tree that Rochester makes his declaration of love and receives Jane's promise to marry him. But the peace of the summer night is suddenly shattered by a thunderstorm; the tree, symbol of their love, writhes and groans, and is found next morning struck by lightning. A month later, on the eve of the interrupted wedding, Jane revisits the same scene. In stark contrast to the previous erotic nature imagery, rich in foliage, flowers and ripening fruit, the description of the tree blasted by lightning anticipates the coming separation, which can yet never be a complete separation, between the lovers:

> . . . Descending the laurel-walk, I faced the wreck of the chestnut-tree; it stood up, black and riven: the trunk, split down the centre, gasped ghastly. The cloven halves were not broken from each other, for the firm base and strong roots kept

them unsundered below; though community of vitality was destroyed – the sap could flow no more: their great boughs on each side were dead, and next winter's tempests would be sure to fell one or both to earth: as yet, however, they might be said to form one tree – a ruin, but an entire ruin. (ch. 25)

Trees are much rarer in the "north-midland shire, dusk with moorland, ridged with mountain" to which Jane goes on leaving Thornfield. But the first night she spends in the open brings her into direct contact with the friendly earth. The heath, rising high on each side, protects her from the cold, and she feels that nature is "benign and good". It is no fault of the moorland that, when to still hot weather succeeds rain, it ceases to be a refuge and becomes instead something to escape from. A refuge is found with the Rivers family at Moor House, and later, in company with Diana and Mary, Jane roams the moors and comes to appreciate their charm. But her chief emotional involvement is with their brother, and the snowdrifts, the jutting crags and mountain torrents associated with their stormy relationship have in reality a greater relevance for the inner action of the novel than the purple moors, though Jane describes the latter with admiration, saying with obvious sincerity: "I saw the fascination of the locality. I felt the consecration of its loneliness . . ." (ch. 30).

But when she sets out to find Rochester again, she returns to the pastoral landscape associated with their love. There is no change in the familiar fields and trees as she approaches Thornfield, but, when she turns the angle of the orchard wall, expecting to see the stately front of the mansion, she discovers that it has now become the ruin she had once seen in her dreams. The "grim blackness" of the stones shows that it has been destroyed by fire. But Rochester still lives, though maimed and blinded, in his other manor of Ferndean some thirty miles away. Trees now regain their importance in the nature imagery, for Ferndean is buried in dense woodland to the very gates: "Even within a very short distance of the manor-house you could see nothing of it; so thick and dark grew the timber of the gloomy wood about it" (ch. 37).

Ferndean is not another Eden, but neither is it a complete wilderness. The sombre evening of Jane's arrival is followed by a sunny morning, and she leads Rochester to cheerful fields, beyond the boundary of the wood, where there are flowers in the hedgerows. But the way home lies in the shade of the trees. And when Rochester expresses his bitter sense of his present helpless condition, and Jane reassures him with her belief in a brighter future, it is a tree image which occurs to both of them as the natural symbol of their thought:

> "I am no better than the old lightning-struck chestnut-tree in Thornfield orchard," he remarked ere long. "And what right would that ruin have to bid a budding woodbine cover its decay with freshness?"
>
> "You are no ruin, sir – no lightning-struck tree: you are green and vigorous. Plants will grow about your roots, whether you ask them or not, because they take pleasure in your bountiful shadow; and as they grow they will lean towards you, and wind round you, because your strength offers them so safe a prop". (ch. 37)

It has been remarked that the description of the almost impassable woods that surround Ferndean reminds the reader of "the savage country, where the woods were wilder and thicker" to which, in the opinion of the child Jane Eyre, the elves for whom she had vainly searched on her walks must have gone on leaving England.[12] The reminder is apposite, for running through the imagery of earth in the novel is a vein of poetry deriving from folklore and ballad. The child shut up in the red-room sees in her own reflection in the mirror a resemblance to the "tiny phantoms, half fairy, half imp" of her nurse's tales. A lingering belief in the world of faery remains dormant in the mind of the eighteen-year-old girl, and is stirred momentarily into life by the sudden appearance, at dusk in a country lane, of a huge dog, a "lion-like creature", who reminds her of descriptions she had heard of the "North-of-England spirit, called a 'Gytrash'". The dog proves to be Rochester's Newfoundland, Pilot, and later, in conversation with his owner, Jane reaffirms her reluctant belief that the fairies have now disappeared for good: "The men in green all forsook England a hundred years ago."

References to the supernatural beings of folklore do not, on that account, cease but henceforth it is Rochester, not Jane, who is responsible for them. His terms of endearment for her include "elf", "fairy", "sprite" and "changeling". And Jane, who rejects any endearments which recall the sultan-like condescension of Zamorna to his favourites, does not take him to task for using these. The context shows that what Rochester sometimes has in mind is Jane's dexterity in teasing him, like some "malicious elf" – a deliberate manoeuvre, on her part, to keep him from "the bathos of sentiment". But there is none the less an undercurrent of deeper meaning in his words, a sense that Jane has a natural affinity with the elements, that she does at times appear to be the "strange . . . almost unearthly thing" that he calls her in all earnestness when he declares his love. Jane possesses indeed, like her creator, the mysticism of the Celt, and the Romantic's intuitive understanding of the significance of folklore. It is evident that she is also well acquainted with the world of Shakespeare's fairies. It is not purely coincidental that she should sigh for the help of "some gentle Ariel" to endow her with a spirit's wisdom, or that Rochester should once call her his "mustard-seed". If she cannot, like Prospero, control the elements, she has something of his skill to interpret them. And on Midsummer eve the orchard at Thornfield becomes, for a fleeting moment, as full of enchantment as "a wood near Athens".

But it is fire and air, the nobler elements, which have the most active role in *Jane Eyre*. Temperamentally Jane's closest affinity is with fire, and its importance is great throughout the novel. As David Lodge has demonstrated,[13] literal references abound and their frequency is not explicable solely on the realistic grounds that domestic fires were an essential part of a North Country setting. As in *The Professor* but with much more intensity, and on a far wider scale, they also correspond to emotional values. The exclusion of the child Jane from the domestic hearth at Gateshead signifies her pariah-like condition, and forces her to seek a consolatory charm in visions of snow and ice. In the damp cold of Lowood the fireside, though far from easy of access, is a humanising influence when it can be reached, and is associated, for Jane, with the friendship of Helen Burns and the kindly hospitality of Miss Temple. At Thornfield the fireside is of great thematic importance from the moment of Rochester's arrival. When Jane, after her fateful walk to Hay, returns to the "grey hollow, filled with rayless cells", she finds the great house, till then only half alive, illumined by genial firelight. Its glow accompanies her first interview with Rochester, and later, when she talks with the supposed gipsy, the uncertain flickering of the

flames on the hearth reflects the ambiguity of Rochester's position and her own perplexity. In the Moor House section "the
redness and radiance of a glowing peat-fire" is one of the
attractions that draws the destitute Jane, when she gazes
through the window into the Rivers' home. When she is finally
admitted, she finds its warmth reflected in the kindness of Diana
and Mary Rivers, though not in the attitude of their brother,
who conceals his feelings beneath "the ice of reserve". At Ferndean, when she finds Rochester again, it is by "a neglected
handful of fire", burning low in the grate, and one of her first
actions is to revive it, thus transforming the cheerless room, as
her presence will transform his life.

But fire, a source of comfort and cheer when it burns on the
domestic hearth, is also, when unleashed, an agent of havoc and
destruction. Lightning blasts the great chestnut tree. The flame
of a candle is sufficient to set Rochester's bed alight, and disaster
is only prevented by Jane's prompt action. But she is absent
when, by the same agency, fires are started in the upper and
lower storeys which shortly engulf the whole mansion in one
mass of flame. The incendiary, Rochester's mad wife, perishes in
the disaster, in spite of his attempt to save her. Thornfield itself
is reduced to a blackened ruin. Its master survives, but as a
"sightless Samson", maimed and blinded.

Figurative references to fire are, as David Lodge says, "almost
entirely restricted to Jane and Rochester",[14] both essentially
creatures of passion. It is Jane's passion for liberty which makes
her, as a child at Gateshead, "break out all fire and violence", in
protest against the tyranny to which she is subjected. At Thornfield she compensates for a monotonous life by listening to the
tale continually narrated by her imagination, "a tale . . . quick-
ened with all of incident, life, fire, feeling, that I desired and had
not in my actual existence" (ch. 12). The advent of Rochester
arouses in her both physical passion and a passionate recognition of the spiritual affinity between them. Metaphors of fire,
applied to Jane's temperament, become more frequent in the
Thornfield section. In the gipsy episode Rochester tells her:
"You are cold, because you are alone: no contact strikes the fire
from you that is in you" (ch. 19). After the orchard scene, fire
imagery comes naturally to him as he recalls the passion with
which she affirmed her love and claimed her right to be heard:
". . . I have seen what a fire-spirit you can be when you are

ndignant. You glowed in the cool moonlight last night, when
you mutinied against fate, and claimed your rank as my equal"
(ch. 24).

But Jane, though passionate, also possesses conscience and
reason. She first learns that passion uncontrolled can be dangerous when, as a child, her momentary triumph over her heartless
aunt is soon followed by the realisation of its futility. In retrospect, it is fire imagery that the mature Jane chooses to express
her assessment of the situation:

> A ridge of lighted heath, alive, glancing, devouring, would
> have been a meet emblem of my mind when I accused and
> menaced Mrs. Reed: the same ridge, black and blasted after
> the flames are dead, would have represented as meetly my
> subsequent condition, when half an hour's silence and reflec-
> tion had shown me the . . . dreariness of my hatred and hating
> position. (ch. 4)

At Lowood the Christian teaching of Helen Burns and the sweet
reasonableness of Miss Temple help her to master the anger
aroused in her passionate nature by unjust treatment. When
later she returns to Gateshead to visit her dying aunt, she can
say: "The gaping wound of my wrongs . . . was now quite
healed; and the flame of resentment extinguished" (ch. 21).

But it is far more difficult for her to combat the danger which
she senses in her passionate adoration of Rochester. First she
fears to let a secret love kindle within her. Then she is obliged to
recognise its existence and its power. But Rochester, studying
her character from her face, concludes that she will be able to
control the passions, elemental in strength as they are, by
following "the guiding of that still small voice which interprets
the dictates of conscience". When he declares his love and asks
her to marry him, the possibility of a conflict between conscience
and passion seems to be averted. But the revelation of the
existence of his mad wife forces such a conflict on Jane, and her
decision to leave him excites him to violent opposition. To
express the tension of the struggle between them, she turns
naturally to images of fire:

> He seemed to devour me with his flaming glance: physically, I
> felt, at the moment, powerless as stubble exposed to the

draught and glow of a furnace – mentally, I still possessed my soul, and with it the certainty of ultimate safety. (ch. 27)

In her previous solitary struggle, alone in her room, after seeing the maniac at Thornfield, Jane had remembered the Psalmist overwhelmed in mighty waters. In her more desperate conflict with her lover, she uses fire imagery which also has Old Testament overtones, a sure indication of its deep significance.[15]

But it is Rochester, whose creation owed much to Byron and something to the Angrian Zamorna, who has the most fire in his nature, and figurative references to the element occur naturally to Jane when speaking of him. Almost from the first, however, she senses that the fire in his nature is partly held in check, and that there is something disquieting in its latent power. She feels as though she had been wandering "amongst volcanic-looking hills, and had suddenly felt the ground quiver . . .". Rochester himself uses the same metaphor when he says to her, after the night when Mason has been stabbed: "To live, for me, Jane, is to stand on a crater-crust which may crack and spue fire any day" (ch. 20). In lighter vein, when telling the child Adèle in a fable of his intended marriage, he says they will live on the moon, "in one of the white valleys among the volcano-tops", where they will be warmed by the fire that rises out of the lunar mountains.

The immediate significance of this metaphor is evident: the volcano which may erupt at any time is the secret of his concealed marriage, thanks to which the duration of his happiness with Jane must always be menaced. But in a wider sense this imagery underlines the volcanic nature of all passion, and its peculiar dangers for the Romantic temperament, prone to allow it to develop unrestrained and to burst forth suddenly in its full violence. Chateaubriand, the ancestor of European Romanticism, had included the ascension of Etna and a meditation beside its crater as an inevitable part of the wanderings of René. Charlotte Brontë herself, in her juvenilia, had often shown passion as a fiery and destructive force, especially in the career of Zamorna. But Zamorna, a half-mythical being, enjoyed the immunity of the gods of mythology from the consequences of his actions – they were felt only by his victims. This is not the case with Rochester. It was his creator's intention to show him as possessing "a thoughtful nature and a very feeling heart".[16] It is certainly true that he not only desires Jane but loves her for what she is. The ordeal by fire through which he has to pass is spiritual as well as physical. It leaves him finally admitting his share of responsibility for the suffering caused by passion uncontrolled. But he does not become, like St John Rivers, a man who has renounced human love and the warmth of the domestic hearth. Had she married Rivers, Jane knew she would have been obliged to keep the fire of her nature "continually low", "to compel it to burn inwardly and never utter a cry, though the imprisoned flame consumed vital after vital". She has no such fear in marrying Rochester, but to describe the happiness of their union she uses not fire imagery but the language of the original Eden: "No woman was ever nearer to her mate than I am; ever more absolutely bone of his bone and flesh of his flesh."

To think of fire and warmth also suggests thoughts of the heat of the sun. But the sun had been the emblem of Zamorna, as the "burning clime" had been the climate of Angria, indissolubly connected with the predominance of passion. In *Jane Eyre* Charlotte Brontë confirms her emancipation from Angria by ascribing a tropical location to the drama of Rochester's disastrous marriage,[17] and reducing the whole West Indian episode to a hated memory, recalled by him only in a desperate attempt to convince Jane of his complete repudiation of the sensual and sexual licence it represented. Only Bertha Mason herself, obviously of Angrian lineage, whose incendiarism ultimately brings disaster, survives as a proof that the past, even if abjured, must still be atoned for.

With the dangers of the "burning clime" in mind, Charlotte Brontë is at pains to stress the beneficence of a sun that does not burn too fiercely. Epithets like "serene" and "placid" are chosen to describe sunshine. During the midsummer idyll at Thornfield it acquires a deeper radiance, approaching the meridional, but never the tropical: "It was as if a band of Italian days had come from the South, like a flock of glorious passenger birds, and lighted to rest them on the cliffs of Albion" (ch. 23). But such radiance is transitory, and in general sunlight seems mellow rather than brilliant. Figurative references reflect a similar serenity. A smile can be "the real sunshine of feeling", and Jane borrows a verse of Moore's to describe the tranquil pleasure of enjoying the esteem of others; it is like " 'sitting in sunshine calm and sweet': serene inward feelings bud and bloom under the ray" (ch. 32).[18]

The elemental imagery of *Jane Eyre* owes much to fire, but much also to air. Air is the most intangible of the elements, which both complements fire and transcends it. It had always possessed, in its varying aspects, a strong fascination for Charlotte Brontë. The poems of her early juvenilia had had as their principal theme the beauty of the sky and all that was most closely connected with it, clouds, winds, the flight and the song of birds. The sky, too had been the setting for visions, whose glory passed the bounds of Nature's law. This intense sensitivity to the pageantry of the sky had been responsible for some of the most evocative writing in the later prose juvenilia. In *Jane Eyre* it has become part of the sensitivity of Jane herself and plays an essential part in the whole complex of the nature imagery.

In her imaginative response to the voice of the wind, which she shows from childhood onwards, she comes nearest to her response to the fascination and sometimes the danger of fire. The wind, like fire, is ambivalent in its action. At Lowood, on a winter evening, its "disconsolate moan" rouses the unhappy child to a sort of "strange excitement": ". . . reckless and feverish, I wished the wind to howl more wildly, the gloom to deepen to darkness . . ." (ch. 6). At Thornfield, on the fateful Midsummer eve, the waft of wind which comes sweeping down the laurel walk seems at first to bode no ill, but it is the precursor of the thunderstorm which blasts the great chestnut tree. A month later, on the gale-swept evening before the interrupted wedding, the wind seems almost to arrogate to itself the dominant role in the action:

> I sought the orchard: driven to its shelter by the wind, which had all day blown strong and full from the south. . . . Instead of subsiding as night drew on, it seemed to augment its rush and deepen its roar: the trees blew steadfastly one way, never writhing round, and scarcely tossing back their boughs once in an hour; so continuous was the strain bending their branchy heads northward. . . . It was not without a certain wild pleasure I ran before the wind delivering my trouble of mind to the measureless air-torrent thundering through space. (ch. 25)

But while literal references to the wind are frequent, figurative references, also comparatively frequent in the case of fire, are almost entirely lacking. The relation between Jane's emotions and the natural phenomena is here in fact so close that the intervention of metaphor or simile could only tend to falsify it. The storm wind in the orchard does not merely echo her chaotic feelings: it expresses and channels them. Charlotte Brontë herself had often experienced similar sensations. Years before, listening in her exile at Roe Head to the blast "pouring in impetuous current through the air" and recognising it for the same that was sweeping the moors at home, she had written: "Glorious! that blast was mighty . . . O it has wakened a feeling that I cannot satisfy . . .".[19]

The aspiration for liberty, for the power of soaring untrammelled through space suggested by the wind is responsible in part for the frequent mention of birds in *Jane Eyre*. There is sometimes, of course, a practical reason for mentioning them: they are part of the country scene. Thornfield has its rookery, and the summer woods their nightingale. Jane has the sympathy with the animal creation which was characteristic of the Brontës themselves and, as an unloved child, finds an outlet for her affections in feeding a hungry robin. But it is the metaphoric allusions which are most significant here. At an early stage Rochester, sensing the imprisoned aspirations of Jane's nature, compares her to a captive bird: "I see at intervals the glance of a curious sort of bird through the close-set bars of a cage; a vivid, restless, resolute captive is there; were it but free, it would soar cloud-high" (ch. 14). Later he himself, in his helpless and blinded condition, is compared by her to an eagle maimed and in captivity: "The caged eagle, whose gold-ringed eyes cruelty has extinguished, might look as looked that sightless Samson" (ch. 37).

The sky itself is a constant presence in *Jane Eyre*. For her creator it had long been both a book in which, as Mrs Gaskell saw, she could read the meaning of the clouds and the signs of the coming weather, and a loved companion. On Jane's first morning at Thornfield there is "a propitious sky, azure, marbled with pearly white". But blue skies, like settled sunshine, are relatively rare, except during the "Italian days" of the brief idyll. Sunset receives more attention than sunrise and the moon, in her rising and her course through the heavens, receives more than either. Lunar imagery is indeed an essential part of the art and the meaning of *Jane Eyre*, and as such has already attracted

critical attention, notably in the searching study of Robert B.
Heilman.[20] The moon seems to be more closely interwoven with
the fate of Jane than any of the other natural phenomena.

She makes, indeed, an unfriendly first appearance as "the cold
and ghastly moon" of one of Bewick's vignettes, probably connected in the child's mind with the darker side of folklore. But
moonlight seems a benevolent presence at Lowood, associated
with the friendship of Miss Temple and the peaceful death of
Helen Burns. It is during her last two vacations at Lowood,
however, that Jane paints the strange water-colours that reveal
the hidden turmoil of her nature, and in one of these there is a
hint of moonlight. While two are concerned with shipwreck and
the spectre of death in polar regions, one is a "vision of the
Evening Star". In the foreground is a hilltop, from which rises
the figure of a woman. Her forehead is crowned with a star and
her eyes shine "dark and wild", while her hair streams like a
cloud. On her neck lies "a pale reflection like moonlight", and
"the same faint lustre" touches "the train of thin clouds" behind
her. There is an erotic quality about this imagery, and a sense of
mystery, neither of which could have been conveyed so success-
fully without the pale reflection that anticipates the rising moon.

In the introductory stage of the love idyll the presence of the
moon is as indispensable as music to a ballet. "Pale yet as a
cloud, but brightening momently", she sheds her light on the
first meeting of Jane and Rochester. For Jane this meeting
appears at the time only an episode, but one which makes return
to a life of stagnation doubly unwelcome. Instinctively she
postpones re-entering Thornfield and turns for comfort to the
night sky. But the rising of the moon and her majestic progress,
as powerfully evoked as in Chateaubriand's painting of moonrise
above the forests of the New World, suggests, like his own lunar
scene, no momentary experience but a moment in a cosmic
drama, in which the spectator is inevitably involved:

> . . . both my eyes and spirit seemed drawn from the gloomy
> house . . . to that sky expanded before me, – a blue sea ab-
> solved from taint of cloud; the moon ascending it in solemn
> march; her orb seeming to look up as she left the hilltops, from
> behind which she had come, far and farther below her, and
> aspired to the zenith, midnight-dark in its fathomless depth
> and measureless distance: and for those trembling stars that

followed her course, they made my heart tremble, my veins glow when I viewed them. (ch. 12)

As the relationship between Jane and Rochester develops, the moon seems at times to exercise a kind of protective surveillance over the lovers. It is the moonlight shining through the uncurtained window which awakens Jane, and alerts her to the danger threatening her master, on the night when his mad wife's attempt to stab her brother nearly betrays his secret to the house-party assembled at Thornfield. The moon is present, too, on the Midsummer eve when the lovers plight their troth. But when the Eden-like spell of the orchard is suddenly shattered by the summer thunderstorm, its light is inevitably obscured. On the stormy evening before the interrupted wedding, it appears only at intervals between the clouds, and Jane feels that it shares in the forebodings to which she herself is a prey. When the planet is seen momentarily in the cleft between the split boughs of the chestnut tree, it appears to have lost both its serenity and its pure brilliance: "her disk was blood-red and half overcast; she seemed to throw on me one bewildered, dreary glance, and buried herself again instantly in the deep drift of cloud" (ch. 25). With increasing darkness, rain comes "driving fast on the gale", but gradually the moonlight returns: "the moon had opened a blue field in the sky, and rode in it watery bright". This seems the signal for the return of Rochester, who had been absent on business, and ultimately, when Jane has confided to him the mystery that has disturbed her, the night regains its serenity, the wind falls and the moon shines peacefully.

All these varying facets of the moon in the novel, scenic beauty, cosmic grandeur, fluctuations which seem to have a correspondence with the emotions and the aspirations of Jane herself, do not exhaust the significance of her role, which has still deeper implications. For there is also in *Jane Eyre* a supernatural dimension, which does not contradict nature but transcends it, a dimension in which the author profoundly believes but to express which she can only use symbols. Inevitably, in her choice of such symbols, she looks primarily to the least material of the elements, air and especially, in the domain of air, to the night sky:

We know that God is everywhere; but certainly we feel His presence most when His works are on the grandest scale spread before us: and it is in the unclouded night-sky, where His worlds wheel their silent course, that we read clearest His infinitude, His omnipotence, His omnipresence. (ch. 28).

It is inevitable, therefore, that in seeking to express the two supreme spiritual crises in the life of her heroine, Charlotte Brontë should look to the moon for her symbol. It had already symbolised many things in the life of the young Jane Eyre: the dreams and fears of childhood, the sexual awakening of adolescence, the hopes and tortures of young love, the worship of beauty and the mysterious, the response to cosmic grandeur. But on the night when Jane faced in dreams, as she could not yet bear to do in reality, the moral necessity for actual separation from her love, the moon was to be the instrument of an unexpected revelation.

Significantly the catalytic dream begins with a recurrence to her childish fears in the red-room at Gateshead, when she had seen an unexplained light glide to the centre of the ceiling and superstitiously imagined that it must herald a ghostly apparition. But this time the scene changes to the night sky, and the light to that of the moon emerging from clouds and heralding an angelic apparition which inspires no fear:

. . . the roof resolved to clouds, high and dim; the gleam was such as the moon imparts to vapours she is about to sever. I watched her come – watched with the strangest anticipation; as though some word of doom were to be written on her disk. She broke forth as never moon yet burst from cloud: a hand first penetrated the sable folds and waved them away; then, not a moon, but a white human form shone in the azure, inclining a glorious brow earthward. It gazed and gazed on me. It spoke to my spirit: immeasurably distant was the tone, yet so near, it whispered in my heart – "My daughter, flee temptation!" (ch. 27)

The vision remains a vision, but when Jane wakens she has received strength to implement her decision to leave Thornfield.

The second fateful moment of decision in her life comes when, hypnotised by his fanatical zeal, she is on the point of agreeing to marry her cousin St John Rivers without loving him, on the eve of his departure for India. The scene takes place late one evening, in the home of the Rivers. The one candle is dying out, and the room is "full of moonlight". Jane has just prayed for guidance in her still lingering doubt when suddenly she is conscious of an inexpressible feeling that thrills through her being, acting on her senses "as if their utmost activity hitherto had been but torpor". She sees nothing, but she hears Rochester calling her name. Instinctively she rushes into the garden of Moor House, crying out in response that she will come, and asking: "Where are you?". The experience determines her to return to Thornfield to discover the truth about his present situation. When she is finally reunited with him at Ferndean, she learns that he, too, on the same night, at the same hour, had been praying, had involuntarily uttered her name, and had himself heard her response.

In both these crucial experiences the presence of the moon is essential, but there are significant differences between them. In the first its role is purely symbolic. The vision Jane sees in her "trance-like dream" comes from beyond time and space. In the second the May moon shines brightly, and even the almost blind Rochester, in distant Ferndean, is aware by "a vague luminous haze" of its presence. He is also aware that Jane's question "Where are you?", uttered in response to his call, seems "spoken amongst mountains", for he hears "a hill-sent echo repeat the words". It is clear that nature mysteriously participates in the communication between the distant lovers. Charlotte Brontë seems herself to have believed in the possibility of such communication, which she had introduced in a more primitive form, not untouched by superstition, into her first love story "Albion and Marina". When someone questioned in conversation with her the validity of the crucial and mysterious vocal communication in *Jane Eyre*, she replied, as Mrs Gaskell remembered, "in a low voice, drawing in her breath": "But it is a true thing; it really happened".[21] Clearly, in this experience, the supernatural has collaborated with nature. Its origin was not only in human need but in suppliant prayer, and Rochester's reference to the "hill-sent echo" has been thought to recall Wordsworth's poem "Yes, it was the mountain Echo", which culminates in the belief in echoes of divine origin heard by the "inward ear".[22] The voice Jane hears speaks to her spirit as well as to her senses, and when she learns from Rochester how he had heard her reply to his call, she feels that the coincidence is "too awful and inexplicable to be communicated or discussed". The revelation in the "room full of moonlight" comes both from nature and from the supernatural, and with it the essential action of *Jane Eyre* is complete.

We know, from her own words, that nature, and the elements, did not lose their importance for Jane in her married life. But she ceased to find in them chiefly the participants and the symbols of her own emotions and aspirations. Henceforward it was also and above all for Rochester, who could no longer see for himself with clear outward vision, that she sought to interpret their beauty and their wonder: " . . . never did I weary of gazing for his behalf, and of putting into words the effect of field, tree, town, river, cloud, sunbeam – of the landscape before us; of the weather round us – and impressing by sound on his ear what light could no longer stamp on his eye" (ch. 38).

8   *Shirley*

After the success of *Jane Eyre* Charlotte Brontë felt an increased confidence in her powers. But she also felt that the fame she had acquired had imposed upon her "a double responsibility".[1] Among the chorus of praise she had not been deaf to the dissentient voices. G. H. Lewes, while greatly admiring the novel, found "too much melodrama and improbability" in the story. Elizabeth Rigby, in a highly unjust attack, considered that the heroine's individualism was socially subversive. No one recognised the originality of the treatment of nature, though some admired the descriptions. It is not surprising that Charlotte Brontë, conscious of the resources of her genius, should have chosen, for her next novel, a subject which offered less possibilities of melodrama, and at the same time involved a much wider spectrum of society and showed she had a balanced attitude to social issues.

Elizabeth Rigby had accused her of having "the tone of the mind and thought" which fostered "Chartism and rebellion at home", as well as revolution abroad.[2] At the time economic depression was causing a resurgence of the Chartist movement of the early 1840s, which was particularly in evidence in the West Riding. The subject seemed to offer a remarkable opportunity to give a balanced social picture. Charlotte Brontë sympathised with the underprivileged, but she was in fact very far from sympathising with anarchy, and firmly believed in the need for order. But the topicality of the Chartist issue made it too controversial a theme. She preferred to place the action of her tale in the days of the Luddite movement, which presented an evident analogy with Chartism but was sufficiently far in the past to be treated more dispassionately. She followed in this the example of her much admired Scott when he was dealing with events in his own country.

Like Scott also she aimed at portraying not simply events in

157

themselves but the social forces which had helped to produce them. *Shirley* shows the attitude of the manufacturers as well as the workers, of the Tory landowners and the Church. So wide a canvas meant a change in the method of narration. Like Scott, and like Thackeray, the contemporary novelist she most admired, she chose, instead of the autobiographical approach of *Jane Eyre,* the third-person narration, better adapted to the scope of a work which presupposes knowledge of a number of differing social groups. But in opting for this method she put it out of her power to maintain the same intimate relationship between the narrator and the physical world, or to give that relationship a similar structural function in the composition of the whole.

This is not to say that nature has not its part in *Shirley.* One of the novel's salient characteristics is that the action is firmly localised in a particular countryside. *Shirley* is a regional novel, to an extent which was then an originality in English fiction. When the Luddite riots took place in Yorkshire, in 1811–12, Charlotte Brontë's father was clergyman at Hartshead, only a few miles away from the mill which was the target of a fierce attack, and during her schooldays at Roe Head she herself lived in the same region. The limited area of West Yorkshire in which the action takes place was one very well known to her, and the accuracy of her descriptions[3] was one of the clues that led to the discovery of the identity of Currer Bell. At the centre of the action is Shirley Keeldar's estate of Fieldhead, containing her manor-house, and the adjoining "Hollow" with its stream. Fieldhead is in the parish of Briarfield, and in the same parish is Briarmains, home of the Yorke family. Briarfield has been recognised as largely corresponding to Birstall, where Charlotte's schoolfriend Ellen Nussey lived, Fieldhead as Oakwell Hall, near Birstall, and Briarmains as the Red House at Gomersal, not far away, the home of her other close friend Mary Taylor. The adjoining parishes are Nunnely and Whinbury, both within walking distance of Briarfield, while a high road leads across moorland to the town of Stillbro', which marks the limit of the action and rarely features in it directly. Whinbury is thought to have been Dewsbury and Nunnely Hartshead, which then had an extensive common to the east, while westwards the high ground overlooked the valley containing Kirklees Park, the original of Nunnwood in *Shirley,* not far from Roe Head. The country side in general was, as Mrs Gaskell said, less austere than the region round Haworth: "The soft, curving and heaving landscape . . . gives the stranger the idea of cheerful airiness on the heights, and of sunny warmth in the broad green valleys below."[4]

But *Shirley* is an industrial as well as a regional novel. In the Hollow close to Fieldhead stands, beside the stream, the mill which Robert Moore has rented from Shirley Keeldar, and from the highroad nearby can be seen at night, on the horizon, the "tremulous lurid shimmer" thrown by the furnaces of Stillbro' ironworks. The model for Hollow's Mill was actually the Taylors' mill at Hunsworth, two miles distant, and it was Rawfolds Mill, nearer Roe Head, which was the real target of the Luddite attack in 1812.[5] But if Charlotte Brontë allowed herself a few minor liberties in her topography, she was completely accurate in showing the close juxtaposition of the pastoral and the industrial in the Yorkshire of the early nineteenth century.

From the descriptive point of view, it is on the former aspect that she concentrates. At the outset the exterior of Hollow's Mill is described only by its size, and the interior only as far as Robert Moore's own quarters and the counting-house are concerned. Of the busy interior of the mill on a working day, nothing is seen. Far more attention is given to the appearance of the nearby cottage where Moore and his sister live. Its situation, screened from view by the hedge and high bank of the lane which leads to it, and its trim garden give a pleasant sense of sylvan seclusion. Fieldhead, the old manor-house of the Keeldars with its picturesque and irregular architecture, has a more impressive but equally sylvan setting: spreading oaks rise behind it, and there is a stately cedar on the lawn in front. The village of Briarfield receives little attention, though it is rapidly growing because of the mill in its vicinity. It is the pastoral surroundings that are commented on, the close-shorn fields where the Whitsuntide feast is spread for the children of the Sunday school, the "extensive and solitary sweep" of Nunnely Common, the forest of Nunnwood with its huge old trees. Even on the fateful night when Hollow's Mill is attacked, the reader remains very conscious of its rustic surroundings, for it is by taking a short cut through solitary fields that Shirley and her friend Caroline, the niece of the parson of Briarfield, hope to reach Moore in time to warn him of the approach of the rioters. The mill itself inevitably becomes the focus of interest during the actual attack in the summer night. But when day dawns on the battered mill and its yard, where lie the dead and the wounded, the description begins with a lament for what man's violence has done to peaceful nature:

> It was no cheering spectacle: these premises were now a mere blot of desolation on the fresh front of the summer-dawn. All the copse up the Hollow was shady and dewy, the hill at its head was green; but just here in the centre of the sweet glen, Discord, broken loose in the night from control, had beaten the ground with his stamping hoofs, and left it waste and pulverised. (ch. 19)

Shirley is a regional novel not only in its setting but in its characters. Most of these are Yorkshire born and bred, and the fact that they were recognised as such by Charlotte Brontë's Yorkshire readers is the best proof of their authenticity. Southerners like Donne, the curate of Whinbury, and Shirley's relatives the Sympsons are shocked by their lack of ceremony and their plain-speaking. And Yorkshiremen like Joe Scott, the overseer at Hollow's Mill, are not averse to encouraging such reactions: ". . . we like weel enough to gi'e 'em summat to be shocked at . . .". It is true that Joe's employer, Robert Gérard Moore, is of mixed ancestry, since his father had married the daughter of a firm of Antwerp cloth-manufacturers closely associated with his own, and he had been born and partly reared on the Continent. But, as Joe points out to him, ". . . your father war Yorkshire, which makes ye a bit Yorkshire too; and anybody may see ye're akin to us, ye're so keen o' making brass, and getting forrards." (ch. 5) But it is the family at Briarmains, modelled on Charlotte Brontë's friends the Taylors, who are given the name of Yorke and who best illustrate the close links between this hardy race and their northern background:

> Yorkshire has such families here and there amongst her hills and wolds – peculiar, racy, vigorous; of good blood and strong brain; turbulent somewhat in the pride of their strength, and intractable in the force of their native powers; wanting polish, wanting consideration, wanting docility, but sound, spirited and true-bred as the eagle on the cliff or the steed in the steppe. (ch. 9)

The native force of the Yorkes is, however, channelled into industry. Although Charlotte obviously prefers describing the countryside to the mill, it is the manufacturers and the industrial workers who are at the centre of the decisive action in her novel. A tribute is paid in *Shirley* to the "natural politeness" of the "peasant girls" who are Caroline's Sunday school pupils, and to the sterling qualities of the rustic tenants on Shirley's estate. But they have much less part in the action than the workers at the mill, who are themselves in origin cottagers, thus resembling many of the inhabitants of Haworth, who worked in the local mills. Joe Scott, the competent overseer, has become indispensable to his master and so runs no risk of being put out of work by the new machines. William Farren, on the contrary, has lost his livelihood because of them, and as a reasonable man expresses the predicament of himself and others like him with telling brevity: "Invention may be all right, but I know it isn't right for poor folks to starve." But he is not prepared to join the frame-breakers, led by Moses Barraclough, in using violence. The workers, however, have only minor parts in comparison with the manufacturers. Thanks to her friendship with the Taylors, Charlotte Brontë knew the employers better than their workpeople. It was partly this knowledge that enabled her to give in *Shirley* a balanced account of the social situation which has earned the commendation of the historian Asa Briggs.[6] Moore shares the outlook of the Whig manufacturers, whose trade is being ruined by the effect of the Orders in Council and who oppose the continuation of the war with Napoleon on economic grounds. He needs the new machinery to stave off bankruptcy. Yorke, an extreme radical in theory, is financially more secure, and is more considerate to his workmen. But it is Shirley, the heiress who is both landowner and mill-owner, who attempts conciliation by denouncing the folly of exalting any one class at the expense of another, and by relieving poverty among her tenants. She recognises, however, that conciliation becomes impossible once violent action is taken, and that she herself would fly to the defence of her property, were it attacked.

The social picture is made more comprehensive by the inclusion of those who are a part of provincial society without being personally involved in the industrial disputes. The High Tory Helstone, Rector of Briarfield, who should have been a soldier, supports the war and opposes the Luddites with all the militancy of his nature. Hall, the vicar of Nunnely, is a man of peace, whose genuine Christianity is expressed in practical acts of kindness. Local gentry like the Wynnes are comfortably engrossed with their own affairs. There are also those who have no recognised position in society but who, unlike the Luddites, refrain from open rebellion against their lot: the governess and the tutor, the unmarried woman with no independent means or occupation – a fate which Caroline Helstone fears may be hers.

So wide a canvas inevitably raises the question of the unity of *Shirley* as a novel, since its regional character is not in itself sufficient to ensure this, and even the Luddite theme does not consistently occupy the centre of interest, once the successful defence of the mill has quelled the efforts of the rioters. It is significant that Charlotte Brontë herself had difficulty in finding an appropriate title, selecting at first "Hollow's Mill", and later hesitating between "Fieldhead" and "Shirley", before finally deciding on the latter. Clearly the tragic circumstances which accompanied the novel's composition affected its development. It was interrupted after the deaths of Branwell and Emily, resumed during Anne's illness and finally completed after her death in 1849. Understandably there are shifts of emphasis, and there are obvious irrelevances. But *Shirley* does possess an overall thematic unity. As Andrew and Judith Hook have shown, in their defence of its structure, the conflict between the values in which Charlotte Brontë believes and a hostile reality is extended in this novel "out from the area of individual experience . . . into the broader area of the life of society as a whole".[7] It represents not like *Jane Eyre* the ultimate triumph of Romanticism but its struggle for survival in a world which prefers to ignore its existence.

It might appear that a novel constructed on these lines would offer little scope for any development of the theme of nature beyond the regional aspect already considered, which is inherent in the subject matter. *Shirley* conveys, as has been seen, an authentic impression of a clearly defined locality. The places round which the action centres are carefully described. But such descriptions necessarily lack the individual quality inherent in those of *Jane Eyre*. They may be more realistic, but they are less moving and less poetic. If the treatment of nature in *Shirley* offered no more than this, it would represent a marked decline in originality from that in the earlier novel.

But the approach to nature is not always of the objective and realistic order. As omniscient narrator Charlotte Brontë is entitled to present a scene not only as it appears to the detached observer but as it appears to her characters, whose thoughts she is privileged to read. Not many of them have in fact much leisure for contemplating nature, nor is it likely that they would in any case find much interest in doing so. But the joint heroines of the novel – for *Shirley* has two, the Rector's niece Caroline and the heiress of Fieldhead – have a different attitude. It is into their consciousness that Charlotte obviously enters with most ease, and it is their vision that provides the finest descriptions in *Shirley*, and the moments of most intimate contact with nature.

In selecting her heroines, Charlotte depended partly on living models. She told Mrs Gaskell that it was Emily whom she tried to depict in Shirley, Emily as she would have been, "had she been placed in health and prosperity".[8] Anne, the younger sister, to whom Emily seems to have been closest, was certainly often in her mind when she drew the portrait of Caroline.[9] No doubt, as in all her characterisation, other elements entered into the final creation. Mary Taylor contributed something to the character of Shirley,[10] Ellen Nussey to that of Caroline.[11] But, in her attitude to nature, it is the vitality of Emily that Shirley mirrors and something of her mysticism, as far as Charlotte understood it; in the same sphere Caroline has the delicate sensitivity of Anne and also, increasingly, something of the sensitivity of Charlotte herself, especially in those chapters written in solitude after the death of both her sisters.

The similarities and, at the same time, the differences in the always sympathetic response of both girls to the natural world are seen at their simplest in their attitude to animals. For both, kindness to animals, or the reverse, is an unfailing criterion of character. Both love all animals, but Shirley's favourite is the fierce-looking Tartar, half bulldog and half mastiff, while Caroline's sympathies go rather to helpless and timid creatures; she feeds hungry birds and will not allow a trap to be set for the mouse who steals out of a cranny in the wainscot.

Tartar was obviously modelled on Keeper, the house-dog at Haworth parsonage who became Emily's constant companion. Like the dogs celebrated by the Romantic poets, and by their predecessor Cowper, Tartar is judged worthy of an individual role. He is not romanticised, though there is beauty in the sketch which depicts him at Shirley's feet and which reproduces Emily's drawing of Keeper in youth: "The tawny and lion-like bulk of Tartar is ever stretched beside her; his negro muzzle laid on his fore paws, straight, strong and shapely as the limbs of an Alpine wolf" (ch. 22). However Tartar is actually by this time a canine warrior with many scars, some of them gained in fights similar to that in which Keeper and another powerful dog were involved, and in which Emily Brontë intervened to separate the combatants, while the onlookers stood helplessly by.[12] But in his mature years Tartar has become "an honest, phlegmatic, stupid but stubborn canine character", who loves his mistress and is largely indifferent to others, always provided they do not strike him, in which case all the latent ferocity of his nature is aroused. As a watch-dog he still barks at strangers, and when the obtuse and arrogant Mr Donne, who has come to visit Shirley, responds by unjustifiably striking him, the intruder has to flee for his life up the staircase at Fieldhead. In his own way, Tartar is fighting for his rights against a hostile world, in the only manner open to him.

The fate of an animal, but more particularly of a suffering animal, later has a decisive effect on Shirley's own destiny. In the lane near Fieldhead she tries to help a neighbour's dog, in whom she recognises Phoebe, a pointer often ill-treated by her master, running by in obvious distress. But the creature, too flurried to know her, turns and bites her arm before continuing her headlong course. Soon afterwards a keeper comes in pursuit with a gun, saying the dog is "raging mad". Shirley tells no one, but cauterises the bite with an iron. Ultimately, however, her concealed anxiety begins visibly to affect her health, and she is induced by Louis Moore, the brother of Robert, who is staying at Fieldhead with relatives of hers in his capacity of tutor, to confide her fears to him. The bite has no disastrous consequences, but the episodes marks a turning-point in the relations of Shirley and Louis, who love each other but are each too proud to be the first to admit it. The incident was based on an actual happening. Emily was herself bitten while "calling to a strange dog, running past, with hanging head and lolling tongue, to give it a merciful draught of water".[13] She at once went into the kitchen and cauterised the wound with an iron, but she was even more stoical than Shirley, enduring whatever fears she felt without telling anyone "till the danger was wellnigh over".

Although both Shirley and Caroline are animal lovers, it is not till the advent of Shirley – who does not appear till one third of the novel is completed – that animals receive much attention. It is likewise with the advent of Shirley that the social-pictorial treatment of landscape begins to be complemented by a more intimate approach, in which the physical reality becomes inter-fused with the reactions of the individual. Before the arrival of this new friend, Caroline, who loves Robert Moore but has become convinced that her love is not returned, has lost interest in the country scenes she once enjoyed in his company. But the companionship of Shirley revives her appreciation of the countryside. Together the two girls visit Nunnely Common, and the view from the uplands has a lyric quality hitherto unknown in landscape description in the novel:

> They both halted on the green brow of the Common: they looked down on the deep valley robed in May raiment; on varied meads, some pearled with daisies, and some golden with kingcups: to-day all this young verdure smiled clear in sunlight; transparent emerald and amber gleams played over it. (ch. 12)

Here too their individual preferences again become evident. From the brow of the Common they can see Nunnwood, and Caroline describes with enthusiasm the forest with its great trees and its sheltered depths. Shirley, like Caroline, looks forward to visiting Nunnwood, but what attracts her most is the heath on the ridges of the Common, for the heath reminds her of moor-land:

> . . . she had seen moors when she was travelling on the bor-ders near Scotland . . . they journeyed from noon till sunset, over what seemed a boundless waste of deep heath, and nothing had they seen but wild sheep; nothing heard but the cries of wild birds. (ibid.)

Shirley's revitalising influence on Caroline does not stop at shaking her out of her depression. She holds out the prospect of a summer tour to the Scottish islands, and then expands the proposed itinerary "into the North Atlantic, beyond the Shet-land – perhaps to the Faroe Isles". So far her plans have a realistic basis, but when she adds, for Caroline's further encouragement, "We will see seals in Suderoe, and, doubtless, mermaids in Stromoe", an imaginative element enters the picture, which speedily comes to dominate it.[14] Her words rouse Caroline to dream of northern seas, as Jane Eyre had done on reading Bewick's description of the polar regions. But where Jane had dreamt of "death-white realms", corresponding to her situation and her fears, the older Caroline translates her reawakened longing for a more active life into the vision of a very different northern ocean. She sees it as the reservoir of primeval force, and attempts to envisage "the sway of the whole Great Deep above a herd of whales rushing through the livid and liquid thunder down from the frozen zone . . .". Shirley takes up the theme, imagining that their intended sea-voyage has already begun, and introduces the supernatural in the shape of the promised mermaid, who appears one evening beside their ship, by the light of a harvest moon. One recognises the archetypal image of the woman half seen through the waves which haunted Charlotte, and which had featured in one of Jane Eyre's paintings. But on this occasion it is not a drowned corpse which emerges from the waves but "an image, fair as alabaster", and both the watchers see "the long hair, the lifted and foam-white arm, the oval mirror brilliant as a star" (ch. 13). The mermaid cannot lure women to their death, but she can appal them by her anger as she rises high on the dark wave-ridge.

These seascapes do not correspond, any more than those in *Jane Eyre*, to a concrete reality. Their function is to suggest states of feeling, and modes of thought. But both feeling and thought lend themselves more easily to rational definition. Shirley and Caroline both respond instinctively to the elemental vigour of the ocean world, the first because she herself is the fortunate possessor of great vitality, the second because she longs for it. But such elemental force is normally associated with the sea; the travellers will not be disappointed in their expectations of "ocean-waves . . . like tossing banks of green light, strewed with vanishing and re-appearing wreaths of foam . . .". Such a living ocean does not give the sense of strangeness of the frozen polar wastes of Jane Eyre's imaginings. The mermaid might seem to be closer to the elves and fairies of Jane's childhood world, but it is the adult world that Shirley is thinking of when she addresses the apparition as "Temptress-terror! monstrous likeness of our-

selves!'' With the unexpected analogy she establishes a connection between the romantic vision and the question of woman's
role and, still more, of woman's nature, which is one of the major
themes in *Shirley*. Caroline protests that they themselves are
neither temptresses, nor monsters, but Shirley reminds her
that "there are men who ascribe to 'woman', in general, such
attributes". The mermaid has, after all, something in common
with Thackeray's Becky Sharp in her siren role. The sea vision,
splendid as it is, fades all too easily into the light of common day.

The fellowship between Shirley and Caroline, which introduces a more imaginative approach to nature, is temporarily
interrupted by circumstances. At the very time when they might
have started on the planned northern tour, "an invasion befell
Fieldhead" in the shape of the unexpected visit of Shirley's
relations from the south, in whose home she had been educated.
Their visit is not unwelcome to her because they are accompanied by the tutor Louis Moore. For the sake of the man she loves,
she also shows marked friendship to his brother Robert. But
Caroline, unaware of the true situation, is misled by their
apparent intimacy into believing they are going to marry. Prevented from visiting Fieldhead by the presence of Shirley's
fashionable relatives, she broods over her apparently unrequited
love for Robert till her unhappiness undermines her health. She
contracts a fever, largely psychomatic in origin, and becomes
seriously ill.

During her illness she shows an intense sensitivity to weather
conditions. Till this point in the action the weather had indeed
been by no means ignored in *Shirley* – the contrary would have
been surprising in a Brontë novel – but its chief function had
been to serve, in conjunction with the landscape, as a realistic
background to the action. The rawness of an early February
morning at Hollow's Mill, when work is already about to begin,
reinforces the harshness of the industrial climate. The stillness of
a summer night makes the tramp of marching feet the more
audible to those awaiting the arrival of the Luddites. There is no
organic link here between weather conditions and the emotions
of individual characters. It is otherwise with Caroline during the
hot summer when she lies ill at the Rectory.

At the onset the breeze blowing from the east is credited with
sinister significance, seeming to bring with it a taint of pestilence
from Asiatic lands.[15] Under the influence of the fever Caroline's

thoughts follow strange paths, and she ponders over the connection between feelings and atmospheric conditions:

> "What is that electricity they speak of, whose changes make
> us well or ill; whose lack or excess blasts; whose even balance
> revives? What are all those influences that are about us in the
> atmosphere, that keep playing over our nerves like fingers on
> stringed instruments, and call forth now a sweet note, and
> now a wail – now an exultant swell, and, anon, the saddest
> cadence?" (ch. 24)

In her present state, it is naturally to "the saddest cadence" that
Caroline's nerves are most attuned. In the night wind she seems
to hear a lament, as it passes the casement "sobbing, as if for
sorrow to come".

It is natural that, at a time when her imagination is in the
ascendant, she should also be drawn by the mysterious spell of
moonlight. One night, when the moon "floating in deep blue
space . . . watched her unclouded", she pictures the effect of its
rays on the world without. Instinctively her thoughts go to the
churchyard beyond the Rectory garden, and to the church itself,
where she knows that the moonlight must be shining through the
east window full on the family monument. But thoughts of the
mystery of death are dramatically diverted by the intervention of
maternal love. Caroline learns that her nurse is also the mother
from whom she has been separated since her infancy, and the
discovery gives her a motive for living. It was the intervention of
maternal love that had given Jane Eyre strength to surmount as
dire a crisis, and there, too, the revelation had been closely
associated with the presence of moonlight, though Jane's experience had only been possible in a "trance-like dream". The
importance given to the presence of the moon is all the more
striking because *Shirley* is the novel where Charlotte Brontë
declares herself most firmly committed to the unromantic world
of "Monday morning". A scene like this is in fact eloquent of
"the special scenic and tonal vividness to which the moon
inspires her".[16] But it is only possible in *Shirley* when she is
portraying characters with the sensitivity of her two heroines.
Nor does Caroline ever reveal fully, except during her illness,
how close she feels herself to the elemental in nature.

But the west wind blows and the "livid cholera-tint" passes from the face of nature, Caroline recovers, and ultimately finds that her love is reciprocated by Robert Moore. Before this can happen, however, Moore has to suffer the humiliation of being scornfully rejected by the heiress of Fieldhead, to whom he has proposed marriage without loving her, and has further to endure a long illness, after he has been shot at in revenge for his pursuit of the ringleaders after the Luddite attack on his mill. It is when he is being nursed back to health at the Yorkes' house that he and Caroline are able to meet again, thanks to the help of young Martin Yorke, who, in spite of the strict seclusion in which the invalid is kept, manages to gratify Caroline's longing to visit him.

Martin, though quite as intractable as the rest of his family, secretly indulges in the romantic dreams of early adolescence, and is reading "a contraband volume of Fairy tales" in a wood, on his way home from school on a winter evening, when Caroline comes to him with her anxious enquiry about Moore's progress. The legends which absorb him are the prelude to her unexpected appearance and also to the brighter future which awaits her. Such daydreams, however, would no longer be possible to Caroline herself; she has left the shores of Elf-land too far behind her. Ironically, it is now she who will briefly become, for the adolescent Martin, as spell-binding as the Fairy Queen or as one of the band of mermaids of whom he reads. It is the description of the legendary Nereides that fascinates him most. Sea imagery thus occurs again in a context where only imaginative associations can justify its presence. Here is certainly the most powerful vision of the sea that Charlotte Brontë has yet created. Vision as it is, it is also realistic. There is the same northern harshness as before, the "strong tide, boiling at the base of dizzy cliffs", "the reef of rocks, black and rough", stretching far into the water. There is the very smell of the sea in "the wet, wild sea-weed" and the rock-pools where "the brine lies fathoms deep and emerald-clear". Instead of the conventional mermaid, the Nereides seen by "the lone wanderer", at the extreme point of the reef, are "shaped like man, but made of spray, transparent, tremulous, awful". These "foam-women" seem to crystallise the beauty of the foam itself, the "swells, wreaths, drifts of snowy spray" (ch. 32).

Caroline, of whose excessive sensibility Martin Yorke acts, it
has been said, "as a male reflector",[17] is always deeply appreciative of nature, except when her personal problems preoccupy
her to the exclusion of all else. But Shirley's love of nature goes
deeper still. It could hardly be otherwise, in as far as she was
modelled on Emily Brontë. But Charlotte, in seeking to depict
her enigmatic sister as she would have been in health and
prosperity, was attempting a difficult task, and she made it more
difficult by giving Shirley a social role of the first importance in
the novel. Ironically if inevitably, she is more consistently successful in showing her heroine in society than when she attempts
to penetrate into her private world. "Shirley Keeldar, Esquire",
as she likes to style herself, is a refreshing and convincing figure.
"They gave me a man's name; I hold a man's position; it is
enough to inspire me with a touch of manhood . . .". She is
proud to be both landowner and millowner, and genuinely
interested in the supervision of her estate and in the business
affairs she discusses with her tenant Robert Moore. She can
match Helstone in wit and repartee and be as plain-spoken as
Yorke. But her assumed masculinity is a way of asserting her
equality with men; what might seem a pose is in reality motivated by that concern for the position of women which is one of
the central themes in *Shirley*. When she considers the situation
requires it, she can cease to be "Captain Keeldar" and become
again the heiress of Fieldhead, richly dressed, dispensing hospitality and diplomatic flattery with equal assurance and natural
grace.

Shirley in her personal life is a more enigmatic figure. The love
of nature is part of her being, but it does not always manifest
itself as clearly as in the love of animals and the appreciation of
landscape which she shares with Caroline. She seeks a communion with the natural world which goes deeper still. It is this
desire which inspires her proposal of a sea voyage to remote
northern isles, which proves so reviving for Caroline, and fires
the imagination of both. There are times when she can satisfy
this longing more simply in her daily life by choosing to become
completely absorbed in the beauty of the world about her:
"Often, after an active morning, she would spend a sunny
afternoon in lying stirless on the turf . . . no spectacle did she ask
but that of the deep blue sky . . . no sound but that of the bee's
hum, the leaf's whisper." (ch. 13) But her approach to nature is

too dynamic to be satisfied for more than a limited time by such passive contemplation. It contains a mystic element, but hers is an active mysticism, in which both a powerful imagination and passionate feelings have their share.

This mysticism is something she only attempts to express occasionally. On the evening when, after the school-feast, she and Caroline stand watching the sunset from the churchyard, the sight inspires her to elaborate her own vision of nature: "Nature is now at her evening prayers: she is kneeling before those red hills . . . I will tell you what she is like" (ch. 18). The woman figure she describes represents for her both "Eve when she and Adam stood alone on earth" and the mother of the Titans, who bore Prometheus. Caroline protests against what she considers "a hash of Scripture and mythology" and finds this Eve, who is certainly not Milton's Eve, "very vague and vision-ary". This is not surprising, for Shirley is here attempting to combine her own idea of nature with her ideal of woman's nature: her Eve is not the temptress but the universal mother, the life force, Titan source of vitality, daring and courage. These views are expressed in the highly rhetorical language Charlotte Brontë judged appropriate to Shirley's rare moments of self-revelation. Nature personified was one of the archetypal figures in her own work, having first appeared in the early poem "The Violet", and later contributed to Jane Eyre's picture of the Evening Star. She here commands the complete allegiance of Shirley: ". . . I will stay out here with my mother Eve, in these days called Nature."

But there is another element in Shirley's mysticism, of which she does not appear conscious but which Charlotte Brontë, as omniscient narrator, is entitled to disclose: the presence of a spark of genius. After communing with nature by day, and reading some chosen book as dusk falls and the moon rises, she feels "earth an Eden, life a poem", and this joy "gives her experience of a genii-life". But she does not write down her dreams, for she does not realise their rarity: "If Shirley were not an indolent, a reckless, an ignorant being, she would take a pen at such moments; or at least while the recollection of such moments was yet fresh on her spirit: she would seize, she would fix the apparition, tell the vision revealed" (ch. 22).

On one occasion, however, Shirley does take a pen; it is when she writes, as a schoolgirl, the strange essay "La Première

Femme Savante" for her half-Belgian tutor Louis Moore. Inevitably it suggests echoes of the *devoirs* written by the Brontës in Brussels, and the rhapsodic style has affinities with George Sand's *Lélia*. But what was appropriate in a symbolic novel is less so in this context and, even when presented as a translation, this attempted prose poem is not stylistically successful. Thematically, however, it has its importance. The theme is defined as "the bridal-hour of Genius and Humanity", and at the centre of the essay is the girl Eva, a Wordsworthian figure who has grown up in communion with nature, whose nursling she is. But Eva must be united with Genius before she can fulfil her true destiny, and their union must be through mutual love. The strongly erotic tone of the essay is the prelude to the love story of Shirley and Louis Moore, and it has been described as resembling "a mythifying of the Louis-Shirley relation".[18]

It is this relationship which dominates the last part of the novel. Like Caroline, Shirley at heart needs love as well as nature to satisfy her. Her social role enters into the question, and complicates her position, for she values her independence highly and sees no reason to forfeit it for a marriage that might prove unhappy, like most of those of which she hears. She will not marry any man whom she cannot both trust and admire. But increasingly she becomes convinced that Louis Moore is such a man. He has no doubts about his desire to marry Shirley, but feels that the difference in their fortune and social position forbids him in honour to attempt to win her: "Her Gold and her Station are two griffins, that guard her on each side." This view is entirely endorsed by society in general, but Louis finally discovers that such considerations mean nothing to Shirley herself, and that "in love, questions of superiority are ultimately meaningless".[19]

Unfortunately Louis Moore never comes entirely to life as a personality, partly because he is obliged for most of the time to conceal his true feelings. He does, however, confide to a notebook the love and longing he cannot reveal. This is rather out of character and when Charlotte Brontë, abandoning, as she occasionally does, the stance of third-person narrator, invites the reader to "stoop over his shoulder fearlessly, and read as he scribbles", the invitation might present no great attraction if she had not previously invoked, as a framework to the figure of the disconsolate lover, all the charm of a tempestuous moonlit night:

. . . the equinox still struggles in its storms. The wild rains of the day are abated: the great single cloud disparts and rolls away from heaven, not passing and leaving a sea all sapphire, but tossed buoyant before a continued long-sounding, high-rushing moonlight tempest. The Moon reigns glorious, glad of the gale; as glad as if she gave herself to his fierce caress with love. (ch. 29)

In this context, it seems natural that Louis should poeticise Shirley, recognising the fire in her nature and comparing her to some tameless forest creature, "a young lioness or leopardess". Later he complements the definition by calling her "a thing made of an element, – the child of a breeze and a flame, – the daughter of ray and rain-drop, – a thing never to be overtaken, arrested, fixed" (ch. 36).

But the novel ends, as it began, on a realistic note. Shirley and Caroline each marry the man they love, but Shirley only achieves this after alienating her relations, horrified at her choosing the tutor for her husband, and Caroline has to thank the repeal of the Orders in Council, without which Robert Moore would have become bankrupt and could not have thought of matrimony. It is evident that the future will involve both couples in close co-operation with the new industrial society. Robert Moore will build another and larger mill, and his brother, as master of adjacent Fieldhead, will profit financially from a venture which doubles the value of the mill property. Caroline, as the millowner's wife, will busy herself with active philanthropy, and Shirley, as the squire's lady, will support her in this, as she will support her husband in his important social functions as landowner and magistrate. In these circumstances there will not be much time left for country walks or a close communion with nature. There can be no doubt as to which of the two, Caroline or Shirley, will feel the deprivation most.

The story concludes with another personal intervention on the part of the author. We learn how the latter's old housekeeper still remembers at the present day, when Robert Moore's great new mill has long since replaced the original one, how the Hollow near Fieldhead used to look when there was neither mill nor cottage, only an unspoiled nature which still had its supernatural visitants:

". . . I can tell of it . . . when there was neither mill, nor cot, nor hall, except Fieldhead, within two miles of it. I can tell, one summer-evening, fifty years syne, my mother coming running in just at the edge of dark, almost fleyed out of her wits, saying, she had seen a fairish (fairy) in Fieldhead Hollow; and that was the last fairish that ever was seen on this country side (though they've been heard within these forty years). A lonesome spot it was – and a bonnie spot – full of oak-trees and nut-trees. It is altered now."

9   *Villette*

In *Shirley* Charlotte Brontë had shown her power of dealing with wider social issues than in *Jane Eyre*. But, perceptive and judicious as was her view of the social situation at the time of the Luddite crisis, she was at her best only when she wrote of what she knew from direct personal involvement. The vacillations of Shirley between love and independence, the struggles of Caroline to endure existence without either, interest the reader more than their conscientious attempts to pour oil on the troubled waters of contemporary social unrest. In *Villette* Charlotte Brontë thankfully returned to her study of the individual destiny, but she was now equipped to do so from a wider standpoint than in *Jane Eyre*. *Villette* combines the personal with the universal in a way only possible to mature genius.

The greater complexity of the later masterpiece is reflected in the more complex handling of the first-person narration. Where Jane Eyre looks back after an interval of ten years, Lucy Snowe looks back over a lifetime. Jane's narrative follows a chronological order, and we see her reaction to events as they appeared to her at the time. Lucy's is also basically a chronological narrative, but there are concealments and reticences, as well as anticipation of later developments. There is more ambiguity in the interpretation of characters and events. Truth, it has been said, is in *Villette* "something to be discovered".[1] This is also true of the narrator herself. It is only gradually that Lucy Snowe becomes conscious of her real identity.

The ambiguity of her position is mirrored in the name given to her by her creator. Charlotte Brontë hesitated over the choice, changing the surname to "Frost" and then, when the novel was two-thirds completed, deciding to revert to the original "Snowe". To her publishers she wrote, commenting on her choice.

> As to the name of the heroine, I can hardly express what subtlety of thought made me decide upon giving her a cold

name. . . . A *cold* name she must have; partly, perhaps, on the *"lucus a non lucendo"* principle – partly on that of the "fitness of things", for she has about her an external coldness.[2]

It is noteworthy that, as in *Jane Eyre*, Charlotte Brontë gives her heroine a surname with elemental overtones. Snow suggests both air and water, but the final rejection of the alternative, frost, banishes the idea of rigidity associated by Jane Eyre with the frozen wastes of the Arctic North. Snow in itself is not incompatible with softness, as well as with a potentially luminous quality reinforced, in this case, by the selection of the forename.

There are, however, few signs, in the opening chapters, of qualities in Lucy Snowe which would justify these elemental overtones. She seems to have none of the young Jane Eyre's immediate response to world of nature. In her fourteenth year she is already, it seems, a mere "looker-on" at life, though a highly perceptive one, who misses nothing of the emotional drama which takes place in her godmother's house with the advent of a homesick child, a temporary guest, who is only pacified when she becomes the playmate and favourite of the son of the house. Yet there are indications that Lucy's apparent calm is really a defensive weapon, prematurely acquired, to arm herself against the blows of fate, which she has already had good cause to fear. She never mentions her parents; the quiet visits to her godmother are apparently her greatest pleasures, and the possibility of any news from "home" an immediate cause of acute apprehension. Years later, when she is living in *Villette*, the sight of a crescent moon shining through trees arouses latent memories, and it becomes clear that, before calamity had prematurely darkened the scene, she had once been a happy child, responding spontaneously to the sight of natural beauty:

> A moon was in the sky, not a full moon, but a young crescent. I saw her through a space in the boughs overhead. She and the stars, visible beside her, were no strangers where all else was strange: my childhood knew them. I had seen that golden sign with the dark globe in its curve leaning back on azure, beside an old thorn at the top of an old field, in Old England, in long past days. . . . Oh, my childhood! I had feelings: passive as I lived, little as I spoke, cold as I looked, when I thought of past days, I *could* feel. (ch. 12)

The premonition of coming trouble of which Lucy is aware while staying with her godmother is amply justified when she returns to her kinsfolk. No factual details are given of the following eight years, but the archetypal image of the sea as symbol of disaster, familiar from *Jane Eyre*, reappears. After an obviously ironic reference to a supposedly halcyon period when her life was like a ship in harbour, with the steersman stretched on the deck, his eyes closed – an image eerily reminiscent of *The Ancient Mariner* – Lucy speaks of the shipwreck that followed: ". . . there was a storm, and that not of one hour nor one day. . . a heavy tempest lay on us; all hope that we should be saved was taken away. In fine, the ship was lost, the crew perished" (ch. 4).

In the Bretton episode and its sequel, which is only hinted at, but which is none the less real for that, the basic rhythm of the action of *Villette* is established: it consists of a series of variations between periods of calm and periods of mounting unrest.[3] At this stage, however, Lucy, already prematurely disillusioned, shows much the same apparent passivity both in the calm of Bretton and in her attitude to the subsequent period of disaster. It is the initiative of her godmother which procures her the temporary respite of the first, and the initiative of the elderly invalid Miss Marchmont in sending for the now destitute girl, which affords her escape from the second. Her time of attendance on Miss Marchmont marks the apex of her half-involuntary sequestration from nature. She forgets that there are "fields, woods, rivers, trees" outside the "steam-dimmed lattice of the sick chamber". But once again this artificial calm is shattered, and followed by a time of turmoil.

It is nature that gives the signal for the coming change. Seated one evening at the fireside, Lucy is disturbed by the Banshee-like wailing of the gusts that herald the spring equinox. Like all Charlotte Brontë's heroines she is intensely sensitive to the sound and presence of the wind. This is not the summer gale that blows through Thornfield orchard; it is more akin to the tainted wind from the east that is associated with Caroline Helstone's lingering fever; but it is more formidable than either, menacing both the life of the individual and human life on a global scale:

> . . . I had heard that very voice ere this, and compulsory observation had forced on me a theory as to what it boded.

Three times in the course of my life, events had taught me that these strange accents in the storm – this restless, hopeless cry – denote a coming state of the atmosphere unpropitious to life . . . I fancied, too, I had noticed – but was not philosopher enough to know whether there was any connection between the circumstances – that we often at the same time hear of disturbed volcanic action in distant parts of the world; of rivers suddenly rushing above their banks; and of strange high tides flowing furiously in on low sea-coasts. (ch. 4)

Lucy's apprehensions are soon verified in her own restricted sphere. Her mistress, who had been asleep, awakes in a state of unusual excitement recalling her distant youth, the snowy Christmas Eve when her lover was killed in falling from his horse, the long years that followed, centred round his memory. But her excitement is the prelude to a stroke which causes her death. The episode is itself an anticipation of Lucy's own future fate, but the equinoctial gales give it a cosmic quality which transcends its significance for the individual destiny.

Lucy's destiny has, however, yet to be fulfilled and, for the first time, she is forced to act on her own initiative. "It seemed I must be stimulated into action." Here, too, the influence of forces emanating from the physical universe is again experienced. As she walks along a lonely country road pondering her future, on a moonless night, she sees in the northern sky "a moving mystery – the Aurora Borealis". From its presence she draws encouragement: "Some new power it seemed to bring. I drew in energy with the keen, low breeze that blew on its path." It is as a direct result of the encounter with this mysterious force that she forms the bold resolution to seek new surroundings which inaugurates a new phase in her life.

The decision takes her first to London and then across the Channel, in the hope of finding employment with a foreign family. Thus appropriately the new period of stress begins with an encounter with that stormy element, the sea, which here makes its first appearance in Charlotte Brontë's novels as reality and no longer purely as vision. Like the author herself on her second journey to Brussels, Lucy goes on board the night before she sails. As she is rowed out alone across the midnight Thames, she passes several ships before reaching her own. It has been pointed out that their names, the *Ocean*, the *Phoenix*, the *Consort*, the *Dolphin*, imply what she lacks – the complete freedom of non-identity, powers to transcend the elements, a protective male escort – while the name of her own ship, the *Vivid*, is "an apt characterisation of her solitary consciousness of things".[4] It indicates also the keenness of her awakened sensations and of her awakening capacity to live. When she finds herself on the water, exposed to wind and rain, she discovers she is unexpectedly enjoying the situation: "I asked myself if I was wretched or terrified. I was neither." The vibrant note, once struck, persists. The crossing has its concomitants of sea-sickness, ungracious stewardess, exasperating travelling companion – not to mention a destination called Boue-Marine. Yet how buoyant is the tone and how vivid the glimpse of the sea! ". . . deep was the pleasure I drank in with the sea-breeze; divine the delight I drew from the heaving Channel waves, from the sea-birds on their ridges, from the white sails on their dark distance, from the quiet yet be-clouded sky, overhanging all". Even when the ship runs into heavy weather, there is no foreboding fear of disaster: "As dark night drew on, the sea roughened: larger waves swayed strong against the vessel's side. It was strange to reflect that blackness and water were round us, and to feel the ship ploughing straight on her pathless way, despite noise, billow and rising gale" (ch.6).

The "pathless way", which is also Lucy's own, puts a heavier strain on her resources when she pursues her search for a livelihood on foreign soil. The journey in the diligence to Villette, the capital of Labassecour, is followed by an odyssey of wandering through inhospitable streets. At last she finds herself at the door of the pensionnat directed by Mme Beck who, as she has heard from her fellow-traveller Ginevra Fanshawe, herself a pupil at the school, is said to be looking for a nursery governess for her own children. Pleading her cause with the eloquence inspired by her plight, she succeeds in obtaining the post, and enters on another period where material security guarantees at least external calm.

The pensionnat is initially a pleasant refuge to Lucy. But she is, beneath her quiet exterior, fundamentally a creature of feeling and imagination, in spite of the precocious stoicism with which she has attempted to stifle both. The novelty of her recent experiences has roused these essential qualities of her nature to renewed activity, and they demand a satisfaction which cannot be supplied by the ordered routine of the rue Fossette. In the isolation of the nursery she admits to leading two lives, that of thought and that of reality, and to depending on "a sufficiency of the strange necromantic joys of fancy" to counterbalance an outward existence whose privileges are limited to "daily bread, hourly work, and a roof of shelter". Her horizon is enlarged when Mme Beck, aware of her abilities, persuades her, half against her will, to become a teacher in her school. But teaching a classroom of lively Labassecouriennes does not satisfy her inner life, though it testifies to her developing personality.

There are occasions when the hidden self demands almost irresistibly to be heard, and here the action of the elements once more plays a leading role:

> At that time, I well remember whatever could excite – certain accidents of the weather, for instance, were almost dreaded by me, because they woke the being I was always lulling, and stirred up a craving cry I could not satisfy. One night a thunder-storm broke . . . the tempest took hold of me with tyranny: I was roughly roused and obliged to live. I got up and dressed myself, and creeping outside the casement close by my bed, sat on its ledge, with my feet on the roof of a lower adjoining building. It was wet, it was wild, it was pitch-dark . . . I could not go in: too resistless was the delight of staying with the wild hour, black and full of thunder, pealing out such an ode as language never delivered to man – too terribly glorious, the spectacle of clouds, split and pierced by white and blinding bolts. (ch. 12)

The elemental fire and passion of this outburst recalls, though with greater power, the instinctive response of the young Jane Eyre when she heard, in the schoolroom at Lowood, the sound of the rising tempest without. But the solace Jane found in this "strange excitement" had no aftermath of bitterness. Lucy has to pay for it by subsequent hours of desperate longing for a release from her present existence, the effect of which is to confirm her in the stoical resolution to resist all such feelings, which imperil her precarious peace.

Much of her time, during her first months at the rue Fossette, is in fact taken up by her initiation into the life of the pensionnat.

While in *Jane Eyre* society, as far as it exists, is primarily a background to the heroine, in *Villette* it impinges on her personal life at every turn. Mme Beck herself, at first the most important person in this new world and, to the end, the most formidable, is, in Lucy's eyes, the embodiment of reason unsoftened by feeling and, as such, admirable in one way and antipathetic in another. Her own compatriot Ginevra Fanshawe, now spending her last months as pupil at the pensionnat, rouses in her feelings of similar ambivalence. Ginevra is an egoist who uses her beauty, as Mme Beck uses her more solid qualities, to ensure an enviable position in society, but her selfishness and superficiality are partly redeemed by the frankness with which she acknowledges them.

Lucy's preoccupation with the life around her is natural in one whose whole future depends on maintaining her footing in a hitherto unknown community. Similarly the external setting, circumscribed as it is, is important to her. The school with its classrooms and dormitories, the "carré" or central hall which connects them all, become part of her existence, as the quiet old house at Bretton had done in the past. But behind the buildings in the Rue Fossette is a garden – something never mentioned in connection with the Bretton dwelling – and this also becomes a part of Lucy's new life.

This garden, obviously, as in *The Professor*, recalling that of the Heger pensionnat, is of unusual extent for a city garden, and it is believed that a convent once stood on the site. There is a legend attached to its monastic past: it is said that the stone slab at the foot of an ancient pear-tree is the portal of a vault where a young nun had been buried alive for sinning against her vow, and that her ghost still haunts the place. This Gothic tale, reminiscent of the fate of the unfortunate Constance, loved and forsaken by Marmion, is dismissed by Lucy, determined to avoid the snares of the imagination, as "romantic rubbish". But the garden itself has its charms for her. It is an oasis of freshness and verdure "where all is stone around". The arbour known as the "grand berceau" is the favourite resort of Mme. Beck. Lucy characteristically prefers the seclusion of the "allée défendue", a walk forbidden to the pupils because of its proximity to the high wall dividing the garden from the rear buildings of the neighbouring boys' college. As the summer advances, pupils and teachers live more in the garden than under a roof, and even her insular prejudices cannot blind Lucy to the charm of the continental climate: "Settled sunshine seemed naturalised in the atmosphere."

The garden theme is of great importance in *Villette*, though its chief significance is reserved for the later part of the novel. This enclosed space, which is yet open to the sky and the action of the weather, gives Lucy, when she can escape from the schoolroom, her one opportunity for contact with nature. Her favourite time for walking in the solitude of the "allée défendue" is in the early morning, or on summer evenings when the soft air is "mistless as noon". As usual with Charlotte Brontë, the garden is associated with the theme of sexual awakening. The unnaturalness of Lucy's youth, deprived of love, is suggested by the legend of the nun, buried alive, and the eventual threat to her happiness with M. Paul is anticipated by the part played in the legend by the "monkish conclave of the drear middle ages". At this stage, however, it is nothing more sinister than the intrigues surrounding the flirtatious Ginevra which begin to disturb the evening peace of the garden. But the discovery that Ginevra is worshipped by the young English doctor at the pensionnat, but disdains him as bourgeois, preferring the "little dandy" Count de Hamal, arouses in Lucy a passion of indignation at such blindness, which betrays her own unconscious love of Dr John. It is at this stage that she is forced by circumstances – and the despotic little "professor of literature", M. Paul – to act with Ginevra in a school play, before an audience which includes both Dr John and de Hamal. The strength of her feeling ensures the success of her acting, but the next day she resolutely rejects the idea of any further use of the dramatic gift thus unexpectedly revealed, determined to regain her surface calm and remain "a mere looker-on at life".

It proves impossible to maintain this precarious equilibrium in the almost deserted pensionnat during the "grandes vacances". The only pupil left is a cretin, whom Lucy has to look after for some weeks. The feeling and imagination which are the most vital part of her being, and which she has tried to suppress, take their revenge in nights of insomnia and days of intense depression, and she finally falls ill with a nervous fever. The turning-point of this new period of crisis comes, as before, with the equinox, this time the autumn equinox which succeeds the

Indian summer. Though still feverish, she musters strength to venture out and, acting on a sudden impulse, seeks relief from her inner torment, Protestant though she is, in the confessional of an adjacent church. When attempting to return, she is too confused to find the way back. Meeting the full force of the wind, her heart rises to meet its challenge: "I only wished I had wings and could ascend the gale." But physical strength is lacking, and she falls down in a faint, from which she recovers, hours later, to find herself in a haven which is the prelude to another period of precarious calm.

This haven proves to be a small manor-house outside the walls of Villette. Lucy, on regaining consciousness, is astonished to find that it is the replica, in its furnishing, of her godmother's house in Bretton. It does in fact belong to her godmother, Mrs Bretton, and her son Graham, now established, after a period of financial reverses, on the Continent. John Graham Bretton is the "Dr John" of the pensionnat who, summoned to her aid by the priest who had heard her confession, had recognised in her the English teacher of the Rue Fossette and taken her to his own home. Lucy had already been aware of his true identity, though she had concealed it from the reader. It is not long before she herself is recognised as "Lucy Snowe", first by her godmother and then by Graham, who had known her in Villette only as "Mademoiselle", and all but forgotten the quiet schoolgirl of ten years before.

In the calm of the little manor of "La Terrasse" Lucy regains health of mind and body. She even feels sufficiently secure to allow her imagination more latitude, and the Bretton furnishings of her small bedroom provide a foundation for perhaps the most charming sea dream in Charlotte Brontë's work. But, as is fitting in a novel "committed to an essential realism",[5] it is a dream in whose creation the dreamer at first consciously collaborates:

My calm little room seemed somehow like a cave in the sea. There was no colour about it, except that white and pale green, suggestive of foam and deep water; the blanched cornice was adorned with shell-shaped ornaments, and there were white mouldings like dolphins in the ceiling-angles. Even that one touch of colour visible in the red satin pin-cushion bore affinity to coral; even that dark, shining glass might have mirrored a mermaid. When I closed my eyes, I heard a gale, subsiding at last, bearing upon the house-front like a setting swell upon a rock-base. I heard it drawn and withdrawn far, far off, like a tide retiring from a shore of the upper world – a world so high above that the rush of its largest waves, the dash of its fiercest breakers, could sound down in this submarine home, only like murmurs and a lullaby. (ch. 17)

This waking dream seems to become in the end an intuitive exploration of the depths of the subconscious, recalling the surrealist paintings of *Jane Eyre*. But, unlike Jane, Lucy has come to terms with the sea; she has even come to terms with her vision of the sea – a more difficult achievement. She can conceive of a state where one descends into the waters without being engulfed by them, where what threatened to be total submersion turns out to be almost total peace.

But life cannot long be maintained in these submarine depths: the vision owes its rare loveliness and its truth partly to its evident fragility. During her convalescence Lucy is gradually drawn by the Brettons, equable, kind and cheerful, back into the daylight world. They do their best to put some colour into her outwardly colourless existence, taking her to the art galleries of Villette, and to the concert hall. On the latter occasion Graham is abruptly cured of his infatuation with Ginevra, when he sees her laughing at his mother and flirting openly with de Hamal. The result is an easier relationship between himself and Lucy and, realising her solitude, he promises to write to her after she returns to the pensionnat.

The promise is no more than that of a friend, but friendship is all Lucy asks in return for her unacknowledged love. Reason warns her that the eagerly awaited letter may never arrive. When it does come, its arrival synchronises with the introduction of the supernatural in *Villette*. The legend of the nun, previously dismissed by Lucy as "romantic rubbish", suddenly acquires a disturbing credibility when she sees the figure of a nun in the dark garret where she has retired to read the precious letter. The ghostly presence is again hinted at by a mysterious light, in the depths of the same attic, on the evening when Graham calls at the pensionnat to take Lucy to the theatre. It is on this evening that he sees the girl who will later become his wife, and who proves to be his former playmate, the Paulina of Bretton days. In future the eagerly awaited letters come no more to the Rue Fossette. But the appearances of the nun do not on that account cease. They continue to be a focus of disturbance in Lucy's life, but it is now the garden that is the scene of the haunting, and its significance is correspondingly increased.

It is at the foot of the old pear tree which marks the place of the nun's burial vault that she decides to bury the few treasured letters, which have now become only a source of bitter grief. In doing so she is exposed, as she had not been in the dark attic, to the action of the elements. It is a wintry evening after moonrise, but there is a mist which changes the moonlight into "a luminous haze", and she is conscious of an electrical quality in the atmosphere which seems to inspire her with a fortitude similar to that she had felt, a year ago, in England, in the presence of the aurora borealis. This "reinforced strength" is unexpectedly challenged when the moon, emerging from the mist, throws into relief a black-robed, white-veiled figure only a few yards away. But Lucy now has the courage to confront the apparition, which then recedes before her.

Between this appearance of the nun and the next, Lucy travels a long way. Having had the courage to abandon an illusion, she gradually discovers the possibility of a love which is not an illusion. M. Paul, the fiery little professor of literature, assertive, provocative and not infrequently ridiculous, but possessing genuine power of intellect and warmth of heart, understands her as no one else does. It is when their friendship, after a stormy beginning, is already firmly established, unlike the "curious one-sided friendship" between Lucy and Graham Bretton, that the nun is seen by them both, as they are walking in the garden after sunset. This time she suddenly appears from among the branches of a high tree, and sweeps past them in a manner that seems to suggest anger. But M. Paul, too, has seen the ghost, so that Lucy need no longer fear that, as Dr Bretton had suggested, the apparition is "a case of spectral illusion", the creation of her own disturbed mind.

The connection between the nun and the garden has an increasing relevance for her own life. The victim of passion had been buried alive in the vicinity of blossoming and fruit-bearing nature; the old pear tree which marks the spot is dead, "all but a few branches which still faithfully renewed their perfumed snow in spring, and their honey-sweet pendants in autumn". Lucy's burial of her letters, and of her hopes of love, beneath the same tree, suggests as unnatural a fate. She recognises, with the psychological penetration which is at once her safeguard and her torment, that there is still life in her feeling for Graham Bretton. "Sometimes I thought the tomb unquiet . . .". But her growing affection for M. Paul, endorsed by reason as well as feeling, seems increasingly to promise a happier future.

The nun, however, was the victim not only of passion but of the "monkish conclave of the drear middle ages" which, according to legend, decided her unnatural doom. The next appearance of the theme of the nun in *Villette* is linked with the religious issue. Lucy is a Protestant, with a deep distrust of Roman Catholicism, and M. Paul a devout son of the Roman Church. His spiritual director and former tutor in Père Silas, the same priest who had heard Lucy's confession, and whose concern for her had indeed helped to save her life, but who does not wish his pupil to marry a heretic. Mme Beck is equally hostile, though for more personal motives: she wishes to marry Paul herself in order to bind him to her interests. Together they plan to separate him from Lucy. She is despatched one sultry afternoon on an errand to the aged occupant of an old house in the historic Basse-Ville, Mme Walravens. While there she is detained by a violent thunderstorm, during which she is joined by Père Silas, also an inhabitant of the house, which is near his church. The general atmosphere of the place suggests to Lucy a sort of sinister magic, and it is only half in irony that she describes the storm as "spell-wakened". But it had clearly been foreseen by Mme Beck, and indeed by herself, as the probable culmination of the cloudy and sultry weather. The crashing of the thunder and the "red zigzags" of the lightning are the result of electricity in the atmosphere; the magic is that of nature.

But the thunderstorm provides the opportunity for Père Silas to engage Lucy in conversation and to make clear to her that his former pupil M. Paul will never forget his first love, Justine Marie, who had taken the veil when their marriage was opposed by her family, and died in her noviciate. Justine Marie had been the grandchild of the still surviving Mme Walravens, and a portrait of her as a nun hangs in the room where they are talking, and gives additional force to the narrative of the old priest. Both he and Mme Walravens are supported by the loyal and devoted M. Paul out of his own earnings, and this generosity is cited by

Père Silas as another and more mundane obstacle to the possibility of his ever marrying.

The real nun seems to present a graver threat to Lucy than the apparition of the garden. But she now has sufficient confidence to treat M. Paul with a frankness inspired by his own. When told of the revelations of Père Silas, he makes it clear that she has nothing to fear from the memory of Justine Marie, now above earthly rivalries. Attempts are made by Mme Beck to prevent their meeting, but the garden sill offers opportunity for this, since working there in his spare time is one of M. Paul's chief means of relaxation. At such times he is often accompanied by a favourite spaniel, who helps to promote meetings between her master and Lucy by insistently demanding attention from both, and whose presence shows incidentally that the true hero of *Villette* includes love of animals among his virtues.

Eventually Père Silas, a kind man by nature, feels sufficient sympathy for their plight to make persistent efforts to persuade Lucy to abjure Protestantism, but without success. She herself feels no such wish to turn M. Paul from the faith of his fathers, recognising the complete sincerity with which he practises it. For them the problem is solved when they discuss it frankly and find that they both share the same essentials of Christian belief. At this point the future seems to promise a happiness and stability that Lucy had never known before.

Her hopes are abruptly shattered when Mme Beck suddenly announces to the pupils of the pensionnat, in her presence, that M. Paul will give no more lessons, since he is about to leave Europe unexpectedly on business "for an indefinite time". She then employs all her stratagems to prevent Lucy from seeing him again before he sails. The day for his departure comes and goes, and Lucy, worn out by many hours of suspense, is finally given, by Mme Beck's contrivance, a drink intended to induce a drugged sleep. But the narcotic does not have the desired effect. Instead it stimulates her to feverish activity and uncharacteristic daring.

The scenes which follow mark the culmination of this period of renewed stress. They are thus part of the basic rhythm of storm and calm which runs through the novel. Yet they are different from any that preceded them, though they had been briefly anticipated by the submarine dream at La Terrasse. Here the conflict between imagination and reason, which never ceases to agitate Lucy's inner life, even when she appears most calm, reaches a new level of intensity. Imagination suddenly asserts its power over its rival, helped by the action of the drug. Using, as she often does, personification to describe abstractions which to her, as to the actress Vashti, are living realities, Lucy relates how the victorious faculty becomes an imperious mistress: " . . . roused from her rest . . . she came forth impetuous and venturous. . . . 'Look forth and view the night!' was her cry; and when I lifted the heavy blind from the casement close at hand – with her own royal gesture, she showed me a moon supreme, in an element deep and splendid" (ch. 38).

There is, as Robert Heilman has brilliantly shown, a deep significance in this supremacy of the moon in the hour when imagination triumphs.[6] This was no unfamiliar presence in Lucy's life. From childhood, as she herself recalled, she had been familiar with the planet in all its phases. In Villette, as in England, she had watched its nightly course and would, on summer evenings, linger alone in the pensionnat garden "to keep tryst with the rising moon". But she had associated it with the favourites of fortune like Ginevra and Dr John, rather than with her own life. It seemed rarely to shine on her meetings with M. Paul. On this memorable night its immediate effect is to fill her with the desire to escape from the stifling pensionnat to the still green park, not far distant, and to visit there a spot well known to her, a great stone basin filled with water and surrounded by trees; she longs "to come on that circular mirror of crystal, and surprise the moon glassing therein her pearly front". It is no Narcissus-like motive that impels her, but the longing to forget her own restlessness in the peace of nature, a peace which seems to have, on this moonlit night, a supernatural dimension.

Impelled by imagination, Lucy does reach the park, but only to find it transformed into a land of enchantment, brilliant with festal illumination which obscures the moonlight. She soon realises that she has in fact wandered into the festivities accompanying the annual celebration of an event in the history of Labassecour, but imagination invests the fête itself with an aura of fantasy. "On this whole scene was impressed a dream-like character; every shape was wavering, . . . every voice echolike – half-mocking, half-uncertain." Seeking the clarity of true vision, Lucy seems to have stumbled into the uncertainties of the baroque. As she moves towards a quieter corner of the park, where the lamplight is partly replaced by moonlight, she moves towards a partial revelation. Watching, unseen, a group which includes the "secret junta" – Mme Beck, Mme Walravens and Père Silas – she sees them presently joined by M. Paul himself, learns that his sailing has been delayed and concludes, mistakenly, that marriage with a young and living Justine Marie, the granddaughter of Madame Walravens, who also joins the group, is to be his reward when he returns.

She waits for no more proof but leaves the park, congratulating herself on being freed at last from all illusions. But her imagination, stimulated by the moonlight, had guided her well until fear tricked her into a false assumption. As she makes her way back to the pensionnat, down the old streets where the same moon reigns supreme, untroubled by the transient glare of the fête, her imagination responds once more to a presence now felt more deeply as part of the cosmic reality which enfolds all human destiny:

> . . . the beauty of the moonlight – forgotten in the park – here once more flowed in upon perception. High she rode, and calm and stainlessly she shone. The music and the mirth of the fête, the fire and bright hues of those lamps had out-done and out-shone her for an hour, but now, again, her glory and her silence triumphed. The rival lamps were dying: she held her course like a white fate. Drum, trumpet, bugle, had uttered their clangour, and were forgotten; with pencil-racy she wrote on heaven and on earth records for archives everlasting. She and those stars seemed to me at once the types and witnesses of truth all regnant. The night-sky lit her reign: like its slow-wheeling progress, advanced her victory – that onward movement which has been, and is, and will be from eternity to eternity. (ch. 39)

With this vision of mystic brilliance, suggesting the transcendent, ends, as it had begun, what has been called "the most wonderful of Charlotte's nocturnes: the surrealistic park scene that opens the English novel to an extraordinary new perceptiveness and style".[7]

After the sublime, the grotesque. The last appearance of the nun is reserved for the moment of Lucy's return to the pensionnat. But the ghostly figure she finds lying on her bed proves to be simply "a long bolster dressed in a long black stole, and artfully invested with a white veil". The spectral disguise had been used by de Hamal, Ginevra's preferred suitor, when he entered the garden and climbed to the attic for secret meetings with her. It is needed no longer since, as is subsequently discovered, they have eloped together on the evening of the fête. But the discovery of the masquerade cannot alter the importance of the legend of the haunted garden in Lucy's life, nor the psychological relevance of the supposed haunting.

Events move swiftly after this memorable night. At the price of a direct confrontation with Mme Beck, M. Paul asserts his right to see Lucy again before he sails, and she discovers he has delayed his departure only in order to make provision for her happiness during his absence. The house in the Faubourg Clotilde contains a schoolroom, where she will be able to teach her own pupils, but it means more to Lucy than a refuge, it is also an anticipation of her future home. In the course of that one happy day she receives from Paul the assurance that he loves her, and that he will return to her when his mission is accomplished.

The house in the Faubourg is surrounded by gardens, with fields beyond. When the moon looks down in the evening, it is over trees and flowers. In the company of Paul, Lucy can gaze on it at last with the happy sense that there is an affinity between the lunar splendour and her own love. The final garden scene has an Eden-like quality, and they return together beneath a moon which seems not only to smile on human love but to suggest the nearness of the divine: "We walked back to the Rue Fossette by moonlight – such moonlight as fell on Eden – shining through the shades of the Great Garden, and haply gilding a path glorious for a step divine – a Presence nameless" (ch. 41).

Faubourg Clotilde is the happiest haven Lucy has ever known. The three years of her lover's absence pass quickly, cheered by his letters and the anticipation of his return. There comes at length the hoped-for month when he is to sail for Europe. "The sun passes the equinox . . . the wind takes its autumn moan . . .". In the sky, whose signs Lucy has noted "ever since childhood", she reads the menace of danger. Once more, as years before in England, she hears the Banshee-like wailing of the storm, which is not to cease till "the Atlantic was strewn with wrecks". It is the final storm of *Villette*, and it is succeeded by the final calm.

In Charlotte Brontë's last and most realistic novel the elements retain all their importance as instruments of her art. But at the same time one is always strongly conscious of their physical reality as direct manifestations of nature. The winds that sweep through the streets of *Villette*, the thunderstorms that drench them, the sunlight and the moonlight that shine on the enclosed garden are all real, as real as the Channel waves that roll between England and Labassecour, and the Atlantic billows that submerge a never-named ship. The difference between physical reality and dream is always clear to the reader, if not always to Lucy herself. The sea vision at La Terrasse is, as she admits, only a waking dream. The torches of the masquerade may vie for an hour with the moonlight, but they are doomed to extinction, while the moon pursues its majestic course.

Yet the correspondences between the inner life and nature which were the triumph of *Jane Eyre* are not lost in the later masterpiece. Lucy Snowe possesses the intense sensitivity to the action of the elements which characterised Jane Eyre and Charlotte Brontë herself. The power and the sound of the wind, its variations according to the quarter from which it blows, the electricity in the storm, the magnetism suggested by the description of the Aurora Borealis, the sunshine of the continental summer and the softness of its nights, all these are influences which act directly on Lucy's senses. But she also makes, like Jane Eyre, an imaginative response to them. In the climate of *Villette*, however, the response is less spontaneous and more complex. Jane, in her youth and confidence, can make the elements into the servants of her imagination. For Lucy they are sometimes almost her masters. Sunlight and moonlight become all but unbearable to her, in their very beauty, during her solitude in the forsaken pensionnat: "I too felt those autumn suns and saw those harvest moons, and I almost wished to be covered in with earth and turf, deep out of their influence; for I could not live in their light, nor make them comrades, nor yield them affection" (ch. 15). But so much the deeper is her delight when, as above all in the happiness of the Faubourg Clotilde, she feels herself completely in tune with nature's beauty: "The air was still, mild, and fresh. Above the poplars, the laurels, the cypresses, and the roses, looked up a moon so lovely and so halycon, the heart trembled under her smile . . ." (ch. 41).

As in *Jane Eyre* the natural can, at moments of climax, suggest the supernatural and this is true pre-eminently of the appearances of the moon. Although it plays a role throughout the novel, it is at the time of Lucy's growing love for M. Paul that the lunar presence becomes most significant. It is associated with the appearances of the nun in the garden, which for them involve the supernatural. It is the most abiding beauty of the nocturne, the "white fate" that remains when the torches are extinguished. In the farewell scene between Lucy and Paul, it acquires the religious significance which characterised it in the decisive spiritual crises of *Jane Eyre*, and becomes the "White Angel", "such moonlight as fell on Eden", a radiance associated with the divine.

It is when gazing at the night sky that Jane Eyre becomes aware that both nature and man belong to a cosmos divinely ordered. In *Villette* the implications of this common origin are more fully explored. The human drama, restricted as it appears, has a cosmic breadth. It begins and ends with equinox, and contact with the forces of nature, though it may be temporarily obscured, is always restored. Much more clearly than in *Jane Eyre*, it is made evident that all human life has a universal meaning, no less than a cosmic setting, because of the divine origin of both. Jane Eyre sees herself primarily as an individual. Lucy Snowe, looking back at her life, sees it as typical of the many lives for which she finds a natural equivalent in the term "cloud", used as expressive of a general state and not a passing phase. For other lives, illustrated in *Villette* principally by those of Paulina and Graham Bretton, she finds the appropriate correspondence in the word "sunshine". In conversation with Paulina she expresses her sense of a divine purpose controlling both destinies: "I think it is deemed good that you two should live in peace and be happy. . . . Other lives run from the first another course. Other travellers encounter weather fitful and gusty, wild and variable. . . . Neither can this happen without the sanction of God; and I know that, amidst His boundless works, is somewhere stored the secret of this last fate's justice: I know that His treasures contain the proof as the promise of its mercy" (ch. 32).

When Lucy thus expresses her attitude to life, she had not yet experienced her brief period of Eden-like happiness. Even though so short, reckoned in human terms, it was enough to convert courageous resignation into a calm and mature acceptance. But the truest maturity in *Villette* belongs, as Lucy would

surely not have disputed, to M. Paul. As Wordsworth, great
interpreter of nature, revered above all the human heart, so this
true lover of nature and man meditates upon the importance of
each in the eyes of God, the Creator of the cosmos:

"We abase ourselves in our littleness, and we do right; yet
it may be that the constancy of one heart, the truth and faith
of one mind according to the light He has appointed, import
as much to Him as the just motion of satellites about their
planets, of planets about their suns, of suns around that
mighty unseen centre incomprehensible, irrealisable, with
strange mental effort only divined."

Part IV
Emily Brontë and Nature

10 *Poems*

Most of Emily Brontë's poems were written in the decade between 1836 and 1846 and during the same period she was actively engaged with the chronicles of the dream world of Gondal, originally created by herself and Anne as counterbalance to Angria. Since the last part of this period must have coincided with the writing of *Wuthering Heights*, completed by July 1846, it is evident that Gondal remained a permanent part of her inspiration during the years of her maturity. When she decided, in February 1844, to transcribe her poems, she divided them between two notebooks, one of which was headed "Gondal Poems". Each received subsequent additions, and other verses were later discovered, thanks largely to the researches of C. W. Hatfield, whose 1941 edition of Emily's poems more than doubled the original number. Many of these additional poems bore witness, by title, references or signature, to a continuing affiliation with the Gondal sage. Both Gondal and non-Gondal works clearly belong basically to the same inspiration, but in considering her total achievement in verse, it seems natural to observe the distinction introduced by Emily herself.

Like Charlotte and Branwell in their Angrian writings, Emily and Anne chronicled the history of their imaginary kingdom in prose, as well as using it as an inspiration for their verse. The prose chronicles, unlike those of Angria, have not been preserved, but there are brief references to them in the still surviving birthday notes exchanged by the two sisters. The chief source of knowledge of Gondal remains, however, the poems themselves. As has already been indicated, both sisters wrote on companion themes. But the speakers in Emily's verse are more dynamic, their actions more dramatic, and her poems have provided a basis for endeavours to reconstruct the saga as a whole. The task has been attempted by Madeleine Hope Dodds and Laura Hinkley, and, most comprehensively, by Fannie Ratchford in *The Brontës' Web of Childhood* and *Gondal's Queen*. In the latter the poems are arranged as a cycle presenting a sequential account of the life of the central figure. Emily herself observed no continuous pattern in her Gondal transcriptions and such reconstructions inevitably contain an arbitrary element. The result is probably to make the saga more of a unified whole than its author envisaged. L. P. Hartley expressed his doubt as to whether the prose chronicle of the kingdom was ever completed.[1] It was not as a narrative that Gondal chiefly interested her but as another world, which offered her, as Angria did to Charlotte, an escape from galling frustrations and a means of exploring the potentialities of an exceptional temperament and an exceptionally vivid imagination.

But Gondal was not Angria. Unlike her elder sister, Emily did not long for a more sophisticated society, more contact with other cultures, the excitement of passionate love affairs seen against a colourful social background. For both, however, it was essential that the dream kingdom should have a distant setting. Gondal is an island in the North Pacific, whose hardy inhabitants also discover and colonise Gaaldine, an island in the South Pacific, which becomes part of their territory and is ruled by members of the same leading families, those of Brenzaida and Exina. Gondal is a rugged northern country, Gaaldine a tropical one. Together they form the background to the stormy existence of a turbulent race.

Love and war are the ruling passions of the Gondals. It must be admitted that their history, reduced to its bare outlines, appears to have the banality of a libretto rather than the simplicity of an epic, and the situation is further complicated by the fact that the central figure, Augusta, a Gondal princess, is referred to by more than one proper name, as well as by cryptic initials.[2] The first man she loves is killed in battle, the second she forsakes, driving him to exile and suicide, a fate shared by other unfortunates who cross her path. She finds a lover more suited to her in Julius Brenzaida, a Gondal prince who succeeds, by war and treachery, in making himself master of both islands but who is assassinated at the height of his power. After his death she becomes a fugitive, then regains her power as queen but, after some years, is herself assassinated by enemies who have good cause to hate her.

The Gondals, like their creator, prefer the open air to that of cities. It was "the great Glasstown" which was the origin of

Charlotte's imagined world, and subsequently the life of Angria was centred in the new capital Adrianopolis. Gondal, too, has its federal capital Regina, and other cities are mentioned, but they are seen, or rather briefly glimpsed, only in a context of war and violence. The home of the Gondal leaders, when they are neither at war nor captives, is on their country estates. But these feudal mansions are far from possessing the concrete reality of the Angrian manor-houses. They recall rather the generalised outline of the fortress or castle in a ballad. Festal halls that blaze with light, stairs that lead to "galleries dim" are stereotyped details which suggest that Emily, unlike Charlotte, took very little interest in describing splendid interiors. The natural background is the one in which the Gondals are most at home. To be separated from it by dungeon walls is almost as hard a fate for them as to be separated from it by death. Nature does not provoke the same metaphysical questioning as in the non-Gondal poems but it is needed to provide the only setting in which these turbulent characters can live out their destiny.

Its physical characteristics show less variety than those of Angria. In her "National Ode for the Angrians" Charlotte could contrast the various provinces of the confederation with dramatic effect because of their widely differing landscapes. The only geographical distinction in Emily's kingdom is between Gondal and Gaaldine. In theory it is admittedly a considerable one: the first-named island is northern, the second tropical. But in what does the tropical colouring of Gaaldine consist? There is the occasional echo of Byron's Orient in lines like

Palm-trees and cedars towering high
Deepened the gloom of evening's sky;

But it has been pointed out that in this tropical climate September is followed by "Autumn's drear declining".[3] The blue skies and golden flowers mentioned as characteristic of this "Eden isle" can also grace a northern summer. In fact what Gaaldine really suggests is a summer version of Gondal, with the emphasis on the valleys rather than the hills. Gondal itself is pre-eminently a land of moor and mountain, rushing torrents and lakes, but there are sheltered dells in the moorland and woods in the valleys. Clearly it is her own native landscape that is the foundation of Emily's imagined kingdom. For Charlotte to achieve the transposition from Angria to Yorkshire was a gradual and by no means an easy process. Between the Gondal and the non-Gondal poems there are in reality no territorial frontiers. The only real liberty Emily took with her setting had a practical purpose. By dividing the action between two widely separated islands, she increased the dramatic possibilities offered by the Gondal wars, and to the suffering caused by imprisonment was added that caused by exile. The separating sea has itself little independent significance. It is the element that carries the Gondal warriors to conquest, or brings them back, and it is only in the context of their homecoming that the sea voyage is evoked with any real enthusiasm.

> The blast which almost rends their sail
> Is welcome as a friend;
> It brings them home, that thundering gale,
> Home to their journey's end;[4]

Descriptions in the Gondal poems are never prolonged, sometimes even curt in their brevity, but they succeed in conveying a very definite impression. The landscape is a microcosm of the territory in its twin aspects of moorland and valley. The earliest in date of the Gondal transcriptions, "There shines the moon at noon of night", combines both within the scope of a single poem. The background is the moor, which stretches into the distance.

> Till it seems strange that aught can lie
> Beyond its zone of silver sky.[5]

Moonlight, reflected in the waters of a lake, provides the only brightness in the initial stanza. The next introduces the contrast between upland and valley, which becomes also that between moon and sun, winter and summer. The narrator recalls how, years before, she had sat at the same lakeside by her dying lover, mortally wounded in battle, at the close of a summer day when the setting sun was glowing on the heather. The contrast becomes complete when the dying man recalls his own home in Gaaldine, surrounded by woodlands bathed in sunshine. Both these aspects of landscape were essential to Emily Brontë, but it was one country and one climate that she painted – her own.

The descriptive background carries conviction, but the main

emphasis is on the figures in the foreground, and their role is more difficult to evaluate. They are characters who had originally evolved in the course of the Gondal play and belong to a society whose values are still largely those of the saga or the ballad. Yet it is possible, as Mary Visick has shown, to trace a correlation between the Gondal people and the characters of *Wuthering Heights*. They cannot be denied a certain reality, though, in her own words, their "blurred story" is revealed only in "a series of lyric moments".[6] All we really know of these figures is their passionately expressed emotions. Sometimes the emotions ring hollow, and the result is minor verse. When they ring true, they can inspire poems which rise to such heights as the great lament of Rosina for her dead lover. Whether Rosina is synonymous with Augusta, "Gondal's Queen", or not, does not affect the emotional impact of the poem on the reader. What matters is the intensity of her feeling, but something of the effect would be lost without the spontaneous evocation of place:

> Now, when alone, do my thoughts no longer hover
> Over the mountains on Angora's shore;
> Resting their wings where heath and fern-leaves cover
> That noble heart for ever, ever more?
>
> Cold in the earth, and fifteen wild Decembers
> From those brown hills have melted into spring –
> Faithful indeed is the spirit that remembers
> After such years of change and suffering![7]

No conscious thought is given here, as it frequently is in the non-Gondal poems, to the relationship between the speaker and the landscape or, more generally, between the speaker and nature. Yet there is a relationship and it is possible, to some extent, to define it. Most obviously nature represents a principle of stability in the flux of life. The return of the seasons is the means of measuring the passage of the years. But nature itself does not change with time, as man does. It is the "sweet, sweet world", to which he clings with passionate regret when faced by premature or violent death:

> . . . never more at early dawning
> To watch the stars of midnight wane;

To breathe the breath of summer morning
And see its sunshine ne'er again.[8]

Nature is the silent witness. Changing emotions, all intense, characterise the protagonists in the human drama. Sometimes there is harmony between setting and action. There are natural correspondances between childhood and spring, between happy love and summer. In Gondal, however, as in life itself, childhood may be darkened by calamity, love may encounter obstacle or disaster. In such cases the contrast between setting and action reinforces the tragedy of the situation. In "A Farewell to Alexandria" a mother abandons her infant in the same moorland dell where she had loved to linger on summer days, but where now the heather is fast being covered by snowdrifts, harbingers of speedy death for the forsaken child. In "The Death of A. G. A." the assassination of the Gondal queen is preceded by that of two young lovers, her loyal friends, who were her only guard as she wandered on a mountain-side, and it is in these idyllic surroundings that they meet their doom:

The lark sang clearly overhead,
And sweetly hummed the bee;
And softly, round their dying bed,
The wind blew from the sea.[9]

Nowhere is the contrast between nature and the vicissitudes of human life more acutely experienced than by those in captivity. The Gondal poems contain abundant references to prison bars and dungeon floors. The captives immured in such surroundings see no more of winter than the snow whirling through the grating, or of summer than the "green luster" reflected on the wall, that tells of "fields of lovelier green". In such circumstances life is bitter indeed:

What bird can soar with broken wing?

For Emily Brontë, as for all Romantics, the theme of nature is closely associated with that of freedom, and never more evidently than in the Gondal saga.

So close an association has its dangers. Nature itself does not offer complete freedom. The physical universe has its laws, no more questioned in Gondal than anywhere else, for Gondal is the creation of a countrywoman. For man, complete freedom, could he ever attain it, would be anarchy. This is what menaces the elemental inhabitants of Emily's imagined kingdom. Her saga, like all sagas, is founded on love and war. Augusta, "Gondal's Queen", is also "Sidonia's deity", the high priestess of her own cult, following without question the impulses of her nature and sacrificing men to the dictates of her passions. Julius Brenzaida and his rivals of the house of Exina fight, are captured, or die, not for any convincing political ideal – the names "Royalist" and "Republican" serve chiefly to distinguish rival camps – but in a grim struggle for power. Emily is too much of a realist, even in the annals of her imagined kingdom, to conceal the dire consequences of unbridled passion or of bitter civil war. Gondal, it has often been said, is a more moral world than Angria. The amoral Zamorna, in spite of temporary reverses, survives, but Augusta and Julius both die at the hands of an assassin. Yet they themselves seem conscious neither of guilt nor remorse. They retain none the less an epic quality because of the intensity of their passions and because of their unshaken courage.

The dangerous link, in such a milieu, between courage and barbarism cannot be concealed. A ballad like "Douglas's Ride" is exhilarating because it is presented as a ballad, "a song of troubled times". It has amazing pace and fire in a context where these are the essentials. But when an episode from the Gondal wars is described, like the fall of Tyndarum, it is by an eyewitness, a soldier who dwells not on the heat of battle but on the grim aftermath of devastation. The impression left is of horror rather than triumph. An even starker portrait of desolation is presented in "The Fall of Zalona", as the starving inhabitants prepare to abandon their besieged city. More impressive than either, however, is the poem beginning "Why ask to know the date – the clime?", both "the last and one of the greatest of the narrative poems."[10] It opens with deceptive mildness by evoking a pastoral scene, harvest time in perfect autumn weather. But there is something unnatural about this harvest:

> Week after week, from noon to noon,
> September shone as bright as June –
> Still, never hand a sickle held;
> The crops were garnered in the field . . . . [11]

The field has become a battlefield, and the crops are men's lives. In the grim school of civil war, the opponents have become steeled to show no mercy. Even if, by an unforeseen turn of fate, one of the victors is brought to realise his inhumanity, it is no longer in his power to make amends to his victims.

A year earlier, in 1845, Emily had written the most famous of the Gondal poems, "The Prisoner", also dealing with the theme of captivity, but developing into a great vision of freedom, no longer in the political arena but in the inner world of the spirit. The juxtaposition of Gondal setting and superb visionary poetry has attracted criticism, and the understanding of "The Prisoner" has not been helped by the fact that incomplete versions appeared before Hatfield's definitive text restored that of the original.[12] The juxtaposition is indeed unexpected, but not inexplicable. Gondal afforded particular opportunities for exploring both the dramatic situation and the inner anguish of the captive, and this theme was of peculiar importance to Emily, for it came increasingly to signify for her the basic predicament of the human spirit.

Rochelle, the central character in "The Prisoner", finding herself completely cut off from nature and life in her grim dungeon, reacts by aspiring to liberation of the spirit through death, and anticipates this in periods of mystic ecstasy. This is the inspiration of the great stanzas at the centre of the poem. They are addressed by Rochelle to the narrator of the poem, who is one of her captors. His initial indifference to her plight becomes first compassion and then love, which finally wins an equal love from her. Love is one of the dominant Gondal themes, but the fate of these lovers is wrapped in mystery. The action belongs to the recent past, and the narrator's chief comfort now lies in awaiting the visits of a mysterious "Wanderer", who comes nightly across the "waste of winter snow", a situation which seems akin to the vigils of Heathcliff after Catherine's death. But the implications of this situation are of less importance than Rochelle's impassioned attempts at spiritual evasion from her dungeon, which so nearly reach the goal that, at heart, she now most desires.

"The Prisoner" is a Gondal poem, but one senses, in the central verses, that closeness to its creator's thought which is most evident in Emily's non-Gondal poetry. In her imagined world, as in *Wuthering Heights*, she presents a drama, though essentially a lyrical drama. In the personal poems we are nearer to the mind which directed the actors. We do not find biographical details or Rousseauesque confessions, but intensity both of feeling and of thought, for in Emily there was a rare combination of the passionate heart and the meditative mind. In these poems she treated the themes that were closest to her, convinced that truth could be arrived at only by personal experience and personal reflection. The seemingly limited nature of her own experience did not dismay one who was so conscious of her inner resources. When she chose, Emily could turn from the Gondal fiction to her own outwardly circumscribed life and find there the starting-point for a deeper exploration of the problems that tortured her, the hopes that encouraged her and, not least, the nature that surrounded her.

As has been seen, it was basically her native landscape that she used in Gondal. In the personal poems its intrinsic importance is greater, and its regional character more strongly felt. For the Gondal figures it was a necessary background. For her it was the ideal one. Charlotte Brontë was at pains to show, in the prefatory notice to her 1850 selections from Emily's poems, that it was only an imagination like her sister's that could perpetuate "the brief flower-flush of August on the heather, or the rare sunset-smile of June", or find beauty in the moors at their bleakest: "Flowers brighter than the rose bloomed in the blackest of the heath for her; out of a sullen hollow in a livid hill-side her mind could make an Eden."[13] Charlotte's appreciation of her sister's exceptional imaginative power is just, but one senses here that the moors, much as she loved them, never satisfied her as completely as they did Emily. The northern summer was in fact more beautiful to Emily because it was brief, its flowers more precious because they were rare; the undulating stretches of dark moorland were evidence of the abiding presence and reassuring nearness of the earth, and their extent suggested infinity no less than the wide skies above them.

Such a landscape has a universal appeal because it is elemental and timeless. But Emily also gives it in her verse a regional character, not by comprehensive description but by the introduction at intervals of concrete details evocative of the Yorkshire scene. In his searching and lucid study of Emily's poetry Derek Stanford has shown how such objects become "the symbols of regionality – essences of the spirit of place".[14] Inevitably these allusions occur also in the Gondal setting, but it is in the non-Gondal poems that one is most conscious of the pervading spirit of the West Riding moors:

> . . . lovelier than corn-fields all waving
> In emerald and scarlet and gold
> Are the slopes where the north-wind is raving,
> And the glens where I wandered of old.[15]

Such scenes were the breath of life to Emily, but, with her, nature was not only a source of visual delight, it was the starting-point of her thought. She wrote no nature poems as an objective observer, she wrote poems through which runs, sometimes as an under current, sometimes as clearly defined as the two parts in a piece of music, a dialogue between the physical universe and the human soul. But there is a happy time in most lives, and it was so for Emily Brontë, when the dialogue briefly dissolves into complete harmony. The golden age remembered by Wordsworth was also a cherished memory for her. In childhood and early youth, before "shades of the prison-house" began to close upon her, she had enjoyed the freedom of the moors. The world was then truly an Eden, accepted unconsciously and consciously adored. By the time she wrote her earliest recorded verses, however, Eden was no longer inviolate. She could still be, when on the moors, as Ellen Nussey remembered, "a child in spirit for glee and enjoyment",[16] but she was already acutely conscious of the disharmony between joy in nature and the problems of her own life and of human life in general.

This awareness seems to have developed very early. By temperament she was akin both to the primitive and to the thinker, and in such a temperament emotions were strong, and thought itself was not leisurely reflection, it was deeply interfused with emotion and had the same intensity.[17] Beneath the surface calm maintained by her extreme reserve, she went through inner crises whose effects were as indelible as were those of her dreams on the mind of Catherine Earnshaw. It seems possible that the deeply disillusioned attitude to which she gave such early expression may have been due originally to some personal experience of rejection.[18] It is at least certain that when, on the eve of her seventeenth birthday, she was obliged to leave her beloved home for the uncongenial environment of school at Roe Head, she found her exile unendurable. She returned home in less than three months, but the experience must have left her with a sense of insecurity, and a sense of failure equally damaging. 1835 was an unhappy landmark, for in the same year she lost the companionship of Anne, sent in her place to Roe Head, and Branwell returned from his abortive visit to London with a similar sense of failure.

It is not surprising that in the earliest recorded poems, dating from 1836, nature is no longer a paradise full of unshadowed sunlight. A poem written in 1837, when she was eighteen, already testifies, as Jacques Blondel points out in his analysis of her work, to "l'harmonie rompue".[19] Here the song of a bird is at first a source of intense pleasure:

Redbreast, early in the morning
Dank and cold and cloudy grey,
Wildly tender is thy music,
Chasing angry thought away.[20]

But the song becomes associated with the memory of a child lost on the "desert moor". As a result, though still "seraph sweet" in itself, the music is changed to a "shriek of misery" in the listener's ear.

In general, the non-Gondal poems of this period show a series of fluctuations between happiness, which still comes chiefly from nature, and a profound pessimism. Even a passing impression of natural beauty is felt to be worth capturing in its unforgettable freshness:

Only some spires of bright green grass
Transparently in sunshine quivering[21]

But a more foreboding note is often struck, and the natural setting may even be rejected, if it is felt to be out of tune with the speaker's mood:

Wind, sink to rest in the heather,
Thy wild voice suits not me:
I would have dreary weather,
But all devoid of thee.[22]

Underlying these changing moods is an increasing struggle for spiritual equilibrium. Sometimes Emily shows the same reasonably cheerful attitude as in her birthday notes: more often she expresses a profound disillusionment, rarely felt with such intensity at the age of eighteen:

> 'Twas grief enough to think mankind
> All hollow, servile, insincere;
> But worse to trust to my own mind
> And find the same corruption there.[23]

But her next period of exile from home, when she went to teach at Law Hill,[24] though it did nothing to change her views on human nature, acted as a catalyst on her art. Law Hill itself was still "exile afar", but she now had sufficient mastery of her medium to give fuller expression to her feelings. The duration of her stay does not seem to have exceeded six months, but the poems written at Law Hill, or begun there and completed after her return home, show a new depth and a new lyric fullness. Sometimes, inevitably, she turned to Gondal, now becoming an increasingly stormy and war-torn land, but it is when she recalls the landscape of home that her lyricism soars to heights unattained before:

> Yes, as I mused, the naked room,
> The flickering firelight died away
> And from the midst of cheerless gloom
> I passed to bright, unclouded day –
>
> A little and a lone green lane
> That opened on a common wide;
> A distant, dreamy, dim blue chain
> Of mountains circling every side;
>
> A heaven so clear, an earth so calm,
> So sweet, so soft, so hushed an air
> And deepening still the dream-like charm,
> Wild moor-sheep feeding everywhere –
>
> That was the scene; I knew it well,
> I knew the path-ways far and near
> That winding o'er each billowy swell
> Marked out the tracks of wandering deer.[25]

The vision ends there, but not the poem. Even as the speaker is blissfully contemplating the remembered scene, the leisure for doing so is over and the "dungeon bars" reassert their tyranny. This tyranny, however, now begins to encounter opposition from a source hitherto unmentioned in Emily's poetry, a visionary power which comes to her in moments of solitude, bringing with it a sense of liberation from the trammels of ordinary existence. With the appearance of the visionary element her full potential as a poet becomes apparent. The years between the Law Hill exile and the writing of her last, unfinished poem saw her finest achievements in verse, above all in the non-Gondal work. The theme of nature remains, as before, interwoven with that of human destiny. Now, however, it is studied in more depth, provokes more variations and proves to have metaphysical overtones.

It might have been expected that what is essentially a deeply disillusioned view of human existence would ultimately have coloured Emily's attitude to nature itself. But this is never the case. Behind the individual landscape she sees the physical universe, which is not modified by the human situation but follows its own course in accordance with its own laws. In this she finds matter not for resentment or resignation but for profound satisfaction: ". . . over the plain physical fact of the bare life of the earth she had always exalted".[26] She glories in manifestations of the strength of natural forces, seeing them not as agents of chaos or destruction but as expressions of the dynamic energy which is as essential to the functioning of nature as its softer manifestations. As a Northerner she finds mountain winds, rushing torrents and whirling snow even dearer to her personally than summer sunshine and green valleys, though she accepts that both aspects are equally fundamental in the life of the universe.

Nature is independent of man, but man is not independent of nature. No one was more conscious than she of the ties that united her to the physical world. She did not hesitate to express symbolically what she herself felt as a close relationship in imagined dialogue. In "The Night-Wind" the soft breathing of the wind becomes an attempt to distract her from sorrowful thought:

"Have we not been from childhood friends?
Have I not loved thee long?"[27]

In "Shall Earth no more inspire thee", her consciousness of the spell which the physical universe has always exercised over her is acknowledged in words supposed to be spoken by Earth itself:

> When day with evening blending
> Sinks from the summer sky,
> I've seen thy spirit bending
> In fond idolatry.
>
> I've watched thee every hour;
> I know my mighty sway,
> I know my magic power
> To drive thy griefs away.[28]

This poem is a recognition of the power nature has to charm the writer. It is at the same time a recognition that there are limits to that power. In the verses that immediately follow, Earth admits its incapacity wholly to satisfy the "lonely dreamer", while reasserting the value of the consolation it can offer:

> Few hearts to mortals given
> On earth so wildly pine;
> Yet none would ask a Heaven
> More like this Earth than thine.
>
> Then let my winds caress thee;
> Thy comrade let me be –
> Since nought beside can bless thee,
> Return and dwell with me.

What nature cannot offer is a lasting solution to the ills inherent in the human condition. At an early stage Emily Brontë seems to have lost faith in the desires and hopes common to most in youth, and she reaffirmed her indifference to them in her maturer years:

> Riches I hold in light esteem
> And Love I laugh to scorn
> And lust of Fame was but a dream
> That vanished with the morn – [29]

Such detachment can breed misanthropy, but Emily, who could be stoical for herself, remained intensely conscious of the ills and

tribulations of human society, perpetually torn by the inter-
necine strife of warring egoisms. Here, too, nature seemed to
offer no lasting solution. At most she could find a temporary
oblivion in the peace of nightfall:

> The world is going – Dark world, adieu!
> Grim world, go hide thee till the day;[30]

Not all Romantics shared Emily Brontë's pessimism as to
nature's incapacity to repair the harm done by society to mankind in general. Wordsworth, with whom she often showed a
deep affinity, held a different view. After his disillusionment with
the aftermath of the French Revolution and with Godwinian
intellectualism, it was to nature that he turned for healing not
only for himself but for humanity. In early poems like *Guilt and
Sorrow*, he showed lives ruined by the callousness of society, nor
did he ever attempt to conceal its baleful effects. Michael, the
Grasmere shephered, is obliged, in old age, to face hardships he
has done nothing to deserve. But his unfinished sheepfold does
not stand for failure; it is rather a memorial to the power of the
natural affections and the stability of the man whose life is rooted
in his native soil. The portrait of the leechgatherer in *Resolution
and Independence* is an equally impressive tribute to the power of
uncomplaining endurance that can be fostered by a stern but
natural environment. The old man seems himself almost a part
of nature, but proves to be at the same time a human being
whose courage and dignity make the poet's pity for his harsh fate
unnecessary and almost insulting:

> I could have laughed myself to scorn to find
> In that decrepit Man so firm a mind.[31]

Clearly, one does not look for such characters in the world of
Gondal, but in the non-Gondal poems they are equally lacking.
The poet is most often alone with nature, and with her own
thoughts. If she speaks of others, it is usually to mourn former
companions now absent or those whose youthful promise has
never been fulfilled, and whose lives have foundered in disaster.

But of even more concern to Emily Brontë than the ills
inflicted by society of human weakness, are the spiritual limitations inherent in the human condition. Even if, as Wordsworth

at least believed possible, men like Michael and the leech-gatherer are strong enough, thanks to their natural environment, to avoid becoming warped or embittered by what they have to endure, they still have, as individuals, to face the question posed by Catherine Earnshaw: "What were the use of my creation if I were entirely contained here?" Nature unaided cannot provide a solution but may, if interpreted in a metaphysical sense, point the way towards doing so.

Catherine Earnshaw, like her creator, wanted freedom to penetrate beyond the bounds of self and communicate with a wider life. This is what Wordsworth achieved through spiritual communion with nature, as he describes in "Tintern Abbey". That Emily Brontë, in her greatest poems, evoked similar moments of spiritual illumination cannot be questioned. But that she owed as much to nature in the process seems doubtful. For him the spirit which permeates all created things is at the same time a moral force. He describes himself in "Tintern Abbey" as

> . . . well pleased to recognise
> In nature and the language of the sense
> The anchor of my purest thoughts, the nurse,
> The guide, the guardian of my heart, and soul
> Of all my moral being.[32]

Nature in itself rarely seems to present for Emily the same possibilities of spiritual elevation. It is a source of unmixed joy for the child, and affords precious consolation and refreshment to those oppressed by the trials of life, but it cannot offer lasting protection from personal sorrow or the ills of this world. Above all, it cannot change the fact of death. It is her very love of nature which gives the sharpest sting to the intimations of mortality which beset her during the swift passage of time. In her acute anguish at the separation from the physical world which menaces her, she can affirm, in "I see around me tombstones grey", that she desires no after life unless it is "a mutual immortality" to be shared with the maternal earth.

Yet the dream of a sensual infinite could not give lasting satisfaction to one who had been reared in the Christian belief in immortality and who, with all the force of her indomitable spirit, aspired to a higher state of being. For Emily, as for Wordsworth, nature led to vision. But it did not merge into vision; it was temporarily transcended, at privileged moments, by a higher reality with which it could not co-exist. It is with this transcendence of the natural that the most intimate of her peoms are concerned.

It was the period of exile at Law Hill that saw the earliest expression of Emily's personal mysticism:

> I'm happiest when most away
> I can bear my soul from its home of clay
> On a windy night when the moon is bright
> And the eye can wander through worlds of light –
>
> When I am not and none beside –
> Nor earth nor sea nor cloudless sky –
> But only spirit wandering wide
> Through infinite immensity.[33]

Here it is nocturnal nature that is deliberately chosen to provide the necessary prelude, and the concerted effect is one of absence rather than presence; the light has brilliance without colour, the wind is visible only in its movement, there is a sense of the vastness of interstellar space. This negative character provides the transition to the complete immateriality of the spirit's flight; personal identity is temporarily forgotten in the sense of liberation. But this wandering seems too purposeless to belong to a divine cosmos: the vision is as yet too vast for the visionary.

The experience of the transcendent can only be of rare occurrence, however, and nature, with all its normal appeal to eye and ear, as well as to the heart, continues to be a major source of inspiration in Emily's mature poetry. But at times she seems to become aware, with a shock of surprise, of her growing sensitivity to those quieter aspects of the visible world that are most favourable to meditation:

> How still, how happy! Those are words
> That once would scarce agree together;
> I loved the plashing of the surge,
> The changing heaven, the breezy weather . . .
>
> How still, how happy! Now I feel
> Where silence dwells is sweeter far . . .[34]

In these years there becomes apparent a growing preoccupation with the darker side of human destiny and a more sombre questioning of her own. But she is also able to express more fully those moments of liberation through mystic ecstacy which she had already begun to record. In "Aye, there it is! It wakes to-night", the poet is speaking to herself and becomes her own interpreter. It is once again a natural cause, the blast of the storm wind, which precipitates the transition from her imprisoning situation to spiritual freedom, but this is now seen to be because the wind arouses in the listener the full strength of her inner life:

Aye, there it is! It wakes to-night
Sweet thoughts that will not die
And feeling's fires flash all as bright
As in the years gone by!

And I can tell by thine altered cheek
And by thy kindled gaze
And by the words thou scarce dost speak,
How wildly fancy plays.[35]

"Fancy" here signifies imagination, for the Romantics the faculty which could transform, by its creative action, the natural world and whose highest and most mysterious function was "to serve as a link between the known universe and the transcendental realm".[36] It is primarily through the action of the imagination that the poet now experiences union with the rhythm of the universe and mystic anticipation of the freedom that comes with release from mortality:

And thou art now a spirit pouring
Thy presence into all –
The essence of the Tempest's roaring
And of the Tempest's fall –

A universal influence
From Thine own influence free;
A principle of life, intense,
Lost to mortality.

Belief in the imagination was common to all the Romantics, but their estimate of the extent of its action varied, inevitably, with the individual. Wordsworth, the greatest lover of nature, was most concerned with its power to show "ordinary things" in an unusual light. Coleridge was more dependent on the inner vision:

. . . in our life alone does Nature live.

Blake and Shelley, in different ways, both attached supreme importance to the imagination, and Shelley in his *Defence of Poetry* did not hesitate to define poetry itself as the expression of this cardinal quality. An affinity with Shelley has been increasingly stressed by critics in Emily's later poems, and this one has been described as "a kind of Ode to the West Wind".[37] But she preserves, as always, her own individual outlook. Shelley's Ode anticipates the effects of the poet's imagination on mankind:

Be through my lips to unawakened Earth
The trumpet of a prophecy!

Her essential concern is with liberation from mortality.

But there can be a conflict between mystic elevation and the visible, tangible world, of whose power and beauty Emily is still intensely aware. This conflict finds unforgettable expression in the poem to which Charlotte, in the 1846 collection of the sisters' verse, gave the title *Stars*. It begins with the poet's passionate regret that a brilliant dawn has effaced the mystery of the night sky, propitious to imaginative experience; it continues with a nostalgic plea for the return of "Stars and Dreams and Gentle Night", and culminates in a determined yet despairing attempt to ignore the presence of the joyously awakening day. There is no doubt of the reality of the physical background.[38] The stars belong to the physical universe. But they lead to vision because their remoteness evokes the transcendent. The spell is broken with the return of daylight:

Why did the morning rise to break
So great, so pure a spell,
And scorch with fire the tranquil cheek
Where your cool radiance fell?

Blood-red he rose, and arrow-straight
His fierce beams struck my brow:

The soul of Nature sprang elate,
But mine sank sad and low! . . .

O Stars and Dreams and Gentle Night;
O Night and Stars return!
And hide me from the hostile light
That does not warm, but burn . . .[39]

It is the mystic experience which is dominant in Emily's two greatest poems. They are, apart from the Gondal war narrative already referred to, her last. The first of them, "The Prisoner", as seen earlier, is set in a Gondal context, but centres round the seven stanzas in which the captive describes how a supernatural visitant comes nightly to her dungeon with the promise of liberation. Nature still has its part in the inception of the vision. The coming of the "messenger of Hope" is accompanied by west winds and the host of the emerging stars, whose presence is sensed rather than seen. There follows, for the prisoner, a trance-like state, in which the natural world ceases temporarily to exist, and is replaced by a higher reality:

"Then dawns the Invisible, the Unseen its truth reveals;
My outward sense is gone, my inward essence feels –
Its wings are almost free, its home, its harbour found:
Measuring the gulf it stoops and dares the final bound!"[40]

This is the leap from one form of life to another which is spoken of by many mystics and confirms "the authentic nature of the experience which the poet describes".[41] The visionary is now completely distanced from the physical world, and the return to it is torture;

"Oh dreadful is the check – intense the agony
When the ear begins to hear and the eye begins to see;
When the pulse begins to throb, the brain to think again,
The soul to feel the flesh and the flesh to feel the chain!

"Yet I would lose no sting, would wish no tortures less;
The more that anguish racks the earlier will it bless:
And robed in fires of Hell, or bright with heavenly shine,
If it but herald Death, the vision is divine."

The last verse might be interpreted as an expression of the death wish, but this is only possible when it is taken out of context. In the words of C. Day Lewis, the passage as a whole conveys "not a retrogressive yearning for oblivion but something much more positive – a struggle towards a life, and a mode of being, beyond death".[42]

Three months later Emily reached the peak of her vision and the supreme statement of her metaphysical thought in the most affirmative of all her poems:

> No coward soul is mine
> No trembler in the world's storm-troubled sphere
> I see Heaven's glories shine
> And Faith shines equal arming me from Fear
>
> O God within my breast
> Almighty ever-present Deity
> Life, that in me has rest
> As I Undying Life, have powers in Thee . . .
>
> Though Earth and moon were gone
> And suns and universes ceased to be
> And thou wert left alone
> Every Existence would exist in thee
>
> There is not room for Death
> Not atom that his might could render void
> Since thou art Being and Breath
> And what thou art may never be destroyed.[43]

It has been observed that Emily, in her mystic experience, had an attitude of "awe before the numinous" and habitually spoke of the power whose presence she apprehended in symbolic language.[44] Here she addresses herself directly to God, and He is seen to be both imminent and transcendent. Such a belief is neither that of the pantheist nor of the agnostic. The Heaven whose glories shine suggests the Christian cosmos. But if this tremendous poem still leaves one with a sense of the unknowability of God, which is not complemented by any mention of the mediating influence of Christ. Emily omits any reference to the cost at which Heaven's glories became accessible to fallen man.

This is certainly not because she was unaware of the element of corruption in human nature, so often emphasised in her poems. She was no believer in "the noble savage". She believed in the innocence of childhood, and lamented its departure as she lamented the prelapsarian Eden. The problem of the conflict between good and evil, of guilt, remorse, and the after-life, these were questions with which she was permanently concerned, to which she often alluded in her verse and which she as often left unanswered. Her poem "The Philosopher" is a confession of her failure to reply to them to her own satisfaction. They were to become embodied in the human drama of "Wuthering Heights".

But nature, the maternal earth and the encircling sky, did not pose such questions for her. Nature was not life in the absolute sense, and so it could never give her the kind of ecstasy that was hers when she affirmed her triumphant belief in the immortality of the soul. But it was a God-given refuge and source of renewal, a means of returning, if only temporarily, to the original Eden. It was the best loved because the most immediately accessible of her sources of inspiration.

As a lyric poet Emily far outstripped either of her sisters. Hers was no facile inspiration, nor had it ever the sustained flow and fullness normally characteristic of Romantic poetry. She herself, at nineteen, lamented that she had been denied the gift, given to many, to "speak their thoughts in poetry", but she was then already in process of realising her own highly individual lyricism, in which what she felt as a limitation proved to be only the reverse side of her most distinctive qualities. Charlotte Brontë came as near as anyone had done to defining these within the compass of a few words when she described her reaction to the discovery of her sister's poems: "I thought them condensed and terse, vigorous and genuine. To my ear they had also a peculiar music – wild, melancholy, and elevating."[45]

At its best Emily's poetry does possess a remarkable density, only equalled perhaps by Blake. The deeper, and the more deeply felt, her thought, the more sparing she was of words in which to express it. Her language is terse, but forcible and emotive. She frequently uses abstractions – doom, bliss, pride, shame, hope, despair – but there is nothing vague or rhetorical about them, they are felt as part of her own inner life. Their use is balanced by her vigorous use of the concrete: her material terms have substance and breadth of meaning. With what appears to be a limited but is rather a consciously selective vocabulary, she can suggest both the universal and the particular. She never multiplies epithets, but she does introduce at intervals the unexpected word that is as startling in its aptness as in its orginality. She does not fear to be repetitive, where the choice of adjective corresponds to her deepest preoccupations. "Drear", "lone" and "wild" are of frequent occurrence, but so is "glorious"; they reflect the two poles of her private world. She is sparing in her use of metaphor and simile, for she identifies too closely with her inner life and her surroundings to have much need of such intermediaries. When she does use them, they tend to be taken from some process of nature. But in her greatest poems she used symbols to express what could not possibly be expressed in any other way.

Charlotte's reference to the "peculiar music" of her verse seems equally just. She had an intuitive mastery of rhythm and of verbal harmony which is apparent, as Derek Stanford has shown, even in her minor verse, but is most effective when beauty of form and depth of meaning are fused into one. Her metres vary in accordance with her inspiration, but her verse patterns are always flexible, her rhythms full of vigour, and her verbal music rich in assonance and alliteration, both subsumed in a harmony more subtle than either. Charlotte's definition of this "peculiar music" does, however, exaggerate its melancholy. It could also be joyous, as when it echoed the harmonies of nature and "the spontaneous rhythms of natural creation – of animals, birds, and foliage, the moving patterns of winds and waters".[46]

One of the last great poems perfectly expresses the maturity both of her art and her thought, while at the same time it is a farewell to the physical world. Human life, as she sees it, is symbolised by a young tree which, though roughly despoiled of its pristine beauty, revives through the healing power of nature. It blossoms again in all its glory throughout a second spring, but only to succumb suddenly to the blight of death. Its fate is tragic, but tragedy proves, as in "The Prisoner", to be the herald of Eternity:

> . . . Heartless Death, the young leaves droop and languish!
> Evening's gentle air may still restore –
> No: the morning sunshine mocks my anguish –
> Time for me must never blossom more!

Strike it down, that other boughs may flourish
Where that perished sapling used to be;
Thus, at least, its mouldering corpse will nourish
That from which it sprung – Eternity.[47]

11 *Wuthering Heights*

While Emily Brontë's poetic activity, like the writing of her Gondal chronicles, occupied her from adolescence onward, *Wuthering Heights* was the product of her final years. The actual date of its inception is not known, but Charlotte Brontë was able to offer to send the manuscript, together with those of *The Professor* and *Agnes Grey*, to a publisher in July 1846. The previous October had seen an interruption in her poetic activity, coinciding with Charlotte's discovery of her poems, and it seems probable that her writing of a novel intended for publication did not begin before then.[1] To produce such a work in so short a time was a remarkable feat. There is no doubt that she must have been considerably helped by the practice acquired in the writing of the Gondal prose chronicles, and it has been shown that there are undoubted affinities between characters and situations in the Gondal poems and in *Wuthering Heights*.[2] But the actual composition of Emily's only novel indubitably belonged to the period when life at the parsonage was darkened by the increasingly rapid decline of Branwell and, as John Hewish has said, "it is reasonably certain that *Wuthering Heights* and Heathcliff would hardly have been the same without this example of romantic self-destruction so close to its author".[3] The novel is basically the product of a more tragic vision than the poems, and this is inevitably reflected in the treatment of nature, but the theme retains all its vital importance.

Wuthering Heights is a regional novel in a far more intimate sense than any of the works of Emily's sisters. Changes of setting are an essential part of the action of *Jane Eyre* and *Agnes Grey*, and also, despite its misleading title, of *The Tenant of Wildfell Hall*. In *Villette*, as in the earlier *Professor*, the Belgian sections are by far the most important. The only viable comparison is with *Shirley*, whose action takes place within a clearly defined area of the West Riding, the neighbourhood round Roe Head. But *Shirley* is both a regional and an industrial novel. It is worth while recalling that, though the heiress of Fieldhead and owner of Hollow's Mill was partly modelled on Emily, Emily herself found Roe Head unendurable. "Every morning when she woke, the vision of home and the moors rushed on her, and darkened and saddened the day that lay before her."[4] Though Haworth village was one of the centres of the woollen industry, it was the unspoilt nature of the open moorland above, and the hill valleys between its ridges, that she loved, and such is the country that provides the setting for *Wuthering Heights*.

The scenic background is completely convincing, obviously based on close as well as loving observation. Her native moors, and the isolated houses of leading local families, varying in importance from farm to manor, offered models for her landscapes and the homes of her protagonists. Wuthering Heights has been traditionally associated with Top Withens, near Haworth, and Thrushcross Grange with Ponden Hall, the home of the Heaton family in the nearby village of Stanbury. But, like all artists, Emily borrowed material from more than one source. It has been shown by Hilda Marsden that she was also indebted to features of the landscape round the school where she taught at Law Hill. Law Hill was backed by "the vast sweep of upland" which "extends in an unbroken line over the Oxenhope moors towards Haworth . . .",[5] a type of country similar to her own region. In her demonstration of the affinities between the district round Law Hill and the background of *Wuthering Heights*, Hilda Marsden has revealed striking resemblances. The home of the Earnshaw family, obviously larger than the now ruined Top Withens, though resembling it in situation, has grotesque carvings on the front similar to those which distinguished the façade of the now demolished High Sunderland Hall near Law Hill. Thrushcross Grange, more impressive than Ponden Hall and standing in its own extensive park, though with some similar features, has resemblances with Shibden Hall, in the Shibden Valley, below the level of High Sunderland. And the situation of the village of Gimmerton, within walking distance of both the Heights and the Grange, corresponds with that of Southowram, the village of which Law Hill was the highest point.

Out of these various elements Emily Brontë has created her own background. The action is entirely concentrated in one locality. A distance of only four miles separates Thrushcross Grange, in the valley, from Wuthering Heights, and the distance from the park boundary of the Grange to the edge of the moor is considerably less. From the Grange itself the moorland hills are clearly visible, and the salient landmark of Penistone Crag, obviously suggested by Ponden Kirk, the millstone grit outcrop at the head of Ponden Clough, fascinates the younger Catherine, as she gazes at it from the windows of her home. The two houses are the twin poles of the action, but the fact that they are really in such close proximity greatly increases the sense of place which is essential to the novel.

Both houses are strongly rooted in their native soil. The Heights has been the home of the Earnshaws since 1500. The Grange has, in all probability, been the property of the Lintons for as many centuries; there is a carved monument to the family in Gimmerton Chapel. The action begins in the latter part of the eighteenth century, by which time the Industrial Revolution had already begun, though cloth was still woven by hand in the cottages of the West Riding. But there is no mention of hand weavers in the village of Gimmerton. It is the seasonal activities of the country year which determine the routine of life in *Wuthering Heights*.

It is typical of Emily's whole approach to her subject that this routine is taken completely for granted. It receives no detailed description; it is simply referred to where such reference is relevant to the action, and for that very reason is all the more convincing. It is at the beginning of harvest that Mr Earnshaw, after giving orders for the day's work on the farm, makes the fateful journey to Liverpool which results in the advent of Heathcliff. It is while servants and labourers are busy with the hay, on a fine June morning, that news comes of the birth of Hareton Earnshaw, the heir to the Heights. It is on a mellow September evening, when the servant Ellen Dean has been gathering apples in the garden of Thrushcross Grange, that Heathcliff reappears, asking to see her mistress, now married to Edgar Linton. It is at the time of a late harvest that Edgar Linton, staying out till dusk one chill, damp evening to watch the carrying of the last sheaves, catches the cold which is the beginning of his final illness.

Though Emily does not give detailed descriptions of the country year, she describes more fully the two houses which are at the centre of the narrative. It is above all Wuthering Heights which the reader learns to know with an intimacy made possible

by the fact that it is seen at different stages of the action and, in
accordance with Emily's narrative method, through the eyes of
different observers. It is fitting that a stranger, Lockwood,
should be the first to describe it, for to him the features which the
people of the region take for granted have all the freshness of
novelty. Wuthering Heights, as we are made to feel from the
beginning, stands on the defensive against both weather, as its
name suggests, and against all comers. It is both farm and
fortress. On his first arrival Lockwood finds the causeway
guarded by a barrier, which has to be unchained before he can
enter the court. The grotesque carving over the front, and the
date and name above the porch, confirm the antiquity of the
building. Its architecture is essentially functional: ". . . the narrow windows are deeply set in the wall, and the corners defended
with large jutting stones".

Once the threshold is crossed, however, a single step leads to
the "house", a "huge, warm, cheerful apartment" lighted by an
immense fire of coal, peat and wood. The firelight is reflected in
the shining pewter on the shelves of a vast oak dresser, and a
wooden frame suspended overhead and "laden with oatcakes
and clusters of legs of beef, mutton, and ham" confirms the
domesticity of the scene. Warmth and plentiful if homely fare are
characteristic of life at the Heights, and the subsequent reminis-
cences of the servant Nelly Dean show that they have never been
entirely lacking, even when the fortunes of the Earnshaws were
at the lowest ebb. Behind the "house" is the kitchen with its own
glowing hearth and the "scoured and well-kept floor" which was
Ellen's particular care. Upstairs are the bedrooms, reached by
narrow lobbies from which wooden ladders lead to the garrets.
The room occupied by Lockwood, when snowbound at the
Heights, and formerly by Catherine and Heathcliff when children, is furnished with one of the old box-beds in use in such
houses at the time. By her unerring selection of concrete detail,
Emily Brontë conveys a vivid impression of an ancient farmstead
on the Yorkshire moors.[6]

By contrast the reader has a much less clear impression of
Thrushcross Grange, though it is obviously a far more imposing
residence. It is the material luxury of the interior which fascinates Catherine and Heathcliff as children, when they gaze in
from without, and this could belong to any country house of the
period. There is, despite its affluence, a curious air of emptiness

and defencelessness about the Grange. The upstairs parlour and the library are the only rooms that acquire a certain individuality, and that is mainly because of the action connected with them. One has only to compare this rather nebulous picture with the massive reality of Shirley's manor of Fieldhead to become aware how much less importance the country house possesses in itself for Emily than for her sister Charlotte. She is more interested in the view from the windows of the Grange over the park and the valley of Gimmerton than in its stately interior. What is really significant for her is its situation.

The Grange and the Heights are obviously the two most important houses in this remote and sparsely populated locality. It would be natural for their owners to play an active part in the life of the rural community and, when the younger generation were still children, their fathers had done so. But, after the death of Mr Earnshaw, the rhythm of life at the Heights, already disturbed by the advent of Heathcliff, is profoundly shaken by the conduct of his son Hindley. The peace of the Grange, when Edgar becomes its master, is undermined by his ill-fated marriage to Catherine Earnshaw and, after her death a year later, he gradually withdraws into almost hermit-like seclusion. The children of Hindley and Edgar grow up in isolation from their contemporaries, though not from nature, represented for Hareton Earnshaw by the farm and the moors, for Catherine Linton by the wide acres of Thrushcross Park.

This lack of involvement between the individual and the rural community would have been a serious flaw in a novel intended to show them as complementary. But such was not Emily's chief concern. In a brief comparison between *Wuthering Heights* and Hardy's *Return of the Native*, J. F. Goodridge remarks that Egdon Heath "unites more than divides human beings, creating a community out of scattered hamlets . . . their communal tradition . . . alone survives personal tragedies. But in *Wuthering Heights* the moors isolate and divide, and only the strong, passionate individual survives."[7] And it is certainly true that Emily's epic protagonists occupy the centre of the stage, and that Heathcliff is not a native of the moors but a towering figure whose shadow darkens them. There are no scenes of village life in *Wuthering Heights*. The Gimmerton band, "mustering fifteen strong", has, on its one appearance at the Earnshaws' farm, no voice other than that of its instruments and its carols. Yet the rustic chorus which is so indispensable in Hardy's work is not completely absent from Emily's. It is supplied by two characters, Nelly Dean and Joseph. Clearly, this is only part of their function in *Wuthering Heights*, where Nelly herself is the chief narrator, but it is by no means a negligible one.

The portrait of Nelly obviously owed much to Tabitha Aykroyd, who brought the life and tales of the countryside into the Brontë parsonage and who was described by Mrs Gaskell as "a thorough specimen of a Yorkshire woman of her class in dialect, in appearance, and in character".[8] Nelly's roots are in the northern countryside. She does not speak in dialect, like Tabby, but accounts for this by the advantages she has had when housekeeper at the Grange: "You could not open a book in this library that I have not looked into, and got something out of also . . .". But, in spite of occasional lapses into stilted language, she retains, in her speech, the directness, the colloquialisms and often the raciness of her milieu. Unlike the romantic Raphael in Balzac's *Peau de Chagrin*, Emily Brontë was well aware that those who live close to nature express themselves with a frankness disconcerting to the more sophisticated.

Nelly has all the shrewdness and the down to earth commonsense of the intelligent countrywoman, gained, as she says, in a hard school. She has a healthy belief in her own importance, and accepts the material disadvantages involved in being "a poor man's daughter" without falling a victim to the sense of inferiority induced in the class-conscious. She has the country distrust of "foreigners" and points out to the well-meaning but patronising Lockwood that it is for them to earn a welcome, not to expect one: "We don't in general take to foreigners here, Mr Lockwood, unless they take to us first." She has a piety which is on one level, no doubt, superficial, leading her to irritating moralising, but which is founded, none the less, on genuine Christian beliefs. She has a strong maternal instinct which leads her to mother young children, and to sympathise in a practical though never a sentimental manner with the unfortunate. Even the boy Heathcliff, disqualified at first as a foreigner, finishes by appealing to her compassion. It is she who coaxes him into reasonableness, at a moment of crisis during his unhappy adolescence, and if others had had as much feeling and as much good sense as herself, he might never have developed into an agent of doom to the entire Earnshaw household. When he is subsequently rejected and disgraced, it is Nelly who affirms that, as it is Christmas time, he ought not to be deprived of his share of the Christmas fare. An age-long tradition of sanity, justice and hospitality speaks in her protest, wantonly ignored by the exacerbated Hindley Earnshaw: "Nay, sir . . . I suppose he must have his share of the dainties as well as we."

Nelly Dean, though shrewd and benevolent, has her faults, the chief of them being her over-confident intervention in the affairs of the family she serves, without full understanding of the issues at stake. But hers is on the whole a beneficent influence. Her fellow-servant Joseph, on the contrary, seems to incorporate, on his first appearance, all the grimness of the northerner wrestling all year long with harsh weather and an infertile soil. Lockwood, a stranger, is disgusted at the outset by his churlishness. Nelly Dean, who dislikes Joseph, does nothing to attenuate the initial impression given to the reader of a man of singularly harsh character. Rather, she increases it by portraying him also as a grim old Puritan, "the wearisomest self-righteous Pharisee that ever ransacked a Bible to rake the promises to himself and fling the curses to his neighbours". But Joseph, who at first appears almost a caricature, coloured by the Brontë dislike of the "ranting" type of Dissenter, is in fact as essential as Nelly in representing the traditional values of country life.

His loyalty to the family whom he serves is shown by his actions, however harshly he may condemn their faults. When Hindley Earnshaw, on succeeding his father, banishes both him and Nelly from the family sitting-room to the back kitchen, he accepts his lower status without apparent protest. When Hindley's conduct after his wife's death drives the other servants away, he and Nelly are the only ones who will stay in the house. When Nelly has to leave, to accompany Catherine to the Grange on her marriage, Joseph still remains. He becomes the staunch supporter of Hindley's son Hareton, for him "t' little maister", and even when Heathcliff takes possession of the farm, he continues to do his usual heavy share of the work. It is only when Hareton, at Cathy's direction,[9] uproots his treasured currant and gooseberry bushes in the farm garden in order to plant flowers that, in a rage, he declares his intention of leaving the place where he has served for sixty years. The issue appears trivial but, for him, it is not: he sees the values of the Heights, where a living has to be wrested from the land and fertile soil is precious, threatened by an alien way of life. He is in reality indispensable to its welfare, as Heathcliff tacitly acknowledges, and, in the end, he is reinstated as Hareton's tenant beside the hearthstone in the kitchen which is his elysium.

Unlike Nelly, Joseph speaks entirely in dialect. Emily Brontë does not, like her sisters, content herself with a restricted use of dialect features. Even Mr Yorke in *Shirley*, though he is said to prefer "his native Doric to a more refined vocabulary", is sparing in his use of it. But Joseph expresses himself at length in the scenes where he appears, and these are by no means infrequent. His language shows how well Emily knew her region, and suggests she had a wider acquaintance among countryfolk than Charlotte credited her with, for it reproduces both their idiom and their pronunciation with remarkable accuracy.[10] But in speaking his own language Joseph speaks also for the countryman and his values with a rough eloquence not otherwise attainable. Half a century after the publication of *Wuthering Heights*, Halliwell Sutcliffe could still describe him as being "from the first gesture, thought, speech, to the last, the Joseph whom you will find to-day in any of the lone-lying farms about the moors".[11]

It is largely thanks to the presence of Nelly and Joseph that the action of *Wuthering Heights* is seen as firmly situated in a rural locality with its own way of life. They themselves take both for granted, though Nelly, keenly observant, has an eye for natural beauty and can describe a landscape briefly but vividly. The chief interest of the action, however, centres on the families whom they serve, and the relation between the leading protagonists and their natural environment involves deeper and more complex issues, which are indissolubly connected with the significance of the novel as a whole.

From the moment when Lockwood enters the living-room at Wuthering Heights, one is aware of a primitive harshness which is at odds with the domestic comfort afforded by the blazing fire and confirmed by the shining pewter on the dresser. The cause is not difficult to locate. The arch under the dresser is inhabited by "a huge liver-coloured bitch pointer, surrounded by a swarm of squealing puppies", while other fierce-looking dogs haunt other recesses. When temporarily left alone with them by his reluctant host, Lockwood senses their hostility and, mistakenly imagining that they "would scarcely understand tacit insults", retaliates by making faces at them, with the result that they attack him in a pack. He fares no better on his next visit, when his rash attempt to escape out into the snowstorm, on finding the household impossible, is foiled by "two hairy monsters" with the appropriate names of "Gnasher" and "Wolf". Examples of animal ferocity are not limited, however, to the sombre atmosphere of the Heights. More than twenty years before Lockwood's visit there, it had played its part in a crucial episode in the childhood of Catherine and Heathcliff. Suspected of being marauders when they had been seen gazing through a window at Thrushcross Grange, they had been chased by the Linton's bulldog Skulker, let loose on such occasions. Catherine received an injury to her ankle which led to her being nursed for five weeks at the Grange, and thus to the intimacy with the Lintons which was the beginning of the widening gap between herself and Heathcliff.

Animals had, of course, always played a part in the Brontës' novels, as in their lives. But it was the qualities of helplessness and dependence in them, and the affection and fidelity they gave in response to human kindness, which were their principal attraction for Anne, and basically for Charlotte also. Emily, too, showed deep compassion for those who were helpless or wounded, and, as has been seen, a dramatic incident in *Shirley* was suggested by her intervention on one such occasion. But she was more attracted than her sisters by the wildness of the creatures of the moors, and by the traces of wildness latent even in domestic animals, such as she sometimes encouraged her dog Keeper to display. Keeper was the prototype of Shirley's Tartar, and Tartar's great moment comes when he springs at his enemy. But, like Keeper, he acknowledges the authority of his mistress, who at once calms him. He is a domestic animal and, like the members of Byron's menagerie, tame though not tamed.

A much more sinister impression is given by the menagerie at the Heights. It arises from the fact that one senses, in their human master, a relish for violence akin to their own. Heathcliff does not go so far as to allow his dogs to savage Lockwood, who is his tenant, but he is in no hurry to call them off – an office actually performed by the servant Zillah – and, in the nearest he gets to an apology, in fact identifies himself with them: "Guests are so exceedingly rare in this house that I and my dogs, I am willing to own, hardly know how to receive them."

The importance of the animal theme in *Wuthering Heights* had been foreshadowed in one of the essays written by Emily in Brussels. These *devoirs*, though they reflect some of the bitterness of exile, express none the less her own opinions with the openness encouraged by the essay form, even when the convention of an imagined setting is adopted. The "most important and metaphysical" among these essays is "The Butterfly".[12] Here the speaker describes herself as wandering in sombre mood on the edge of a forest. She hears a nightingale singing, but reflects that the beauty of the song may well make the bird the target of human attack by revealing its whereabouts, and so comes to considering the dilemma of all living creatures:

> All creation is equally insane. There are those flies playing above the stream, swallows and fish are diminishing their number each minute: these will become in their turn, the prey of some tyrant of air or water; and man for his amusement or for his needs will kill their murderers. Nature is an inexplicable puzzle, life exists on a principle of destruction; every creature must be the relentless instrument of death to the others, or himself cease to live.[13]

Here, as Richard Benvenuto has said, Emily Brontë anticipates Tennyson's "Nature, red in tooth and claw" and Darwin's *Origin of Species*.[14] In her utter disillusionment, the speaker in "The Butterfly" finds fresh proof of the destructiveness of nature when she picks a flower in full bloom, only to find a caterpillar concealed among its petals, which are already beginning to wither. In a moment of passionate revulsion against the apparent meaninglessness of life she crushes the insect underfoot. Hardly has she done so when she sees a magnificent butterfly flutter through the trees, and the sight becomes for her, in a moment of imaginative vision, the symbol of a new heaven and a new earth, of which the present universe is only the embryo.

There is no reason to doubt the sincerity of this conclusion, unexpected though it is as a sequel to such stark disillusionment. Emily Brontë said what she meant to say, not what she was expected to say, whether her audience was M. Heger or an eventual reading public. But the new world visualised in the closing lines of the essay is the product not of evolution but of revolution, and its birth is preceded by "the funeral pyre of a universe in flames". The theme of "The Butterfly" anticipates

Wuthering Heights in its continuing sombreness until the final note of optimism. It is in the bleak world of the struggle for existence that Catherine and Heathcliff live their tragic lives, once the brief happiness of their childhood is past, and even Cathy and Hareton must taste its bitterness to the last drop of poison.

The violence which is an integral part of *Wuthering Heights* is based on a deep philosophical conviction of the violence which man shares with the animal world. But violence implies force, and force in itself was something that Emily Brontë admired. It is only when force becomes violence deliberately employed for a destructive purpose that it develops into a source of evil. The difference, and it is an essential one, is very evident in the career of Heathcliff. The secret of his magnetism is his vital force, and it is this that carries him through the stresses of his early years. He shows indomitable courage in grappling with the bulldog which attacks Catherine, and bears no grudge against her for her favoured treatment by the Lintons. If he becomes unkempt in appearance and sullen in manner after Hindley Earnshaw has degraded him from adopted son of the house to farm labourer, and deprived him of the lessons he shared with Catherine, the change is not irrevocable, as long as her attitude to him remains the same. It is not till he overhears her saying that to marry him now would degrade her, that he leaves the Heights. But marriage with her is still his aim, and, with this hope in view, he has the strength to "fight through a bitter life" during the three years of which he never gives any fuller account, but from which he returns civilised in appearance, and with money at his command. It is then that he learns of her marriage to Edgar, and the whole strength of his will becomes concentrated on revenge, not on her but on Hindley Earnshaw and the Linton family.

It is from this point onwards that animal imagery is used with increasing frequency to describe Heathcliff.[15] Even Catherine who loves him, calls him "a fierce, pitiless, wolfish man". Isabella Linton, after she becomes his wife, compares him to "a tiger, or a venomous serpent". Nelly Dean sees his despair after Catherine's death as not like that of a man but of a savage beast. Heathcliff himself, when he wishes to insult his enemies, compares them to animals, not, however, to the wild creatures he respects for their strength but to the gentler animals whom he despises. Edgar Linton is "a lamb" that "threatens like a bull", and Isabella a "pitiful, slavish, mean-minded brach". Linton

Heathcliff, his son, is as "puling chicken". Of Hindley Earnshaw, whom he hates most as the author of all his misfortunes, he says brutally, when he dies before the doctor can arrive, that "the beast had changed into carrion".

These metaphors are not rhetorical, or melodramatic; they correspond to the violence which has developed in Heathcliff, and which governs his behaviour to others. It is no longer only the violence shown by men and animals in the struggle for survival; it is the more sinister violence motivated by the deliberate will to wound as well as to destroy; it has degenerated into sadism. Driven by despair, and the insatiable longing for a lost happiness, he wreaks his vengeance on his usually helpless victims in acts of conscious brutality. His first action, on eloping with Isabella Linton, is an attempt (foiled by Nelly Dean) to kill her pet dog, symbol of Grange effeteness in his eyes but, above all, a means of wounding her. He kicks and tramples on Hindley Earnshaw when he is lying unconscious. He is merciless in his treatment of Isabella when she is in his power at the Heights. But his brutality is seen at its starkest when, after a lapse of years, he attacks the younger generation, who are innocent of offence against him. He detests Cathy, as Edgar's daughter, and shows no pity for her. He lures her to the Heights through her affection for his ailing son and succeeds in marrying her to Linton, whom he knows to be dying, in order to secure the mastery of the Grange. When she becomes virtually a prisoner at the Heights, he treats her brutally when she attempts to defy him. He takes a sadistic pleasure in terrifying Linton, whom he despises as a weakling. Only Hareton Earnshaw, though reduced to being a servant in his own house, receives better treatment from his father's enemy because he is fearless by nature and has "none of the timid susceptibility which would have given zest to ill-treatment, in Heathcliff's judgment".

It is not only Heathcliff who, as a result of past wrongs and desperate unhappiness, becomes sadistic. His sadism awakes similar reactions in his victims, though they are not, as a rule, in a position to retaliate physically. After her disastrous marriage Isabella, though reared according to the code of the Grange, finds herself instinctively coveting the pistol, with a spring knife attached to the barrel, with which Hindley Earnshaw, now a wreck of a man, vainly hopes to avenge himself on his enemy..

Linton, too weak to oppose his father, becomes so warped in nature by his taunts that he, too, would enjoy playing the tyrant if he could. Cathy herself, generous and affectionate as she is, becomes temporarily so embittered that she repulses Hareton's attempts at friendship with cruel scorn. Even Lockwood, a well-intentioned stranger, is so shaken by his reception at the Heights that, when obliged to pass the night in the room that had been Catherine's, he betrays in his dreams the violence of his desire for retaliation. The immediate cause of his nightmares is the combined effect of reading the marginal jottings in her books about Hindley's tyranny to herself and Heathcliff as children, and the tapping of a fir branch against the window. But the account of the riot after Jabez Branderham's sermon, in the first dream, echoes the savagery of Heathcliff's dogs. In the second, a more horrifying scene of violence stems from the same subconscious source. Lockwood, who dreams he has broken the window pane to seize "the importunate branch", sees a ghost child outside, crying to be let in. She clings to his hand and, in the effort to shake off her grip, he rubs her wrist on the broken glass till the blood soaks the bedclothes. Here, too, it is his own recent experience of barbarity which accounts for his violence in the nightmare: " . . . his barbarity to the child grows out of the first dream and is an ultimate act of self-assertion and self-preservation – the final terrified retaliation of the dreamer for the physical and emotional outrages he has sustained".[16]

The connection between the animal theme and that of human violence introduces into the novel a note of peculiar sombreness almost entirely absent from Emily Brontë's treatment of nature in her poetry. Only once does she there develop the analogy between man and animal in any depth, and then it is in one of the most tragic of her poems, where she mourns the "blighted name" of a dead and dishonoured friend and strives to find, in such an analogy, grounds for compassion:

> Do I despise the timid deer
> Because his limbs are fleet with fear?
> Or would I mock the wolf's death-howl
> Because his form is gaunt and foul?
> Or hear with joy the leveret's cry
> Because it cannot bravely die?

No! Then above his memory
Let pity's heart as tender be . . .[17]

The tone is compassionate, but the argument is ambivalent. The plight of the man who fails to master his instinctive reactions, whether of cowardice or violence, calls indeed, like that of the hunted animal, for pity, but there is another dimension to his tragedy.

The analogy is, however, exceptional in Emily's poetry. The violent instincts in human nature are shown there in the unbridled passions of the Gondals, and above all in the Gondal wars. But, unless defiled by acts of violence, the physical universe itself remains, both in the poems and in *Wuthering Heights*, a place of beauty and mystery. In both, nature is an unfailing source of strength and consolation, the Eden of childhood, the presence whose "magic power" retains its spell even at the approach of death.

In the poetry, nature had a double aspect: Gondal and Gaaldine, the hills and the valleys. In the novel the contrast is even more strongly felt because Emily is not only evoking the "spirit of place", a "Yorkshire of the inward eye", but an actual West Riding landscape, where the darkness of the moors formed of millstone grit and overgrown with heather accentuates the greenness of the valleys. This contrast between dark uplands and green valley which appears as "a dominant motif in nearly all Emily Brontë's work"[18] had been familiar to her since childhood. Both aspects are essential, and repeat the polarity between the Heights and the Grange, though it is the moors that dominate the landscape, as it is the Heights that dominates the action.

Charlotte Brontë was well aware of the importance of this landscape for her sister, saying that "her native hills were far more to her than a spectacle; they were what she lived in, and by, as much as the wild birds, their tenants, or as the heather, their produce".[19] She went on to deduce from this the reason for the excellence of Emily's descriptions of natural scenery, which "are what they should be, and all they should be". Few would quarrel with her verdict, yet in fact straightforward descriptions are rare and almost invariably brief. A few lines suggest the expanse of the moors under snow: ". . . the whole hill-back was one billowy, white ocean; the swells and falls not indicating corresponding rises and depressions in the ground. . ." (ch. 3).

Again a few lines evoke the whole range of the uplands seen from a distance, during a March thaw: " 'The snow is quite gone . . . and I only see two white spots on the whole range of moors: the sky is blue, and the larks are singing, and the becks and brooks are all brim full' " (ch. 13). The contrasting view of the valley is similarly expressed with a modicum of words, as it is seen by Catherine and Edgar Linton: "They sat together in a window whose lattice lay back against the wall, and displayed, beyond the garden trees and the wild green park, the valley of Gimmerton, with a long line of mist winding nearly to its top . . ." (ch. 10).

Such descriptions are always closely related to the action, for *Wuthering Heights* is essentially dramatic. It is for this reason that they are brief, for the pace of the drama is swift. Anne Brontë's heroines are naturally reflective; they take time to meditate on their surroundings. The action in Charlotte's novels is more dramatic, but her heroines have time to observe their changing environment closely, time, above all, to dream about it. There is only the one landscape, with its dual aspects, for the narrators in *Wuthering Heights* to describe, and they seldom pause to do so in any detail, once they have rapidly established the main scenic features. Sometimes what they describe is simply a series of actions, but the very nature of the terrain can emerge from such accounts with astonishing vividness, as when Isabella tells of her escape from the Heights: ". . . I bounded, leaped, and flew down the steep road; then, quitting its windings, shot direct across the moor, rolling over banks and wading through marshes: precipitating myself, in fact, towards the beacon-light of the Grange" (ch. 17).

Occasionally, however, there are descriptions, in almost microscopic detail, of scenes which, in themselves, seem to possess no special interest to warrant such attention. There is the spot "where the highway branches off on to the moor", which is marked by a sandstone pillar serving as guide-post, whose weather-worn appearance is delineated with the most careful precision. There is the high bank on one side of the formal walk in the Grange park, where "hazels and stunted oaks, with their roots half exposed, held uncertain tenure". Though covered with bluebells in the spring, it appears singularly drab and colourless when described on an afternoon in late October. Such colour as is provided by the surroundings is autumnal, "a bit of moss, or a tuft of blanched grass, or a fungus spreading its bright orange among the heaps of brown foliage". The unusual fullness of detail is, however, justified in the economy of the narration by the impression made by these particular scenes on the chief narrator, Nelly Dean. For her they are, like Wordsworth's "spots of time", landmarks in a spiritual landscape. The sight of the stone pillar, where she had played as a child with Hindley Earnshaw, her foster-brother, summons up a vision of Hindley as he had been then, and the subsequent encounter with his young son Hareton, her former nursling, confirms her worst fears as to the effects of Heathcliff's domination at the Heights. The high bank where the trees, insecurely rooted, have been blown nearly horizontal by strong winds, had long been a favourite resort of her other nursling, Cathy, but it no longer has sufficient attraction to keep her from leaving the shelter of the park, and from the fateful encounter with Heathcliff which marks the end, for many months, of her youthful happiness.

The focus of interest in *Wuthering Heights* is never on nature in itself but always on its significance for the actors in the drama, and especially for the main protagonists. The most memorable descriptions occur not in the course of the narrative but in the course of the dialogue. To think of nature in *Wuthering Heights* is to think of Catherine's frenzied longing, in her delirium, to be "among the heather on those hills", of her delight at the lapwing's feather which she finds, or imagines she finds, among those pulled from the rent in her pillow, which awakens cherished memories: "Bonny bird; wheeling over our heads in the middle of the moor". It is to think of the younger Catherine's description of the difference between lying on the moor throughout a hot July day, "with the bees humming dreamily about among the bloom", as her cousin Linton prefers, or "rocking in a rustling green tree", as she herself loves to do, with a west wind blowing, and birds "pouring out music on every side" and "the moors seen at a distance . . . but close by great swells of long grass undulating in waves to the breeze; and woods and sounding water, and the whole world awake and wild with joy" (ch. 24). These are landscapes seen only with "the inward eye", but so close is the felt bond between man and nature that they seem as visible and tangible as the physical reality.

The relationship goes deeper, however, than the imaginative reproduction of sense impressions. Catherine's fevered vision of the moors expresses her sense of spiritual exile. Cathy's contrasting accounts of the ideal way of spending a summer day show both the spiritual distance between herself and Linton and her own position, poised between conflicting impulses. Nature in *Wuthering Heights* is both profoundly real and closely allied to the contrast between spiritual forces which underlies the whole work. Lord David Cecil, in his memorable essay, saw the novel as illustrating the philosophical belief that "the whole created cosmos, animate and inanimate, mental and physical alike, is the expression of certain living spiritual principles – on the one hand what may be called the principle of storm – of the harsh, the ruthless, the wild, the dynamic; and on the other the principle of calm – of the gentle, the merciful, the passive and the tame".[20] Such a reading has the advantage of emphasising the significance of the correspondences between the family at the Heights and the wildness of the moors, and between the family at the Grange and the calm of the valley. But his interpretation of the novel includes the belief that Emily Brontë was not concerned with moral standards, seeing Heathcliff as no more responsible for his actions than "a mountain torrent diverted from its channel". This, as has been convincingly argued, is not a view likely to have been endorsed by the novelist herself.[21] The natural symbolism she uses is not intended to show her characters as one with nature, but to show how their relationship with nature constantly throws light on their own feelings and actions.

For her, as for Charlotte, nature means essentially the elements and the weather, but her landscapes, real or imagined, produce a different kind of impression from those of her sister. In Charlotte's novels the landscapes are like symphonies, in which one can distinguish the parts played by the elements as recurring themes. In the epic drama of *Wuthering Heights* one is overwhelmingly conscious of the presence of earth and sky as forming together one vast stage – vast at least in its potential significance – the same stage on which life began.

Dominating the foreground is the earth, in its dual aspect of hill and valley. But the foundation of rock which underlies both is never forgotten by Emily. She does not mitigate its harshness; she exults in it. Penistone Crags are "bare masses of stone, with hardly enough earth in their clefts to nourish a stunted tree", but they are also "golden rocks" in the setting sun. Their presence arouses varying reactions in the different actors in the drama and these in turn shed light on their inner lives. Nelly Dean prefers the moorland heather to the rocks, and the trees of the valley to the heather. But Catherine Earnshaw, in an unforgettable image, associates their primordial function with the depth of her love for Heathcliff: "My love for Linton is like the foliage in the woods: time will change it, I'm well aware, as winter changes the trees. My love for Heathcliff resembles the eternal rocks beneath: a source of little visible delight, but necessary" (ch. 9). Her daughter Cathy Linton, born at the Grange, is attracted by the distant view of Penistone Crags, and by the moors in summer. But she is not really in her element there, any more than the flowers she transplants to the Heights. She belongs to the green valley, which is also part of the archetypal landscape. There is no divisive sea in this landscape, any more than in the original Eden. There are no wide lakes, as in Gondal. There is only the beck, fed by the streams draining the marshland, which follows the bend of the valley, whose sound can be heard from the Grange, when it is not drowned by the murmur of the summer foliage, and from the Heights "on quiet days, following a great thaw or a season of steady rain". The sound of its flow is audible on the day when Catherine dies. Eighteen years later, when Heathcliff is himself nearing death, the same sound can be distinctly heard through the open window. It suggests the nearest approach to peace their restless natures can know.

As always with Emily Brontë, the sky and the weather are essential to her scene, but there is no obtrusive weather symbolism. It is part of nature, and the reader accepts it as such, and as a rule is hardly conscious of how much it contributes to the human drama. But the bitter cold of a northern winter, when the sky is full of whirling flakes driven by gusts of wind, helps to suggest Lockwood's moral as well as his physical dilemma when he is snow-bound at the Heights, just as the mellowness of a September evening mirrors Catherine's short-lived serenity during the first months of her marriage to Edgar Linton. It is on "a fresh watery afternoon" in late autumn with "a cold, blue sky . . . half hidden by clouds" that Cathy, alarmed by her father's illness, first realises the precariousness of her happiness at the Grange. But there are no weather descriptions of any great length, not even of the violent thunderstorm on the fatal evening when Heathcliff leaves the Heights and Catherine, refusing in her distress to take shelter from the drenching rain, becomes seriously ill. Yet the parallel between the storm, which wreaks such damage in its brief duration, and the moral electricity in the tormented natures of the fated pair is clear enough, even if such a correspondence had not been expressed a few hours before, by Catherine herself in unforgettable imagery: "Whatever our souls are made of, his and mine are the same, and Linton's is as different as a moonbeam from lightning, or frost from fire" (ch. 9).

It is lightning, not sunshine, which is opposed to the moonbeam. The sun rarely seems to shine on Catherine and Heathcliff, except at their last meeting. It is rather the blazing fires on the hearth at the Heights, the focus of comfort in a northern farmstead, which seem also best to suggest the fire in their natures. But Catherine's comparison of Edgar Linton's calm temperament with the moonlight comes to mind when Nelly Dean recalls the presence of the moon on the night when Heathcliff reappears, to shatter the peace of his home: "It had got dusk, and the moon looked over the high wall of the court, causing undefined shadows to lurk in the shadows of the numerous projecting corners of the building" (ch. 10). There is a striking contrast between the brevity of this account and Charlotte's emotionally charged and lyrical treatment of the same theme in her nocturnes. Yet Emily achieves her aim no less effectively, conveying in a single sentence the implicit menace of the lurking shadows that the moonlight cannot dispel. The moon shines, too, on the evening when Lockwood pays his last visit to the Heights, after Heathcliff's death, but it then looks down on the happiness of the young lovers, Cathy and Hareton. Here also the description remains concise, but powerfully conveys how the steady radiance illuminates the natural scene, bringing out the familiar presence of the earth as well as the beauty of the sky:

> . . . I turned away and made my exit, rambling leisurely along, with the glow of a sinking sun behind, and the mild glory of a rising moon in front – one fading, and the other brightening – as I quitted the park, and climbed the stony by-road branching off to Mr. Heathcliff's dwelling. Before I arrived in sight of it, all that remained of day was a beamless amber light along the west: but I could see every pebble on the path, and every blade of grass, by that splendid moon. (ch. 32).

The fact that Emily chose as her title "Wuthering Heights" suggests that, of all the elements, it is the wind, and especially the storm wind, that epitomises the spirit of her novel. For all the Brontës it was indissolubly associated with their home and their childhood. Anne loved the north wind.

No other breeze could have so wild as swell. Charlotte, hearing it in the schoolroom at Roe Head, was at once conscious that it was also heard by her family at Haworth, as it swept down from the moors. She was all her life peculiarly subject to the influence of the equinoctial gales, and they sound in the great finale of *Villette*. Emily explains the meaning of "wuthering" as "a significant provincial adjective", descriptive of "the atmospheric tumult" to which the situation of the Heights is exposed in stormy weather. The power of the north wind blowing across the high ground immediately behind the house is shown by the "excessive slant" of the few stunted trees, but the corollary of this situation is the "pure, bracing ventilation" enjoyed by its inhabitants. For Emily, even more than for her sisters, this air was both literally and metaphorically the breath of life. In her delirium at the Grange, Catherine feels that her chance of life depends on the window being opened, midwinter as it is, to admit the cold blast: "Oh, if I were but in my own bed in the old house!. . . And that wind sounding in the firs by the lattice. Do let me feel it – it comes straight down the moor – do let me have one breath!"

Yet, at the close of the novel, we learn that the focus of action, in the future history of the Earnshaws and the Lintons, will be shifted to the valley. On New Year's day Cathy and Hareton will marry, and leave the Heights for the Grange. Since only four miles separate the two domains, and the couple will retain the ownership of both, this does not mean that the moors and the farmstead, with Joseph as tenant, will cease to be part of their lives. It is the Earnshaw name that will survive. But Cathy has inherited Edgar Linton's best qualities, his capacity, wrongly scorned by Heathcliff, for love, loyalty and devotion, his appreciation of literature. Hareton, deliberately denied the chance of literacy by Heathcliff, and taught to despise it, comes, through his love for her, to accept its necessity.[22] "Wuthering Heights" is no apologia for the "noble savage". But there is little danger that either of them will make the library at the Grange a refuge from reality, as Edgar Linton had done in the past, and as his daughter might have done without her searing encounter with

life and death at Wuthering Heights. Above all, both will continue to value and enjoy their natural environment. Hareton
may prefer the moors, and Cathy the wooded valley, but there
will no longer be a man-made barrier between the two constituent parts of the landscape.

The conclusion of the novel, however, belongs to its dominant
characters. After leaving Wuthering Heights for the last time,
half envious of the happiness of the young lovers, Lockwood
pauses on the way home to visit the graves in Gimmerton
kirkyard which, both from Nelly Dean's narrative and his own
encounters with Heathcliff, now have a special significance for
him:

> I sought, and soon discovered, the three headstones on the
> slope next the moor: the middle one grey, and half buried in
> heath; Edgar Linton's only harmonized by the turf and moss
> creeping up its foot; Heathcliff's still bare.
>
> I lingered round them, under that benign sky: watched the
> moths fluttering among the heath and harebells, listened to
> the soft wind breathing through the grass, and wondered how
> anyone could ever imagine unquiet slumbers for the sleepers
> in that quiet earth.

Complete peace, both of man and nature, could hardly be
more perfectly suggested. But the speaker is Lockwood, and his
judgment is in fact a protest against the rumours, just repeated
to him by Nelly Dean, that the ghosts of Heathcliff and Catherine have been seen on the moors. Nelly herself calls such rumours "idle tales", but recalls her recent encounter near the
Heights with a little shepherd lad who has been frightened out of
his path by the sight of "Heathcliff and a woman, yonder, under
t'nab". *Wuthering Heights* had begun with the association between
nature and the supernatural: the snowstorm and the ghost of the
child Catherine at the window in Lockwood's dream. The ghosts
of Catherine and Heathcliff appear in the closing scene, "on a
dark evening threatening thunder", but only by hearsay. Lockwood rejects the story completely, Nelly, a countrywoman, not
quite so completely. But the last word is with the silent graves.

The action throughout *Wuthering Heights* has two dimensions,
the natural and the supernatural. Emily Brontë leaves her

readers to draw their own conclusions as to the relations between them. The different narrators express their different viewpoints; there is no authorial voice. It is only from the text itself that one can deduce, if not definitive conclusions, at least indications as to the relationship between nature and the human soul which is at the basis of her fiction, no less than of her poems.

By placing her story in the only world she thoroughly knew and understood, which was a rustic and, to a large extent, a primitive one, she had a valuable resource in the use of folklore. This was something familiar to all the Brontës. Anne could catch the echo of the ballad tone. Charlotte borrowed some of the magic of folklore in *Jane Eyre*, and there is a ghost in *Villette*, though one that proves to have a rational explanation. In *Wuthering Heights* Emily introduces folklore, like Scott, because it is part of the world in which the characters live. "Ah, they put pigeons' feathers in the pillows – no wonder I couldn't die'!",[23] says Catherine in her delirium, and her conviction of approaching death is strengthened by seeing her face in the mirror. But she also dreams of returning to the Heights, though she knows it now means that she and Heathcliff must "pass by Gimmerton Kirk, to go that journey". Her opening of the window is both a spontaneous gesture and an anticipation of death, reflecting the custom of doing so in order not to hinder the flight of the spirit. The window is open when Heathcliff is found dead at the Heights, and the image represents throughout the novel one of the frontiers of the unknown.[24] Death for the primitive imagination is very close to the mysterious forces of nature.

But Catherine Earnshaw is both primitive and complex. Centuries of Christian tradition, as well as a wild moorland childhood, have made her what she is. She uses religious language when she tries to define her relationship with Heathcliff: "If all else perished, and *he* remained, *I* should still continue to be; and if all else remained, and he were annihilated, the universe would turn to a mighty stranger: I should not seem a part of it" (ch. 9). There is an evident resemblance between this speech and Emily's declaration of faith in her poem "No coward soul is mine", written in the same year the novel was completed:

> Though Earth and moon were gone
> And suns and universes ceased to be

And thou wert left alone
Every Existence would exist in thee[25]

But the poem is addressed to God. Catherine stakes everything on her relationship with Heathcliff, her spiritual affinity.
At fifteen, she believes she can preserve that relationship while
marrying Edgar Linton. At eighteen, and as Edgar's wife, she
finds, after the unforeseen and unhoped-for return of Heathcliff,
when physical desire is added to their torment, and sexual
jealousy to the hatred between the two men, that she has
expected the impossible. Heathcliff is no longer absent, but their
separation is complete, and their very love temporarily embittered. As a result Catherine loses the will to live. She no longer
feels part of the physical world around her. Her true desire now,
like that of Rochelle in "The Prisoner", is for death. But for her,
death suggests release on two different planes. She longs, as her
delirium reveals, to return, unfettered, to the paradise of her
moorland childhood with Heathcliff. But when she is actually
approaching death, still faithful to her love for him, but tormented by his passionate reproaches, she aspires to a more
complete release: ". . . the thing that irks me most is this shattered prison, after all. I'm tired, tired of being enclosed here. I'm
wearying to escape into that glorious world, and to be always
there; not seeing it dimly through tears, and yearning for it
through the walls of an aching heart; but really with it, and in it"
(ch. 15).

After her death, it is for Heathcliff that the universe "turns to a
mighty stranger". Life is made possible for him only by the belief
that her spirit still lives, and is near him. On the evening of her
burial he tries to open the coffin, but is stopped by the sense of
her presence beside him, though he knows that "no living thing
in flesh and blood was by". Heathcliff, like Catherine, is both
primitive and complex. As a primitive, he believes in ghosts. As
the descendant of Milton's Satan and Byron's Manfred, he
rejects heaven. He spends his tremendous vital force in revenge,
unleashing the power of evil in himself and others, but always
haunted himself by his belief in the ghost of his lost love: "When
I sat in the house with Hareton, it seemed to me that on going
out, I should meet her; when I walked on the moors I should
meet her coming in" (ch. 29). The tension ultimately proves too

much, even for him. After eighteen years, at the moment when his revenge is almost complete, he looses the capacity for anything but straining towards the moment of reunion with Catherine. Convinced that he is about to reach his objective, he becomes finally so obsessed by a strange exaltation that he no longer cares to eat or drink. Realising that death is approaching, he does not, like Catherine, look forward to any "glorious world", but he has at last come to include, like her, peace in his idea of bliss. The previous autumn, when Edgar Linton had died, he had visited the corner of the kirkyard, near the moor and the marsh, and invaded by peat mould, where the sexton was digging the new grave beside Catherine's. This time he had opened her coffin and looked on her passionless features, preserved by the action of the peat mould, and since then his deepest wish is at heart less to walk the moors with her ghost than to sleep beside her.[26]

Gimmerton Kirk stands midway between the Heights and the Grange. On his final visit to the graveyard Lockwood notices how the state of the church building has deteriorated in the months since he last saw it. This is not surprising, since after Edgar's death Heathcliff had become master of the Grange, and the fate of the chapel where the Lintons had worshipped must have been as indifferent to him as was religion in general. There is a chapel with a minister in the village itself, and he apparently raises no objection to his servants going there on Sundays when their work is done. But he gives orders that he must be buried in Gimmerton kirkyard, because it is there that Catherine is buried. It is there, in consecrated ground, that Lockwood finds the three headstones, in the corner nearest to the moor.

Wuthering Heights has received many differing interpretations, and there will no doubt be many more.[27] It would be an optimistic critic who could hope to do justice to all its qualities. Yet it is difficult to see how any interpretation can ignore the role of nature, or limit it to the purely physical. The cosmic forces that govern the world of *Wuthering Heights* are the spiritual forces of love and hate, good and evil. Both are at work in the physical universe. Emily Brontë's drama is a mystery play rather than a myth. Even Heathcliff, who rejects heaven because he has been rejected in youth by everyone except Catherine, and who sees nature only as a part of their love, yet believes in ghosts. Catherine finds nature satisfying, as long as she can identify it with the childhood paradise, more imagined than remembered, that she shared with Heathcliff. But when their separation breaks her heart, nature can no longer hold her, and her true home becomes "the endless and shadowless hereafter . . . where life is boundless in its duration, and love in its sympathy, and joy in its fulness" (ch. 16).

Yet till the last Catherine never entirely loses her love of nature. The first crocuses of March can still make her eyes shine with delight, a few weeks before her death, because they were always the earliest flowers at the Heights and remind her of "soft thaw winds, and warm sunshine, and nearly melted snow". But at the height of her youthful vitality, "half savage and hardy, and free", she seems almost the spirit of nature itself, dynamic, irresistible, unknowable, but never wantonly destructive. She curbs the destructive impulse in Heathcliff, after he had set a trap over the lapwings' nest, thus starving the nestlings: "I made him promise he'd never shoot a lapwing after that, and he didn't." This seems almost an anticipation of the "new earth" that accompanied the "new heaven" at the conclusion of Emily's vision in "The Butterfly". Years before she had visualised the spirit of nature in a ballad-like poem which seems curiously in tune with this aspect of Catherine:

It was about the middle night,
And under such a starless dome
When, gliding from the mountain's height,
I saw a shadowy spirit come.

Her wavy hair, on her shoulders bare,
It shone like soft clouds round the moon;
Her noiseless feet, like melting sleet,
Gleamed white a moment, then were gone . . .

"This is my home, where whirlwinds blow,
Where snowdrifts round my path are swelling;
'Tis many a year, 'tis long ago,
Since I beheld another dwelling . . .

"The shepherd had died on the mountain side,
But my ready aid was near him then:
I led him back o'er the hidden track,
And gave him to his native glen . . .

"And the scattered sheep, I love to keep
Their timid forms to guard from harm;
I have a spell, and they know it well,
And I save them with a powerful charm."[28]

Conclusion

The relationship of the Brontës to nature was a close one. They owed to this source the most spontaneous pleasures of their childhood, and when they discovered, as they did at an early age, the imaginative pleasures of literature, it was the Romantics that they found most congenial, and nature is one of the key words of Romanticism. For the Romantics it involved not only the physical world but the whole question of man's relation to nature, which came to mean, as *The Prelude* testifies, his relation also to his fellow men, to the spiritual forces of his own nature, to God.

Anne was very much a Brontë in following the guidance of her individual temperament, but she was the least turbulent of the family. She shared Emily's love of home, of the moors and of freedom and, like her, had no desire to live anywhere but in the country. In her exile at Thorp Green, however, she turned to "Reason, with conscience by her side" to support her in the difficult life which did not undermine her Christian faith but which tested her endurance to the utmost. It was here, rather than in revolt, that she instinctively felt her strength to lie. The "moral world" became more important to her henceforward than the physical one, and the nature lyricism of her earlier poems gave place to the allegorical use of nature in the later ones. In her novels, written after her return to a home still loved but now lacking "domestic peace", the emphasis is on character analysis and moral values. Yet it would be false to conclude that Anne ever lost her love of nature, or that it ceased to provide her with inspiration as an artist. In the most joyous of all her lyrics, composed "on a wild bright windy day",[1] she temporarily forgets reason, and experiences that spiritual fusion with the forces of the universe which was at the heart of Romanticism. In her novels the best of her descriptions are not the carefully realistic passages; they are those where, moved by great happiness or great sorrow, her heroines attain a similar exalted state.

247

Such are the morning seascape in *Agnes Grey* and the moonlit sky
which is the sole witness of Helen Huntingdon's conflict with
despair. Here allegory is transcended by symbolism. But Anne
would not have been faithful to her nature, had she allowed such
moments to be other than exceptional. Hers was a controlled
and reflective art, less challenging than that of her sisters, at
least in intention, and nearer to the eighteenth century than
theirs. Her poem "Vanitas Vanitatis, Omnia Vanitas" has been
compared in thought to Johnson's "Vanity of Human Wishes".[2]
But at heart Anne's truest affinity is with the Christian stoicism
of Wordsworth's lonely heroines, Margaret of "The Ruined
Cottage" or Emily Norton of "The White Doe of Rylstone", who
finds friendship and understanding in the inoffensive and trust-
ing animal who becomes the chief companion of her solitude.

Charlotte Brontë, like her sister, loved the moors, and freedom. But it was clear from the Angrian saga that she also
experienced from childhood the desire for wider horizons and a
more sophisticated and cosmopolitan culture. A quiet country
life did not possess the same inherent attractions for her as for
Anne. But nature in itself did possess for her from the first an
intense attraction, and above all nature in its universal aspects,
the elements, the seasons and the weather, the sun and the
moon. Her most successful Angrian descriptions are those where
she paints what she herself knows, not an exotic landscape but a
spring morning in fields fresh with dew, summer moonlight in
the garden of a country house, a winter hurricane of wind and
rain in the uplands. There is a growing sense, in such passages,
of the correspondences between nature and the emotional climate. But the crudities and heady passions of Angria prevented
such correspondences from having their full effect. Growing
maturity, and growing artistic awareness, enabled Charlotte to
develop their functional importance, so that the use of elemental
imagery became a major feature of her art. But her art was never
artifice; she had been aware from a child of the depth of her
instinctive response, both sensual and spiritual, to the forces of
the universe. In her first novel the creative imagination is too
firmly subordinated to reason to allow her to develop this faculty
as she might have done, though its presence is evident. Imagination, her bridge between the visible and the invisible worlds,
triumphs in Jane Eyre, with the result that feeling, thought and
elemental nature are interwoven in a symphonic whole. In

Shirley, which is both a regional and an industrial novel, there is not the same structural unity. Such unity would only have been possible if Charlotte could have achieved a fusion between the forces of nature and those of science, but, for her, poetry fled from the Hollow when the mill was built. It survives, however, and with it her own original vision of nature, in Caroline's moonlight reveries, and in the dreams of Shirley herself, that "creature of light and air". *Villette*, her most mature work, is a tale of the spring and autumn equinox both in nature and in a human life, and of the fluctuations between them, told by a narrator who has forgotten nothing, but who has lived long enough to reach the period of winter calm, illuminated by the clarity of the winter sky.

Emily was, of the three Brontë sisters, the one to whom her native landscape meant the most. The nine months she spent at the Heger pensionnat were her longest period of absence from home, only endured because it offered the means of acquiring qualifications which should ensure her being able to remain at Haworth in the future. In Charlotte's words, "she was never happy till she carried her hard-won knowledge back to the remote English village, the old parsonage-house, and the desolate Yorkshire hills".[3] They were never desolate to her. Yet, much as she loved them, she was, of the sisters, the one who was most tragically aware that nature could not ultimately satisfy all the aspirations of the human spirit, in spite of the deep affinities between them. She was torn between her love of nature, especially in its wildest moods, and her sense that, when most under its "mighty sway", she might be furthest from that communion with the absolute which, as a mystic, she passionately desired. She could convey the essence of her native landscape in unforgettable verse, but her later poems celebrated not only the maternal earth but her debt to Imagination, her longing for the "Spirit" who could resolve the warring tensions within her, above all her vision of the "messenger of Hope" who

. . . offers, for short life, eternal liberty.

Wuthering Heights also is concerned with the affinities, and the tensions, between the natural and the supernatural, but this time in a firmly localised setting. Emily is the only Brontë to give a realistic impression of the way of life of the yeoman farmer and the farm servant, and is less concerned that Charlotte or Anne with the life of the country house in itself. But at the same time she stages, within a limited area of heath and valley, a cosmic drama. The elements share in the action and, as children, Catherine and Heathcliff ask no more than to participate in the universal rhythm of nature. Natural harmony is destroyed, for them, by the unnatural separation which cannot kill their love but makes it a source of torment. The house on the moor becomes a lost paradise to Catherine, an inferno to Heathcliff. Nature can no longer help them, only what lies beyond nature. But the wind breathes softly over their graves, under a benign sky.

It has been said that the more original an artist is, the longer he must wait to be appreciated at his just value. This has proved true of the Brontës. Anne, long underestimated and later despised for being tamely conventional when she was in fact being loyal to her deepest convictions, is now recognised increasingly as a gifted novelist and a poet of moving sincerity. Nearer to the eighteenth century than her sisters, she is most a Romantic in her attitude to nature, but in this field she cannot rival the achievement of Emily or Charlotte. They both share the same deep response to the physical universe, the same intuition of the spiritual links between their own natures and the elements, and for both elemental imagery is an organic part of their art. These qualities they shared also with the great Romantics, but they were strikingly original in giving them as free expression in their fiction as in their verse. This originality was ignored by contemporary critics, more concerned with "Gothic" features in the plots than with the more subtle underlying harmonies. For critics of the modern novel, this approach to nature, closely linked as it is with the intensity of the imaginative faculty, is of particular interest, not least because it can at times plumb the depths of the subconscious and produce surrealistic effects.

The place of elemental imagery in the novel has now long been recognised, and the insights of Freud and Jung have contributed to its exegesis. In the mid-twentieth century the French philosopher Gaston Bachelard even chose the four elements as "a convenient framework on which to hang his discussion of the different types of poetic imagination".[4] Any such investigation must inevitably be influenced to some extent by individual taste. But it is certain that the numerous examples of elemental imag-

ery found both in Romantic literature and in that of the twen-
tieth century are eloquent of its significance for modern art. It is
hazardous to attempt too definitive a classification in such
matters, and certainly the very essence of the Brontës' own
approach was freedom. They recognised the mobility of the
human spirit, as they recognised the flux of nature. But freedom
is not chaos: underlying all their works is the conviction that the
world of phenomena is only a veil which half conceals and half
reveals the world of the spirit, the ultimate theme of all Romantic art, and of any art with a lasting relevance for humanity.

Notes

CHAPTER 1: THE COMMON HERITAGE

1. See John Lock and W. T. Dixon, *A Man of Sorrow*, 2nd edn (London and Connecticut, 1979).
2. *Collected Works of the Rev. Patrick Brontë*, ed. J. Horsfall Turner (Bingley, 1898) p. 47.
3. Ibid., p. 19.
4. Ibid., p. 91.
5. Ibid., p. 89.
6. Christopher Fry, "Genius, Talent and Failure", BST XVII, pt. 86.
7. Cit. Lock and Dixon, p. 83.
8. *Collected Works of the Rev. Patrick Brontë*, pp. 205–6.
9. Ivy Holgate, "The Cottage in the Wood", BST XIII, pt. 67.
10. *Collected Works of the Rev. Patrick Brontë*, pp. 125–6.
11. Ibid., pp. 135–6.
12. Ibid.
13. Lock and Dixon, op. cit., p. 315.
14. Gaskell, ch. 3, p. 52.
15. Ibid., p. 49.
16. See John Hewish, *Emily Brontë* (London, 1969); Tom Winnifrith, *The Brontës and their Background* (London, 1973); L. J. Dessner, *The Homely Web of Truth* (The Hague, 1975).
17. See Clifford Whone, "Where the Brontës Borrowed Books", BST XI, pt. 60.
18. Cit. Gaskell, ch. 7, p. 131.
19. Scott, *The Black Dwarf, Waverley Novels*, vol. 5, (Edinburgh, 1896) p. 40.
20. "The Cout of Keeldar" is quoted in the notes (no. LI) to *The Lady of the Lake, Scott's Poetical Works*, ed. J. Logie Robertson (Oxford, 1931) pp. 300–1.
21. "The Death of Keeldar", ibid., p. 755. See also Lew Girdler, "Charlotte Brontës *Shirley* and Scott's *The Black Dwarf*", *Modern Language Notes*, LXXI, (Mar. 1956).
22. See intro. and notes to *The Lay of the Last Minstrel, Scott's Poetical Works*, pp. 52, 68.
23. See Winifred Gérin, *Emily Brontë* (Oxford, 1971) p. 15.

24. *Jane Eyre*, ch. 32. *Marmion* was published in 1808.
25. *Jane Eyre*, ch. 25, "with a sullen moaning sound", *Lay of the Last Minstrel*, I xiii I; ch. 31, "The air was mild; the dew was balm", ibid., III xxiv 3-4 (adapted); ch. 34, "Looked to river, looked to hill", ibid., V xxvi I. See *Scott's Poetical Works*, pp. 5, 19, 37.
26. *Shirley*, ch. 2, "rode lightly in", *Lay of the Last Minstrel*, IV xii 13; ch. 22, "the clouds of battle-dust and smoke", *Marmion*, VI xxv 27 (adapted). See *Scott's Poetical Works*, pp. 24, 164.
27. See The *Professor*, ch. 23 and "The Covenanter's Fate", *Scott's Poetical Works*, p. 696.
28. See *Wuthering Heights*, ch. 9 and notes to *The Lady of the Lake*, *Scott's Poetical Works*, pp. 298–9.
29. See Hewish, op. cit., p. 53.
30. See Clarendon edition of *Jane Eyre*, ed. Jane Jack and Margaret Smith (Oxford, 1969), note on p. 596.
31. See F. S. Dry, *The Sources of Wuthering Heights* (Cambridge, 1937) pp. 4–5, 45–6.
32. Q. D. Leavis, "A Fresh Approach to *Wuthering Heights*", in F. R. and Q. D. Leavis, *Lectures in America* (London, 1969) pp. 99–100, 101.
33. Preface to 1st and 2nd cantos of *Childe Harold's Pilgrimage*, *The Poetical Works of Lord Byron* (Oxford, 1904; reprint 1953) p. 179.
34. *Letters and Journals of Lord Byron: with Notices of His Life*, by Thomas Moore, 3rd edn vol. I (London, 1833) p. 325.
35. *Childe Harold's Pilgrimage*, II lxii 1–3, *Byron's Poetical Works*, p. 204.
36. Ibid., III xiii 1–7, p. 211.
37. Ibid., III xciii 1–4, p. 222.
38. Ibid., II lxxxvii 7–9, p. 207.
39. See W. Gérin, "Byron's Influence on the Brontës", *Keats–Shelley Memorial Association*, Bulletin, XVII, p. 3.
40. Moore, op. cit. vol. 2, p. 234.
41. Cp. Hewish, op. cit., p. 37 and Gérin, op. cit., p. 38.
42. Moore, op. cit., vol. 3, p. 92.
43. *Jane Eyre*, ch. 5, "stony street", *Childe Harold* III xxii 2; ch. 21, "wild and wide", *Parisina* xiv 363. See Byron's *Poetical Works*, pp. 212, 334.
44. *Shirley*, ch. 8, "first of a thunder-shower", *Childe Harold* IV cxl 7; ch. 22, "red rain", *Childe Harold* III xvii 7; ch. 26, a man's "morning star", cp. *The Giaour*, ll. 1127–30. See *Byron's Poetical Works*, pp. 245, 211, 262.
45. *Agnes Grey*, ch. 3:

They may crush, but they shall not subdue me!
'Tis of thee that I think, not of them.

Cp. "Stanzas to Augusta" iii 6–8 (adapted), *Byron's Poetical Works*, p. 89.

46. *Wuthering Heights*, ch. 3, "hear me *this* time", cp. *Manfred* II iv 147–8:

> . . . let me hear thee once –
> This once – once more!

Byron's Poetical Works, p. 401.

47. *Wuthering Heights*, ch. 9. Cp. "Ode to Napoleon Buonaparte" vi, *Byron's Poetical Works*, p. 73.

48. Moore, op. cit., vol. 2, p. 19.

49. See Ann Lapraik Livermore, "Byron and Emily Brontë", *Quarterly Review*, CCC, 1962 and *Byron's Poetical Works*, pp. 91–4.

50. See Helen Brown, "The Influence of Byron on Emily Brontë", *Modern Language Review*, XXXIV, 1939.

51. C. W. Hatfield, *The Complete Poems of Emily Jane Brontë*, (New York and London, 1941) 5, p. 31.

52. Cit. Gaskell, ch. 8, pp. 150–1.

53. *Wordsworth's Poetical Works*, ed. Thomas Hutchinson, new edition revised by Ernest de Selincourt (Oxford, 1974) p. 163.

54. Ibid., p. 377.

55. Ibid., p. 164.

56. Preface to 2nd edn of *Lyrical Ballads*, ibid., p. 735.

57. See *Shirley*, ch. 2; *Villette*, ch. 34; *The Tenant of Wildfell Hall*, ch. 25.

58. See *Shirley*, ch. 19; "Sonnets on Liberty" XVI, *Wordsworth's Poetical Works*, p. 244.

59. See *Jane Eyre*, chs 35, 37 and F. B. Pinion, *A Brontë Companion* (London, 1975) p. 113.

60. See *Wuthering Heights*, ch. 32. Cp. "Miscellaneous Sonnets" I i, *Wordsworth's Poetical Works*, p. 199.

61. See F. E. Ratchford, *The Brontës' Web of Childhood* (New York, 1941) p. 47.

62. See Derek Stanford, in Ada Harrison and Derek Stanford, *Anne Brontë. Her Life and Work* (London, 1959), Part Two, pp. 167–8.

63. Edward Chitham, *The Poems of Anne Brontë* (London, 1979) 32, p. 101.

64. Hatfield 93, p. 96.

65. Ibid., 112, p. 121.

66. Ibid., 143, p. 152.

67. Ibid., 114, p. 124.

68. Jonathan Wordsworth, "Wordsworth and the Poetry of Emily Brontë", BST XVI, pt. 82.

69. Preface to 2nd edn of *Lyrical Ballads*, *Wordsworth's Poetical Works*, p. 734.

70. See F. B. Pinion, op. cit., p. 197.
71. See Edward Chitham, "Emily Brontë and Shelley", in Edward Chitham and Tom Winnifrith, *Brontë Facts and Brontë Problems* (London, 1983).
72. See F. S. Dry, op. cit., p. 31.
73. Patricia Thomson, *George Sand and the Victorians* (London, 1977) p. 76.
74. See ibid., ch. 5.

CHAPTER 2: NATURE IN THE JUVENILIA

1. Read by them in a translation of Galland's French text of 1706. See W. Gérin, *Charlotte Brontë* (Oxford, 1967) p. 26.
2. See ibid., p. 27 and Jane W. Stedman, "The Genesis of the Genii", BST XIV, pt. 75.
3. "A Romantic Tale", *The Professor, Tales from Angria, etc.*, ed. Phyllis Bentley (London and Glasgow, 1954) p. 54.
4. Ibid., p. 55.
5. "The Search after Happiness", ed. T. A. J. Burnett (New York, 1969) p. 23.
6. Ibid., pp. 27–8.
7. *Complete Poems of Charlotte Brontë*, ed. C. K. Shorter with bibliography and notes by C. W. Hatfield (London, 1923) no. xxxii, p. 87.
8. "Characters of the Celebrated Men of the Present Time", see Bentley, op. cit., p. 61.
9. *Complete Poems of Charlotte Brontë*, no. xxxix, p. 110.
10. See ibid., pp. 123–6 and W. Gérin, *Charlotte Brontë*, p. 47.
11. See Jane W. Stedman, "Charlotte Brontë and Bewick's 'British Birds'", BST XV, pt. 76.
12. *Complete Poems of Charlotte Brontë*, no. 1, p. 133.
13. See W. Gérin, op. cit., p. 45.
14. Cit. F. E. Ratchford, *The Brontës' Web of Childhood*, p. 68.
15. See W. Gérin, op. cit., p. 49.
16. See Ratchford, op. cit., p. 39.
17. *The Spell*, ed. G. E. MacLean (Oxford, 1931), p. 105.
18. Cit. *The Professor, Tales from Angria, etc.*, ed. Bentley, p. 396.
19. *Complete Poems of Charlotte Brontë*, no. lxvi, p. 174.
20. The references are to Pendle Hill and Boulsworth Hill. See Charlotte Brontë, *Five Novelettes*, ed. W. Gérin (London, 1971), notes on pp. 202, 212.
21. "Passing Events", *Five Novelettes*, p. 61.
22. "Mina Laury", ibid., p. 127.
23. "Captain Henry Hastings", ibid., p. 216.

24. Ibid., p. 244.
25. Cit. Gaskell, ch. 8, p. 173.
26. "Caroline Vernon", *Five Novelettes*, p. 288. Spelling and punctuation as in original, see W. Gérin, General Introduction, pp. 22–3.
27. Ibid., p. 290.
28. Cit. Ratchford, op. cit., p. 149.
29. "Captain Henry Hastings", *Five Novelettes*, note on p. 236.
30. Ibid., p. 240.
31. Ibid., p. 209.
32. Cit. Ratchford, op. cit., p. 87 – it has been noted by Dr Alexander that the "rising sun" emblem has mythic associations for Charlotte Brontë, who knew of the ancient Persian cult of Zoroastrianism, as well as of the Apollo myths. See Christine Alexander, *The Early Writings of Charlotte Brontë*, p. 240.
33. "Mina Laury", *Five Novelettes*, p. 138.

CHAPTER 3:   POEMS

1. See p. 42.
2. See *The Poems of Anne Brontë: a New Text and Commentary*, Edward Chitham (London, 1979), Introduction, p. 33 and Joseph Le Guern, *Anne Brontë*, vol. 1 (Paris, 1977) pp. 240–3.
3. Chitham 5, p. 63.
4. Ibid., 2, p. 54.
5. Ibid., 5, p. 64.
6. Ibid., 51, p. 132.
7. See Le Guern, op. cit., vol. 2, p. 534, note 12.
8. Chitham 44, p. 122.
9. Ibid., 53, p. 137.
10. Ibid., p. 139.
11. Ibid., 30, pp. 99–100.
12. Ibid., 32, p. 102.
13. Ibid., 21, p. 88.
14. Ibid., 18, p. 82.
15. See Chitham, Introduction, pp. 15–16, 19.
16. Ibid., 31, p. 100.
17. See "The Doves", *Poetical Works of William Cowper*, ed. H. S. Milford, 4th edn (Oxford, 1934) pp. 303–4.
18. See Chitham, op. cit., Commentary on the Poems, p. 177.
19. Ibid., 24, p. 93.
20. Ibid., 33, p. 104.
21. Ibid., 43, p. 123.
22. Ibid., 42, p. 118.

23. See Derek Stanford, in Ada and Derek Stanford, *Anne Brontë. Her Life and Work*, Part Two, p. 193.
24. Chitham 57, p. 152. The poem is dated November 1847–17 Apr. 1848.
25. "Ode on Intimations of Immortality", *Wordsworth's Poetical Works*, p. 462.
26. Chitham 58, p. 161.
27. Ibid., 10, p. 73.
28. D. Stanford, in A. Harrison and D. Stanford, op. cit., p. 210.
29. Chitham 15, p. 78.
30. Ibid., 21, p. 88.

CHAPTER 4: *AGNES GREY*

1. The connection between *Passages in the Life of an Individual* and *Agnes Grey* is considered as certain by W. Gérin and as highly probable by W. Craik and F. B. Pinion. It is questioned by T. Winnifrith and rejected by J. Le Guern.
2. Charlotte Brontë to W. S. Williams, 21 Dec. 1847.
3. George Moore, *Conversations in Ebury Street* (London, 1930) p. 222.
4. See Inga-Stina Ewbank, *Their Proper Sphere* (London, 1966) p. 65.
5. Cp. Chitham 2, p. 54.
6. F. B. Pinion, *A Brontë Companion* (London, 1975) p. 242.
7. The drawing, now in the Parsonage Museum, is dated 13 Nov. 1839 and belongs to the last part of Anne Brontë's time at Blake Hall.
8. See Ewbank, op. cit., p. 70.
9. Ibid., p. 56.

CHAPTER 5: *THE TENANT OF WILDFELL HALL*

1. Sir Linton Andrews, "A Challenge by Anne Brontë", BST XIV, pt. 75.
2. The original of Wildfell Hall is thought to have been Ponden Hall. See *The Tenant of Wildfell Hall*, intro. W. Gérin, ed. G. D. Hargreaves (Penguin Books, 1979) p. 497, note 3.
3. See ibid. Hargreaves suggests that, for "the actual district of Wildfell", Anne may, however, have been thinking of "the Yorkshire Wolds, south of Scarborough", which would fit "the relative proximity of the sea".
4. Cp. p. 84.
5. Charlotte Brontë to James Taylor, 22 May 1850.

6. See Terry Eagleton, *Myths of Power* (London, 1975) p. 131.
7. Diary paper, 31 July 1845. Cit. W. Gérin, *Anne Brontë*, p. 209.
8. See W. Gérin, op. cit., p. 256.
9. See Le Guern, op. cit., vol. 2, p. 687.

CHAPTER 6: POEMS AND *THE PROFESSOR*

1. "Passing Events", *Five Novelettes*, p. 61.
2. Charlotte Brontë to the Rev. Henry Nussey, 11 Jan. 1841.
3. See F. B. Pinion, *A Brontë Companion*, pp. 91–2.
4. *Complete Poems of Charlotte Brontë*, no. vi, p. 36.
5. Preface written by Charlotte Brontë and included when the novel was published posthumously in 1857. *The Professor, etc.*, p. 4.
6. See Laura Hinkley, *The Brontës: Charlotte and Emily* (New York, 1945) p. 19.
7. See Cynthia A. Linder, *Romantic Imagery in the Novels of Charlotte Brontë* (London, 1978) pp. 18–21.
8. See Robert Keefe, *Charlotte Brontë's World of Death*, (University of Texas Press, 1979) ch. 3.
9. It has been thought to show the influence of Charlotte Brontë's study of the French Romantics, in particular Bernardin de Saint-Pierre and Lamartine. See J. N. Ware, "Bernardin de Saint-Pierre and Charlotte Brontë", *Modern Language Notes*, XL, June 1925, and Lawrence Jay Dessner, "Charlotte Brontë's 'Le Nid': An Unpublished Manuscript", BST XVI, pt. 83.

CHAPTER 7: *JANE EYRE*

1. See M. H. Scargill, "'All Passion Spent': a Revaluation of *Jane Eyre*", *University of Toronto Quarterly*, XIX, Jan. 1950.
2. Earl A. Knies, *The Art of Charlotte Brontë* (Ohio University Press, 1969) p. 137.
3. Charlotte Brontë to W. S. Williams, 14 Aug. 1848.
4. See David Lodge, "Fire and Eyre: Charlotte Brontë's War of Earthly Elements", in *The Brontës*, ed. Ian Gregor (New Jersey, 1970), p. 115.
5. Ibid., p. 116.
6. See Eric Solomon, "*Jane Eyre*: Fire and Water", *College English*, XXV, Dec. 1963.
7. See Robert B. Heilman, "Charlotte Brontë, Reason and the Moon", *Nineteenth-Century Fiction*, XIV, Mar. 1960; Donald H. Ericksen, "Imagery as Structure in *Jane Eyre*", *Victorian Newsletter*,

no. 30, Fall, 1966; Mark Schorer, *The World We Imagine* (London, 1970) pp. 91–4.

8. See L. E. Moser, S. J., "From Portrait to Person: A Note on the Surrealistic in *Jane Eyre*", *Nineteenth-Century Fiction*, XX, Dec. 1965.
9. Milton, *Paradise Lost*, II, 673, 667.
10. Psalms, 69, i–ii (adapted).
11. E. M. Tillyard, *The Elizabethan World Picture*, cit. Lodge, op. cit., p. 116.
12. See Donald H. Ericksen, loc. cit.
13. See David Lodge, op. cit., pp. 117–25.
14. Ibid., p. 125.
15. See Isaiah, 47, xiv.
16. Charlotte Brontë to W. S. Williams, 14 Aug. 1848.
17. See Kathleen Tillotson, *Novels of the Eighteen-Forties*, (Oxford Paperbacks, 1962) pp. 286–7.
18. Moore, *Lalla Rookh*, Third Day, 1.346. See *Jane Eyre*, Clarendon ed., p. 605.
19. Roe Head Journal, cit. W. Gérin, *Charlotte Brontë*, p. 565.
20. Robert B. Heilman, loc. cit.
21. See Gaskell, ch. 19, p. 445.
22. See F. B. Pinion, op. cit., p. 113.

CHAPTER 8: *SHIRLEY*

1. Gaskell, ch. 18, p. 414.
2. Elizabeth Rigby, Review of *Jane Eyre*, *Quarterly Review*, LXXXIV, Dec. 1848.
3. See H. E. Wroot, "The Persons and Places of the Brontë Novels", BST III; F. B. Pinion, *A Brontë Companion*, Part III, People and Places in the Novels.
4. Gaskell, ch. 6, p. 96.
5. See Pinion, op. cit., p. 126.
6. See Asa Briggs, "Private and Social Themes in 'Shirley'", BST XIII, pt. 68.
7. Penguin edition of *Shirley*, 1974, ed. Andrew and Judith Hook, intro., p. 20.
8. Gaskell, ch. 18, p. 414.
9. See J. M. S. Tompkins, "Caroline Helstone's Eyes", BST XIV, pt. 71.
10. See Ivy Holgate, "The Structure of 'Shirley'" BST XIV, pt. 72.
11. See Gaskell, ch. 6, p. 101.
12. See John Greenwood's diary, cit. W. Gérin, *Emily Brontë*, pp. 146–7.

13. Gaskell, ch. 12, p. 274.
14. See Clarendon edition of *Shirley*, ed. Herbert Rosengarten and Margaret Smith (Oxford, 1979), note on p. 765, for possible influence here of Scott's novel *The Pirate*.
15. There was actually a cholera epidemic in the summer of 1849, when *Shirley* was being written. See *Shirley*, Clarendon edition, note on p. 775.
16. Robert B. Heilman, "Charlotte Brontë, Reason and the Moon", *Nineteenth-Century Fiction*, XIV, Mar. 1960, p. 290.
17. R. B. Martin, *The Accents of Persuasion* (London, 1966) p. 113.
18. Inga-Stina Ewbank, *Their Proper Sphere*, p. 200.
19. Ibid.

CHAPTER 9: *VILLETTE*

1. Earl A. Knies, *The Art of Charlotte Brontë*, p. 181.
2. Gaskell, ch. 25, p. 583.
3. Cp. Andrew Hook, "Charlotte Brontë, the Imagination and *Villette*", in *The Brontës*, ed. Ian Gregor, p. 146.
4. Penguin edition of *Villette*, 1979, ed. Mark Lilly, intro. by Tony Tanner. See intro., p. 29.
5. Andrew Hook, loc. cit., p. 143.
6. See Robert B. Heilman, "Charlotte Brontë, Reason and the Moon", loc. cit.
7. Ibid., p. 287.

CHAPTER 10: POEMS

1. See L. P. Hartley, "Emily Brontë in Gondal and Gaaldine", BST XIV, pt. 75.
2. Augusta's full name is Augusta Geraldine Almeda. She is also referred to as Rosina. Laura Hinkley, however, differs from Miss Ratchford in believing that Augusta and Rosina are two different characters.
3. See Herbert Dingle, "An Examination of Emily Brontë's Poetry from an unaccustomed angle", BST XIV, pt. 74.
4. *The Complete Poems of Emily Jane Brontë*, ed. C. W. Hatfield, 166, p. 194.
5. Hatfield 9, p. 33.
6. See Mary Visick, *The Genesis of Wuthering Heights* (Stroud and Connecticut, 1980 edition) p. 32.

7. Hatfield 182, pp. 222–3.
8. Hatfield 42, p. 60.
9. Hatfield 143, p. 154.
10. See Jonathan Wordsworth, "Wordsworth and the Poetry of Emily Brontë", BST XVI, pt 82.
11. Hatfield 192, p. 244.
12. See Jonathan Wordsworth, loc. cit.
13. Charlotte Brontë, Selections from Poems by Ellis Bell (first published 1850), *The Professor and Poems*, p. 444.
14. Derek Stanford, in Muriel Spark and Derek Stanford, *Emily Brontë, Her Life and Work* (London, 1953), Part Two, p. 156.
15. Hatfield 91, p. 91.
16. Cit. C. K. Shorter, *Charlotte Brontë and her Circle* (London, 1896) p. 179.
17. See Stanford in M. Spark and D. Stanford, op. cit., pp. 165–6.
18. See Margaret Lane, *The Brontë Story* (London, 1953), p. 198.
19. See Jacques Blondel, *Emily Brontë* (Clermont, and Presses Universitaires de France, 1955) p. 159.
20. Hatfield 7, p. 32.
21. Ibid., 20, p. 46.
22. Ibid., 24, p. 47.
23. Ibid., 11, p. 36.
24. The date of this period has been much discussed. It is generally supposed to have taken place in 1837/8, but the latest evidence supports the date 1838/9. See Chitham, "Early Brontë Chronology", in Edward Chitham and Tom Winnifrith, *Brontë Facts and Brontë Problems* (London, 1983) pp. 21–8.
25. Hatfield 92, pp. 94–5.
26. D. Stanford, in M. Spark and D. Stanford, op. cit., p. 181.
27. Hatfield 140, p. 147.
28. Ibid., 147, p. 164.
29. Ibid., 146, p. 163.
30. Ibid., 157, p. 184.
31. *Wordsworth's Poetical Works*, p. 157.
32. Ibid., p. 165.
33. Hatfield 44, p. 63.
34. Ibid., 93, p. 96.
35. Ibid., 148, p. 165.
36. Lilian R. Furst, *Romanticism in Perspective* (London, 1969) p. 147.
37. John Hewish, *Emily Brontë*, p. 59.
38. Cf. Herbert Dingle, art. cit., BST XIV, pt. 74. Dingle mentions *Stars*, dated 14 Apr. 1845, as an example of the impressive agreement sometimes found in the "A" poems transcribed by Emily (i.e.

those not in her "Gondal" notebook) between the weather conditions described (here abundant starlight, then the rising sun) and those noted for the same period by a contemporary recorder of the weather living near Haworth.

39. Hatfield 184, p. 226.
40. Ibid., 190, p. 239.
41. Mildred A. Dobson, "Was Emily Brontë a Mystic?", BST XI, pt. 58.
42. C. Day Lewis, "The Poetry of Emily Brontë", BST XIII, pt. 67.
43. Hatfield 191, pp. 243–4.
44. See Dobson, loc. cit.
45. Charlotte Brontë, "Biographical Notice of Ellis and Acton Bell", (1850), cit. *Wuthering Heights and Agnes Grey*, intro., p. xliv.
46. D. Stanford, in M. Spark and D. Stanford, op. cit., p. 209.
47. Hatfield 183, pp. 224–5.

CHAPTER 11: *WUTHERING HEIGHTS*

1. See Introduction to Clarendon edition of *Wuthering Heights*, p. xvi.
2. See Mary Visick, *The Genesis of Wuthering Heights*.
3. J. Hewish, *Emily Brontë*, p. 100.
4. Charlotte Brontë, Selections from Poems by Ellis Bell (first published 1850), *The Professor, etc.*, p. 444.
5. Hilda Marsden, "The Scenic Background of 'Wuthering Heights'", BST XIII, pt. 67.
6. See Q. D. Leavis, "A Fresh Approach to 'Wuthering Heights'", in F. R. and Q. D. Leavis, *Lectures in America*, Appendix A, "The Northern Farmer, Old Style".
7. J. F. Goodridge, *Emily Brontë: Wuthering Heights* (Studies in English Literature, no. 20), (London, 1964) p. 60.
8. Gaskell, ch. 5, p. 80.
9. In references to *Wuthering Heights* Catherine Earnshaw is referred to as "Catherine" and her daughter as "Cathy".
10. See Clarendon edition of *Wuthering Heights*, Appendix VII, "The Dialect Speech in *Wuthering Heights*".
11. Halliwell Sutcliff, *By Moor and Fell in West Yorkshire*, (London, 1899) p. 31.
12. Richard Benvenuto, *Emily Brontë* (Boston, 1982) p. 78.
13. *Five Essays Written in French by Emily Jane Brontë*, trans. Lorine White Nagel (University of Texas Press, 1948) p. 17.
14. See Benvenuto, op. cit., p. 78.

15. For the use of animal metaphors, see M. Schorer, *The World We Imagine* (London, 1970), Part I, section 3, pp. 32–3.
16. Edgar F. Shannon, Jr., "Lockwood's Dreams and the Exegesis of *Wuthering Heights*", *Nineteenth-Century Fiction*, XIV, Sept. 1959, pp. 98–9.
17. Hatfield, 123, pp. 132–3.
18. Jacquetta Hawkes, "Emily Brontë in the Natural Scene", BST XII, pt. 63.
19. Charlotte Brontë, Preface to the 1850 edition, *Wuthering Heights*, p. lv.
20. Lord David Cecil, "Emily Brontë and 'Wuthering Heights'", *Early Victorian Novelists* (Penguin edition, 1948), p. 119.
21. See Miriam Allott, "The Rejection of Heathcliff?", in *Wuthering Heights: A Casebook*, edited by Miriam Allott (London, 1970) pp. 186–7, and Inga-Stina Ewbank, *Their Proper Sphere*, pp. 95–8.
22. See Robert C. McKibben, "The Image of the Book in *Wuthering Heights*", in *The Brontës*, edited by Ian Gregor, 1970, pp. 34–43.
23. See Q. D. Leavis, op. cit., Appendix C. "Superstitions and Folklore".
24. See Dorothy Van Ghent, "Dark 'otherness' in *Wuthering Heights*", in *Wuthering Heights: A Casebook*, pp. 177–82.
25. Hatfield, 191, p. 243.
26. A possible source of this episode may have been "The Bridegroom of Barna", an anonymous short story in *Blackwood's* in Nov. 1840. But Emily Brontë does not use necrophilia in the Gothic sense, See Ewbank, op. cit., pp. 149–50.
27. See J. Hillis Miller, "*Wuthering Heights* and the Ellipses of Interpretation", *Notre Dame English Journal*, vol. 12, 1980.
28. Hatfield, 95, pp. 100–1.

CONCLUSION

1. Note on MS of poem in Anne Brontë's handwriting. See Chitham 21, p. 88.
2. Chitham 45, p. 123 See Commentary on the Poems, pp. 187–8.
3. Charlotte Brontë, intro. to Selections from Poems by Ellis Bell (first published 1850), *The Professor, etc.*, p. 445.
4. Mary Ann Caws, *Surrealism and the Literary Imagination, A Study of Breton and Bachelard* (The Hague, 1966) p. 18. The studies by Gaston Bachelard on the poetic imagination are *La Psychanalyse du*

feu (Paris, Gallimard, 1934); *L'Eau et les rêves* (Paris, Corti, 1942); *L'Air et les songes* (Paris, Corti, 1943); *La Terre et les rêveries de la volonté* (Paris, Corti, 1948); *La Terre et les rêveries du repos* (Paris, Corti, 1948).

Selective Bibliography

TEXTS

The edition used for the Brontë novels and Mrs Gaskell's *Life* is the Haworth edition, edited by Mrs Humphry Ward and C. K. Shorter (reprinted by John Murray, 1920–2). References to Mrs Gaskell's *Life* are abbreviated to "Gaskell". The editions used for the Brontë poems are: *The Complete Works of Emily Jane Brontë*, ed. C. W. Hatfield (Columbia University Press, 1941); *The Complete Works of Charlotte Brontë*, ed. C. K. Shorter, with bibliography and notes by C. W. Hatfield (London, 1923); *The Poems of Anne Brontë. A New Text and Commentary*, Edward Chitham (London, 1979). References to poems give the number of the poem, followed by the page number e.g. Hatfield 92, p. 93.

The following have also been consulted:

The Rev. Patrick Brontë's Collected Works, ed. J. Horsfall Turner (Bingley, 1898).

Charlotte Brontë: *Five Novelettes*, ed. Winifred Gérin (London, 1971).

The Professor, Tales from Angria, etc., ed. Phyllis Bentley (London, 1954).

The Search after Happiness, a Tale by Charlotte Brontë, ed. T. A. J. Burnett (New York, 1969).

The Spell: an Extravaganza, by Charlotte Brontë, ed. G. E. MacLean (Oxford, 1931).

CRITICAL AND BIOGRAPHICAL STUDIES

Alexander, Christine, *The Early Writings of Charlotte Brontë* (Oxford, 1983).

Allott, Miriam, *Emily Brontë: Wuthering Heights*, Casebook Series (London, 1970).

Allott, Miriam, *Charlotte Brontë: Jane Eyre and Villette*, Casebook series (London, 1973).

Benvenuto, Richard, *Emily Brontë* (Boston, 1982).

Blondel, Jacques, *Emily Brontë: Expérience Spirituelle et Création Poétique* (Paris, 1955).

Burkhart, Charles, *Charlotte Brontë: a Psychosexual Study of her Novels* (London, 1973).

Cecil, Lord David, *Early Victorian Novelists: Essays in Revaluation* (London, 1934).

Chitham, Edward and Winnifrith, Tom, *Brontë Facts and Brontë Problems* (London, 1983).

Craik, W. A., *The Brontë Novels* (London, 1968).

Dessner, L. J., *The Homely Web of Truth* (The Hague, 1975).

Dingle, Herbert, *The Mind of Emily Brontë (London, 1974)*.

Eagleton, Terry, *Myths of Power: a Marxist Study of the Brontës* (London, 1975).

Ewbank, Inga-Stina, *Their Proper Sphere: a Study of the Brontë Sisters as Early-Victorian Female Novelists* (London, 1966).

Gérin, Winifred, *Anne Brontë: a Biography* (London, 1959).

Gérin, Winifred, *Charlotte Brontë: the Evolution of Genius* (Oxford, 1967).

Gérin, Winifred, *Emily Brontë: a Biography* (Oxford, 1971).

Goodridge, J. F., *Emily Brontë: Wuthering Heights* (London, 1964).

Gregor, Ian, ed., *The Brontës: a Collection of Critical Essays* (New Jersey, 1970).

Harrison, Ada and Stanford, Derek, *Anne Brontë: Her Life and Work* (London, 1959).

Hewish, John, *Emily Brontë: a Critical and Biographical Study* (London, 1969).

Knies, Earl A., *The Art of Charlotte Brontë* (Ohio University Press, 1969).

Lane, Margaret, *The Brontë Story: a Reconsideration of Mrs. Gaskell's Life of Charlotte Brontë* (London, 1953).

Leavis, F. R. and Q. D., *Lectures in America* (London, 1969). Includes Q. D. Leavis, "A Fresh Approach to *Wuthering Heights*".

Le Guern, Joseph, *Anne Brontë (1820–1849); La Vie et l'Oeuvre*, 2 vols. (Paris, 1977).

Linder, Cynthia A., *Romantic Imagery in the Novels of Charlotte Brontë* (London, 1948).

Lock, John and Dixon, W. T., *A Man of Sorrow: the Life, Letters and Times of the Rev. Patrick Brontë* (2nd edn, London and Connecticut, 1979).

Lodge, David, *The Language of Fiction* (London, 1966). Includes "Fire and Eyre: Charlotte Brontë's War of Earthly Elements".

Martin, Robert B., *The Accents of Persuasion: Charlotte Brontë's Novels* (London, 1966).

Maurier, Daphne du, *The Infernal World of Branwell Brontë* (London, 1960).

Pinion, F. B., *A Brontë Companion: Literary Assessment, Background and Reference* (London, 1975).

Ratchford, Fannie E., *The Brontës' Web of Childhood* (New York, 1941).

Ratchford, Fannie E., *Gondal's Queen: a Novel in Verse by Emily Jane Brontë* (Austin, 1955).

Schorer, Mark, *The World We Imagine* (London, 1970).

Shorter, Clement K., *Charlotte Brontë and Her Circle* (London, 1896).

Simpson, Charles, *Emily Brontë* (London, 1929).

Spark, Muriel and Stanford, Derek, *Emily Brontë: Her Life and Work* (London, 1953).

Van Ghent, Dorothy, *The English Novel: Form and Fiction* (New York, 1961; first published 1953). Includes "Dark 'Otherness' in Wuthering Heights".

Visick, Mary, *The Genesis of Wuthering Heights* (2nd edn, Stroud and Connecticut, 1980).

Winnifrith, Tom, *The Brontës and Their Background: Romance and Reality* (London, 1973).

Winnifrith, Tom, *The Brontës* (London, 1977).

ARTICLES IN PERIODICALS, ETC.

For articles in *Brontë Society Transactions* (referred to as "BST"), see chapter notes.

Allott, Miriam, "The Rejection of Heathcliff?", *Essays in Criticism*, VIII, 1958.

Burkhart, Charles, "Another Key Word for *Jane Eyre*", *Nineteenth-Century Fiction*, XIV, Sept. 1961.

Burkhart, Charles, "The Moon of *Villette*", *Explicator*, XXI, Sept. 1962.

Ericksen, Donald H., "Imagery as Structure in *Jane Eyre*", *Victorian Newsletter* no. 30, Autumn 1966.

Gérin, Winifred, "Byron's Influence on the Brontës", *The Keats–Shelley Memorial Association*, Bulletin XVII.

Heilman, Robert B., "Charlotte Brontë, Reason and the Moon", *Nineteenth-Century Fiction*, XIV, Mar. 1960.

Hook, Andrew D., "Charlotte Brontë, the Imagination and *Villette*", in *The Brontës*, ed. Ian Gregor (New Jersey, 1970).

McKibben, Robert C., "The Image of the Book in *Wuthering Heights*", in *The Brontës*, ed. Ian Gregor (New Jersey, 1970).

Miller, J. Hillis, "*Wuthering Heights* and the Ellipses of Interpretation", *Notre Dame English Journal*, XII, 1980.

Moser, L. E., "From Portrait to Person: a Note on the Surrealistic in *Jane Eyre*", *Nineteenth-Century Fiction*, XX, Dec. 1965.

Scargill, M. H., "All Passion Spent': a Revaluation of *Jane Eyre*", *University of Toronto Quarterly*, XIX, Jan. 1950.

Shannon, Edgar, "Lockwood's Dream and the Exegesis of Wuthering Heights", *Nineteenth-Century Fiction*, XIV, Sept. 1959.

Solomon, Eric, "*Jane Eyre*: Fire and Water", *College English*, XXV, Dec. 1963.

Index